ALSO BY BETTE HAGMAN
and published by Henry Holt

The Gluten-free Gourmet (1990)

More from the Gluten-free Gourmet (1993)

The Gluten-free Gourmet Cooks Fast and Healthy (1996)

The Gluten-free Gourmet Bakes Bread

BETTE HAGMAN

The Gluten-free Gourmet Bakes Bread

More Than 200 Wheat-free Recipes

Henry Holt and Company | New York

Henry Holt and Company, LLC
Publishers since 1866
115 West 18th Street
New York, New York 10011

Henry Holt® is a registered trademark
of Henry Holt and Company, LLC

Published in Canada by Fitzhenry & Whiteside Ltd.,
195 Allstate Parkway, Markham, Ontario L3R 4T8.

Library of Congress Cataloging-in-Publication Data
Hagman, Bette.
The gluten-free gourmet bakes bread: more than 200 wheat-free recipes /
Bette Hagman.
p.   cm.
Includes bibliographical references and index.
ISBN 0-8050-6077-4
1. Gluten-free diet—Recipes.   2. Wheat-free diet—Recipes.
3. Bread.   I. Title.
RM237.86.H337   1999   98-31908
641.5'63—DC21   CIP

Henry Holt books are available for special promotions and premiums.
For details contact: Director, Special Markets.

First Edition 1999

Designed by Kelly Soong Too

Printed in the United States of America
All first editions are printed on acid-free paper. ∞

3   5   7   9   10   8   6   4   2

*This book is dedicated to my testers throughout the
years who worked quietly and without acclaim to improve
food for fellow celiacs, and especially to Virginia and Genevieve.*

Contents

Foreword

Celiac disease, or gluten-sensitive enteropathy, is a lifelong intolerance to gluten occurring in genetically predisposed individuals who mount an immunological response to an environmental factor. Dermatitis herpetiformis can be regarded as celiac disease of the skin. The offending agents are the gliadin fractions of the gluten molecule, which are found in wheat. Similar proteins, prolamines, are found in barley and rye. Oats, formerly considered toxic, were recently shown to be tolerated by some patients with celiac disease and dermatitis herpetiformis. However, oats should be avoided because there are small amounts of prolamines in oats and there is the possibility of contamination with other grains during production and processing. Children with celiac disease, on a gluten-free diet, have normal longevity and health. Undiagnosed adults have an increased mortality compared to the general population, mainly due to an increase in the incidence of malignant disease. The increased mortality returns to normal after a period of about five years on the gluten-free diet. Adherence to the diet has also been demonstrated to reduce the increased rate of malignancy.

The gluten-free diet is therefore necessary for life. This diet is also the only therapy currently available for uncomplicated celiac disease. Compliance is difficult in this day and age partially because of inadequate food labeling, a preeminence of fast foods, and a lack of awareness about the disease among food preparers. In addition, when the diagnosis is established in one family member, other first-degree relatives (parents, siblings, and children) should have serological blood tests for celiac disease. This is because at least 10 percent of these family members will have the disease, although at this stage they might be asymptomatic. In view of this, the diagnosis must be well established. The gold standard of diagnosis is a duodenal biopsy. The biopsy also provides a baseline; further biopsies may be necessary to document adequate response to the diet because symptoms rapidly improve on a gluten-free diet, and recurrent or persistent symptoms may need to be explained.

The recommendation by physicians, nutritionists, naturopaths, and osteopaths to try a gluten-free diet as a trial of therapy for a set of symptoms, without biopsy confirmation of the diagnosis, should be discouraged.

The majority of patients diagnosed with celiac disease in the United States present with diarrhea, and have positive antibodies to gliadin in their serum and totally flat biopsies. They often have had many years of symptoms, have seen many physicians, and have had a diagnosis of irritable bowel disease along the way. This is, however, the tip of the iceberg. The great majority of celiacs are probably not as yet diagnosed. They are the untested relatives of celiac patients, the patient receiving therapy for osteoporosis, the anemic patient who responds only partially to iron pills, the depressed hypothyroid patient, or even the young patient with a malignancy. Rather than total villous atrophy (destruction of the villi), they may have only partial villous atrophy on the intestinal biopsy.

Celiac disease is not often considered as a diagnosis by the medical community because it is considered a rare disease in the United States. A recent study from Baltimore in which asymptomatic blood donors had their blood screened with antibody tests, which are highly sensitive and specific for celiac disease, revealed 1 in 250 to be positive. This is identical to the figures from Europe, indicating the disease is not rare but in fact is one of the most common genetically determined diseases.

More research needs to be done to establish the true prevalence of the disease in the United States and its many modes of presentation. The result of this research will need to be published in reputable medical journals facilitating the education of physicians. Only research and publication will result in government regulatory bodies listening to the patient population and changing the current status with respect to standardization of blood tests and such important issues as food labeling.

When finally established, physicians regard making a diagnosis of celiac disease as a rewarding process for patients who merely have to change their diet. "Avoid wheat, barley, rye, and oats" are the usual instructions. This is followed by "Here is the phone number of a dietitian." Physicians are wrong in this respect. Patients need to be monitored, vitamin and mineral levels need to be measured, and bone density needs to be quantified because osteopenia and osteoporosis are common, and if present, parameters of calcium absorption need to be assessed.

For the patient the often long and arduous journey to health continues after the diagnosis is finally attained, but with a new twist. Many questions arise: What is gluten? Where is it found? Is any gluten allowed? What if I ingest some gluten? Is it okay if I ingest some gluten and do not experience any symptoms? Do I really need to check with the manufacturers of all my medications for gluten content? What are food starches? What grains can I tolerate? Where do I get all this information?

Most celiacs must become educated consumers. Their education about how to live with celiac disease comes mainly from other patients who have gone through the ordeal of the odyssey of diagnosis, the dismay of the change in lifestyle, and finally the prospects of good health. Bette Hagman's books are an example of how one person can provide an extraordinary educational service to fellow celiacs. Bette's experience and talents have gone a long way to demonstrate how, with imagination, knowledge, and some ability, a restrictive diet can be transformed into a culinary delight.

Peter H. R. Green, M.D., F.R.A.C.P.
Clinical Professor of Medicine
College of Physicians and Surgeons,
Columbia University, New York

Preface

This is not the book I started out to write three years ago. Oh, it was going to be on breads, all right, but I thought the work was all done; I would simply put together a collection of bread recipes from my first three books.

I had been satisfied with those recipes because they were still better than those so-called breads of twenty-five years ago when I was first diagnosed as a celiac and wrapped my sandwich filling in cold rice pancakes and pretended I ate like everyone else. When fellow teachers in the staff room laughed at my lunch, I resolved that something had to be done to make celiac food more appetizing. I never dreamed that I'd be one of the ones to help do so. I thought I was born to write; I certainly was not a born cook. Believe me, I have learned the hard way.

I had never baked yeast bread in my life, and my first attempt could have been used as a doorstop. There were no recipes using rice flour at that time, so when the University of Washington's home economics department came out with a recipe using xanthan gum to give "spring" to the loaf, the results seemed like a miracle. Finally, celiacs had real yeast-tasting bread that we could actually cut and eat. It was heavy, bland flavored, gritty tasting, and dried out quickly—but it was still bread. Later, I experimented and added tapioca, potato starch, and/or cornstarch to the rice flour to lighten the bread in both texture and taste.

In my third book, *The Gluten-free Gourmet Cooks Fast and Healthy,* I introduced bean flour in baking breads, a great improvement in flavor, texture, and nutrition over the rice breads. I could have lived happily ever after with these breads until a lucky coincidence opened up a whole new world of baking. When a box containing twenty-five pounds of Jowar sorghum flour was delivered to me unexpectedly, I hadn't the faintest notion how I was going to use up this new product. I'd tasted a few cakes and cookies made from it but felt that, like rice, it was a flour that needed to be combined with others to produce the best baked products. I tried pairing it with rice flour but wasn't really satisfied with the results. Then, while making a bean dish and pouring in molasses, I remembered my mother calling it "sorghum." A thought occurred to me: Would this sorghum flour be compatible with bean flour?

Success! It took a few tries, but by juggling the amounts around, I found a new flour mix that far surpassed my former Gluten-free Flour Mix in taste and texture, and in uses. By pairing the sorghum flour with bean flours, I discovered that I didn't need any molasses to cut the bitterness, and the flavor was so mild it would accept many variations. It opened the way for better textured breads and all other baking. It also made it easier to convert old recipes to the new mix, for this new bean/sorghum combination would exchange cup for cup with wheat flour in all my old favorites.

With two successful bean flour formulas that turned out bread with a texture to rival wheat ones (springy with no crumbling), I became critical of my rice breads, which didn't compare at all in taste or texture, so I revised the rice formula to a new Featherlight Mix. This wasn't as easy, but finally, using potato flour instead of potato starch, I had a rice formula (Featherlight Rice Flour Mix) that made lighter and tastier rice breads and would still exchange cup for cup with wheat flour.

Now I realized that we needed recipes for all sizes of bread machines or suitable for a single or two bread pans when oven baking. I was always exasperated when I'd spoon out one loaf and then have to put the remaining dough into muffin tins since the time of both rising and baking the muffins was different from the loaves. In all cases possible I created my new recipes in three sizes for all those who, like myself, have a terrible time doing kitchen math to make recipes for different pan sizes.

Then, because many people, like myself, have better control of the proofing time by hand mixing and oven baking, I give directions for that method along with bread machine suggestions. I hope these changes will make the book more useful.

I didn't completely abandon my idea of collecting my old recipes in one place but did this by an addendum at the end of each chapter listing the locations of all the old recipes, including book and page number, so the reader won't have to fumble through three indexes to find an old favorite.

Just before the book was completed, I received a box containing bags of uncontaminated quinoa and millet flour. I've only started to work with these flours but already know that in them we have more protein-rich, flavorful flours to add to our pantry. There are only a few recipes in this book using the flours, but in the future they may become less expensive and more available—thus expanding our choices for new tastes, more nutrition, and better texture in our breads.

I'm excited about the new recipes in this book, and my testers have been raving about them. I hope you will like them, too.

Of course, my real dream is that someday we will be able to pick our breads, rolls, and muffins from the grocery shelf (I'd even settle for the freezer section of the store). But until that time comes, these new and exciting recipes should make for wider choices for anybody with celiac disease or an allergy to wheat.

B.H.

Acknowledgments

This book was a real team effort, combining the work of my testers, the input of three food scientists, and generous donations from several companies that produce or sell gluten-free flours.

The first thanks go to the testers who worked without compensation for over three years. They not only tested my recipes but sent variations, improved the originals, and brought forth suggestions for more mixes or other shapes or uses for the recipes. Two testers, Virginia Schmuck and Genevieve Potts, tested over three hundred recipes and supplied many variations; Vicki Lyles, Karen Meyers, and Eleanor Westling took on extra recipes after they had finished their first twenty. The other seven testers worked under difficult conditions, often with very short deadlines, and I thank them for their quick responses: Debbie Duncan, Mary Gunn, Sheryllyn McClintock, Brigitte Opfermann, Wendy and Elizabeth Percival, and Louise Streule.

When I began this book, although my bread recipes were successful, I had very little understanding of why certain combinations of flours and other ingredients worked and others did not. The cereal chemists Sam Wylde II and Sam Wylde III of Ener-G-Foods spent time at the plant and on numerous phone calls to teach me. Steven Rice of Authentic Foods not only added to my knowledge of the properties and nutrient values of the basic flours but contributed the nutritional analysis for every recipe. Without the generous and invaluable help of these food scientists I would still be tossing in a little of this and that and hoping for success.

In creating new recipes, I figure I average four and a half attempts for every successful recipe. I make between three and nine sets of changes myself before I send a recipe out for testing. Several companies have been generous in supplying the ingredients for these attempts. I want to thank them not only for the many contributions but also for the moral support for this work: Ener-G Foods, Authentic Foods, El Peto Products, Jowar Foods, Inc., Dietary Specialties, and The Gluten-Free Pantry.

This is a book about breads, so unlike my former books, I didn't include much medical information, but I want to thank Cynthia Kupper, R.D., chief executive officer of the Gluten Intolerance Group (GIG) for the medical and nutritional review of the manuscript and for her detailed editing. And special thanks go to Peter H. R. Green, M.D., of Columbia Presbyterian Medical Center, New York, for writing the foreword.

Finally, I have to thank Beth Crossman, my editor, for putting her magic touch to the manuscript and bringing order out of my chaos.

My thanks to all the *bread* team!

The Gluten-free Gourmet
Bakes Bread

The Celiac Story

This title is a deliberate misnomer, for there is no single celiac story. Celiacs come in all sizes, all ages, with a variety of stories. Because after reading my comments about my struggle for diagnosis, eating habits, and coping, so many of my readers wrote to me that they had experienced something different, I have collected a variety of their stories for you.

And yet, in a way, the stories are all the same in their search for a diagnosis, their lack of knowledge about celiac disease, their struggle to cope with the diet, and, often, their desire to help others in some way, whether it was in writing, starting a support group, cooking and experimenting, or another way of spreading the word about this debilitating disease that has had so little publicity.

You notice I don't use the word "rare," for no one now associated with celiac disease or gluten intolerance, as it is often called, thinks this is in any way as rare as was once believed. The European countries have proved through studies that instead of the one in three thousand they had thought might be celiacs, the number is probably closer to one in three hundred. And here in the United States, in the fall of 1997, Dr. Allesio Fasano spearheaded a drive to try to assess the closeness of our population of celiacs to that of the European statistics.

Among the many interesting stories are those of two celiac women diagnosed over twenty-five years ago who are both registered nurses by profession.

Betty was diagnosed in Seattle in 1959, just a few years after the recognition of gluten as the villain in our diets. She feels she had probably been a celiac from childhood, and her first memories of being sickly are that when the family had the usual Saturday outing for shopping and a treat of ice cream cones and cookies, she would have stomach and leg aches before they arrived home. Her parents thought she was just overly excited and tired.

Through the following years of working, marriage, and the birth of four children, she was not aware of any food bothering her. Although her height was normal, she was always thin and hungry with lots of bloating. She suffered from constipation until the last months before diagnosis when she had persistent diarrhea, which caused such weakness that she was hospitalized. At five feet six inches tall she weighed just seventy-nine pounds, and soon after entering the hospital, fell into a coma that lasted five days.

During her stay in the hospital, she was told about a doctor from the University of Washington, Cyrus Rubin, who was doing research on gastroenterology. Dr. Rubin had invented a "capsule" on the end of a tube that could remove a section of the intestine for biopsy. This procedure was the forerunner of today's diagnostic endoscopies and, as Betty was the first patient in that hospital to have this done, the room was filled with nurses and doctors, watching while she swallowed the capsule for this dramatic breakthrough in diagnosis.

Betty says there were "no support groups or celiac organizations and no literature on the disease at this time. All the help I got was that my doctor told me to use rice flour for all my baking." Although feeling stronger, she still had stomach distress, but through persistent checking of her food, she finally determined that she was also allergic to rice; she therefore turned to soy and potato starch for baking. The results weren't very tasty, and when bean flour was introduced, even though she was now in her seventies, she became one of my testers.

Virginia, in a remote town in New Mexico, had always been a sickly baby and grew so slowly that her mother had to take her birth certificate to their school to prove she was old enough for the first grade. Her mother always assumed it was something she ate but never lived to hear a doctor suggest to Virginia (then thirty-two) that she could have celiac sprue and warn her not to eat wheat. The doctor did not perform any tests but went by the then accepted premise that, since taking away the gluten in her hospital diet had stopped the vomiting and diarrhea, she was probably a celiac. Virginia, glad of some answer after all the years of suffering with stomach problems, received no more help than this. She went home to eat Rye Krisp. It wasn't until a diagnosis of diabetes the following year that she began a serious search for help with the celiac diet. She found a booklet from the Canadian Celiac Association that offered a bread mix made with wheat starch (then considered acceptable).

She never met another celiac and at times wondered how she could have such a rare disease. When, after a time, she decided to go off the diet, she became so ill that she vowed she would never do that again.

She thought she was sticking to the doctor's orders, but twenty years later she read in *The Gluten-free Gourmet* that she was still getting a lot of gluten in her diet from hidden glutens and that the Canadian and United States celiac organizations had put wheat starch on the forbidden list. She realized how much better she felt when she was truly gluten free and also how much easier it was to control completely her blood sugar for diabetes.

Virginia's sister, Genevieve, healthy looking and almost twice her size, lived nearby and frequently cooked her sister gluten-free treats while continuing to eat wheat-filled foods. But Genevieve, too, had stomach distress, which eventually was diagnosed as reflux.

She admits, "I had no idea my reflux and other digestive problems, along with poor dental health, a thyroid condition I'd battled for years, and the goiter I'd had as a child, could be related to my sister's diarrhea and vomiting symptoms. It wasn't until I traveled with my sister to a celiac conference and lived three days on the gluten-free meals they provided that I realized by eliminating gluten I had fewer digestive problems."

Her reflux required annual endoscopies, so when she learned that reflux could indicate celiac disease, she asked the doctor to take a biopsy for this at her next annual "scope session." When the doctor's office called to report "no cancer," she accepted the findings without question for a while but later wrote for a copy of the biopsy. She found on the report terms she had learned through her study of the disease were a red alert for celiacs: "blunted villi," "inflammation of the duodenal lamina propria," and "chronic duodenitis." When she asked the doctor what these meant, he appeared challenged and suggested that, since she was neither anemic nor underweight, she couldn't be a celiac. "Besides," he said, "no one can stay on that diet."

A new doctor looked at the medical records and confirmed her feelings that she truly was a celiac. Now, after a year on the diet, she feels much better, has more energy and a more positive outlook. An operation for a hiatial hernia eliminated all the acidy reflux symptoms.

Virginia and Genevieve were so grateful to find help and support that they have spread the word about celiacs in their remote New Mexico community, and with the help of several doctors and health food stores, they have discovered six more celiacs—some recently diagnosed but others living, as Virginia did, with the thought of being alone with a rare disease.

Steve, a forty-seven-year-old, writes, "As with many celiacs, my road to diagnosis was long. Bouts of diarrhea started when I was thirteen and continued, with a few disappearances, until starting the gluten-free diet" thirty years later.

In his thirties, Steve was diagnosed with irritable bowel syndrome, or pre-ulcerative colitis due to stress. For ten years antispasmodics gave relief but no cure. Then he started developing little blisters on elbows and knees, which the doctor suggested came from slivers of the wood he used at work. Cortisone cream helped, but finally the terrible itching and pain that had now spread to his buttocks and scalp drove him to see a naturopath. He suggested they were toxins coming out of the body or perhaps eczema. The nutrition information that he recommended included increased amounts of whole wheat flour, wheat, and oat bran.

By now Steve realized his condition was worsening and that he never felt good. "There was no quality of life."

Finally, thirty years after the first bouts of diarrhea, he was referred to a dermatologist who diagnosed dermatitis herpetiformis (DH) and put him on dapsone. In two weeks most of the blisters had all but disappeared, and the dermatologist suggested that some people with DH also have celiac disease and that a gluten-free diet was required in addition to the dapsone. Steve says, "I have since learned that he was not current and that everyone who has DH is a celiac."

When a biopsy confirmed the celiac disease, the dietitian to whom he was referred had trouble understanding the diet. It wasn't until he joined a support group that he received helpful information. "This is the most useful tool for helping with the gluten-free diet," he said. "I resisted joining for a while but then decided to give it a try. I was surprised at the warmth and caring attitude of those attending. You no longer feel isolated; there are other people like you; information and ideas are shared; you do not have to reinvent the wheel yourself." Steve is now an active member of the group and spends a lot of his time helping others.

The above stories are of adults finally finding a diagnosis, but what about those too young to speak for themselves? I received two stories of babies and one of a young child.

Both Molly and Kevin were such sick babies that doctors thought they were going to die. Their parents were desperate.

At twenty months, Molly looked like a starving baby on the nightly news: bloated tummy and no fat on her shoulders or thighs. Over the previous three months she had been seen by more than fifty doctors at two major medical centers, where she had undergone an interminable number of tests. Finally, a friend of the family four hundred miles away called to suggest that the parents consider gluten intolerance as the culprit. That afternoon a doctor stepped back and looked at the child rather than at her chart. "You know what?" he told Molly's mother. "She *does* look like a sprue kid." A biopsy confirmed the diagnosis of celiac disease. After two weeks on a gluten-free diet, Molly was an alert, smiling, hungry baby. She continues to thrive seven years later.

Molly was not the only child in her family to suffer during those scary months before her diagnosis. Her two older sisters were jealous, confused, and afraid. They even worried that they had somehow made Molly sick. Molly's mother, a writer named Debbie Duncan, recognized there was a real need for a picture book for and about siblings of sick kids, so she wrote *When Molly Was in the Hospital: A Book for Brothers and Sisters of Hospitalized Children*, illustrated by Nina Olli Kainen, M.D. (Rayve Productions, Inc., 1994), to help both parents and siblings understand the complex emotions involved when a child is seriously ill.

The outcome of Kevin's story is somewhat different. His parents were frantic with worry as Kevin became sicker and sicker, too young to tell them where he hurt. They just knew he was going to die, until the doctor diagnosed celiac disease and told them to eliminate gluten from his diet. The change in the baby was fantastic. When the doctor said that celiac was genetic and suggested first-degree relatives should be tested, they took the blood tests even though they were certain neither of them could be celiac because they didn't have any symptoms. The results were astonishing. Kevin's mother tested positive for antibodies; her endoscopy confirmed that she was a "silent" celiac. Now both Kevin and his mother share the gluten-free diet, and because she found her condition before she became as ill as her son, she is the first to advocate testing for first-degree relatives.

Elizabeth, a perfectly normal (even extra tall) six-year-old became tired and irritable when she started kindergarten. The mother assumed this was anxiety and stress. When she noticed strange bowel movements with soft, light-colored, floating stools, she called the doctor, who calmed her by suggesting there were a lot of bugs going around. In two months Elizabeth's health deteriorated until she had lost several pounds and her bones protruded. She seemed to be disappearing before her parents' eyes. Elizabeth's grandmother had heard of another child with celiac disease and so suggested this. The doctor, who had never diagnosed a case, sent them to a gastro-enterologist. They were told to take a fecal fat test by measuring and recording every-thing Elizabeth consumed and collecting her stools to compare fat input with output in order to calculate the efficiency of her body.

Her mother wrote, "While we were wrapping the toilet in plastic wrap to collect the specimens and record the results, I found myself telling Elizabeth that if she ate all the bread with all the butter, she could have a Snickers bar and ice cream. It was almost surreal." The fecal fat test showed Elizabeth was absorbing only 22 percent of the food she ate, while the average person absorbs at least 95 percent. She was liter-ally starving. Blood tests and a biopsy confirmed the doctor's (and grandmother's) suspicions of celiac disease. After three days on the gluten-free diet, the difference was amazing.

Elizabeth, now going on eight, is very knowledgeable about her disease. She understands her diet, reads labels, and teaches fellow students about celiac disease. She even carried her endoscopy report to class for show-and-tell.

While Elizabeth's diagnosis was fast (only two months), I received a letter about a ten-day diagnosis at about the same time. Jane, a thirty-nine-year-old British woman working at a university in Turkey, wrote, "When I moved to Ankara from the south coast where I worked, I thought I'd contracted the 'Turkish tummy bug.' I didn't pay much attention for it's not unusual for foreign teachers, but it seemed strange because I'd already been in the country two years without illness. After a year of almost continual distress, I finally sought medical advice."

She went to an internist who checked her blood and urine, took cardiogram and ultrasound tests; they all proved negative, so she was sent to a gastroenterologist who ordered barium X rays and muttered something about malabsorption and not eating bread. She dismissed this, but when she returned with the films, he said, "I think it's a problem with your willy" and went on to explain about the duodenum. From school biology she remembered the *villi* and realized the misunderstanding was caused by the Turkish "w"/"v" pronunciation problem.

Jane went on: "A zillion questions later he told me that to confirm his diagnosis I needed an endoscopy he was willing to perform there in his 'surgery' (a very slightly converted flat with little equipment) which involved no drugs or tranquilizer and ended with bits of my 'willy' presented to me in a little bottle with instructions to take it to the local medical laboratory for analysis. And there you have it. I kid you not; from my first visit to the doctor until the confirmation of the biopsy results, a maximum of ten days had elapsed. When I hear of the long suffering of others because of misdiagnosis, I realize just what a lucky little celiac I am."

When I first started collecting the stories, I realized that I was getting the history of celiac disease here in the United States, from the beginning before the endoscopy tube was first introduced by Dr. Rubin in Seattle to the recognition that dermatitis herpetiformis (DH) is actually celiac disease (CD); from the beginning of the support groups to the fact that the disease is more readily recognized in Europe than in the United States.

A few years ago the Celiac Disease Foundation surveyed six hundred of their diagnosed members to learn the various diagnoses they had received for their distress before the final one that solved their health problems. The list was rated, with number 1 getting the most answers down to number 20.*

1. Anemia
2. Irritable Bowel Syndrome
3. Psychological (Stress, Nerves, Imagination)
4. Diarrhea

*Data printed in *Celiac Disease Foundation Newsletter*, Fall 1996, volume 6, 4.

5. Irritable Bowel Disease

6. Diabetes

7. Spastic Colon

8. Ulcers

9. Virus (Viral Gastroenteritis)

10. Chronic Fatigue Syndrome

11. Weight Loss

12. Allergies

13. Amebic Parasitic Infection

14. Gall Bladder Disease

15. Thyroid Disease

16. Cancer (Lymphoma, Digestive)

17. Colitis

18. Cystic Fibrosis

19. Lactose Intolerance

20. Reflux

Today, with the serum screening available to doctors, no one should suffer long with a wrong diagnosis. And with the large number of support groups around the nation, help and support are available. No one should feel they are alone with a disease that is not "rare" today.

For more information, including a detailed diet list about celiac disease or to find a local support group, contact one of the following organizations:

American Celiac Society Dietary Support Coalition, 58 Musano Court, West Orange, NJ 07052-4103; phone (973) 325-8837.

Canadian Celiac Association, 190 Britannia Rd. East, Unit 11, Missi, Ontario L4Z 1W6, Canada; phone (905) 507-6208 or (800) 363-7296.

Celiac Disease Foundation, 13251 Ventura Blvd., Suite 3, Studio City, CA 91604-1838; phone (818) 990-2354; fax (818) 990-2379.

Celiac Sprue Association/United States of America (CSA/USA), P.O. Box 31700, Omaha, NE 68131-0700; phone (402) 558-0600.

Gluten Intolerance Group of North America (GIG), 15110 10th Ave. SW, Suite A, Seattle, WA 98166; phone (206) 246-6652.

Internet's Celiac Conference. Send e-mail to celiac@ispace.com.

Help! What Did I Do Wrong?

Of all the letters I receive, the largest number by far contain questions about bread. I know that many readers are intimidated by yeast and frightened by using it for the first time. They have a lot of company. I, too, was overwhelmed by the idea of making my own bread when I was diagnosed, nearly twenty-five years ago. I had mastered muffins (cooking in small pans works better with the gluten-free flours), and turned to yeast breads after the introduction of xanthan gum. I figured that if I had conquered muffins and biscuits, I could do anything. Right? Wrong!

I quickly discovered that baking gluten-free bread successfully is not just cooking. It is truly an act of creation, combining the skills of cook, scientist, and artist. Even now, after years of baking my own bread, both with a machine and by hand, I always feel a surge of pride as I pull a well-rounded, heavenly smelling crusty brown loaf from my oven. Not every loaf is perfect, of course. That is too much to ask when working with an organism as temperamental as yeast in flours as quirky as our gluten-free ones.

In searching for answers to reader questions, I learned a lot. Some of the basics are simple: Always use yeast before the expiration date on the package. Have all ingredients at room temperature (or as warm as the recipe calls for). Don't expect every loaf to rise at the same rate. (In other words, the yeast you use, the flours in the recipe, the other ingredients, the temperature of your kitchen, the humidity, and the altitude will make differences in the working of the yeast and the rising of the unbaked loaf.)

Of course, you can avoid the yeast question by baking self-rising breads using baking powder and/or baking soda. You will find a lot of those in this book. But since yeast breads bring such a sense of satisfaction to the baker and fill such a need in the celiac diet, here are answers to questions I am most frequently asked.

Q. I just took my first loaf of bread out of my new bread machine. I could use it for a doorstop. I followed the recipe exactly as it was in the manual, just replacing the flour with your GF Mix. Help! What did I do wrong?

A. You're not the only one who has tried this. Using recipes formulated for wheat flour simply doesn't work for our gluten-free breads. Our rice or bean breads will need their own recipes, including xanthan gum, extra proteins (in milk, soy, nut, gelatin, or eggs), plus, in most cases, more liquid. Try again using one of the recipes in this book made for your size bread machine. Good luck!

Q. My bread comes out of the pan looking shrunk and crumpled like a hat that was out in the rain. What happened?

A. This sounds like some of the breads I created when I was learning. Now I know the problem might be one of two things. If the bread was well cooked but shrunken, it probably was *overproofed*. In other words, the bread rose to the top of its final height before it started baking, leaving no more yeast action to *oven rise* when the baking started. The yeast was through working and didn't keep the bread up while baking. Next time shorten the proofing time. If making the bread by hand, watch the loaf and don't let it rise to its full height before putting it in the oven. It should not have little bubbles showing (overproofed) but should look more like Mr. Doughboy in the Pillsbury ads.

If using a bread machine, cut the rising (proofing) time if the machine is programmable. If not, you will have to learn to adjust the yeast down slightly until the perfect loaf is achieved for your machine. Sometimes increasing the salt very slightly (25 percent) will lengthen the proofing time. Remember, every recipe will have to be adjusted this way if using a machine.

Another problem in both hand mixing and machine mixing could be that the water was too warm and the yeast worked too fast and burned itself out, thus collapsing while baking.

Q. Why does the top of my bread sink in the middle?

A. This is usually due to the dough being too thin or having too much liquid for the flour to absorb. The dough for our breads is not a heavy dough ball as for wheat breads but a batter-like dough. In your mixer it should resemble cake batter rather than cookie dough. In a bread machine it should be thick enough to show the swirls but thin enough to be smooth and shiny, not dull. This is part of the artistry of making bread—the recognition of just which texture turns out the perfect loaf. Skill at this is best acquired by repeated practice and time. But don't let the failures defeat you. The art is well worth learning, for bread fresh from the oven is absolute bliss.

Q. My last loaf of bread seemed doughy in the center rather than springy. What happened?

A. I can't tell exactly because you didn't tell me what recipe you used. Sometimes heat escapes from the bread machine if you lift the lid too many times, and then the bread is merely underbaked. The same will happen if the oven temperature is lowered.

Often the reason lies in the ingredients in the recipe. Were too many heavy or moist ingredients added? Did you try to use honey instead of sugar? Did you add moist fruits or too many? Lighten up on the additions and see if the center then bakes well. Or try a smaller pan next time even if you have to put some of the dough into muffin tins.

Q. My crusts always seem tougher than a fellow celiac's. Why?

A. Breads made with dairy liquid (milk and buttermilk) have more tender crusts. If you used a water-based recipe, try rubbing the hot loaves with margarine immediately after turning out of the pan. And never leave the bread out after it is cool. Place it in a plastic bag and seal tightly.

Q. My gluten-free bread is drier than wheat bread. Can anything be done about this?

A. We are all aware that rice bread is drier than wheat bread, but some of the new bean breads rival any wheat bread in texture. The low-fat breads will be drier than the ones using fat, and they will definitely dry out faster. Low-sugar breads also dry out more. Store your bread in sealed plastic bags and don't put it in the refrigerator unless necessary.

Q. Can I refrigerate my dough for later baking?

A. Yes, says one of my testers. She had to leave the house just when the bread was finished mixing, so she put the loaf pan in the refrigerator and pulled it out when she came home. The bread rose slowly to the normal proof height and baked well. But don't put the bread in the refrigerator after it has risen and is ready to bake. The creator of Sarah's Bagels says she often mixes these the night before and then refrigerates the dough to bake the next morning. (You can also freeze the dough for later baking.)

Q. You use unflavored gelatin in most of your breads. Why? Is it necessary?

A. It is not necessary and can be eliminated if you have a religious or dietary restriction against it. I suggest it because it adds protein, and yeast combines with it to give elasticity to the bread. Since the gluten protein in wheat must be eliminated in our gluten-free diet, the flours we use for baking don't have much protein; we substitute for it in many ways: dry milk, soy milk, nut milk, egg whites, nut meats, and so forth. Often, when trying to cut down on eggs, milk, or other proteins, something must be added. We find that the gelatin helps to keep the loaf structure stronger and more elastic.

If you can use the milk protein in the dried milk, that may be enough for a fine loaf. But many people cannot tolerate milk or soy, and some cannot have nuts, so I have tried to add protein in different ways. The bean bread recipes in this book do better than rice recipes without the gelatin because the bean flour mixes are higher in protein, but I still include gelatin to achieve a better texture.

Q. You use a lot of eggs. Why? Do we have to use fresh eggs?

A. No, you don't always have to use fresh eggs. Egg whites are an inexpensive and accessible protein, which is why I use them. Whole eggs (use large eggs) add flavor as well as spring to the bread. The egg white is the most important in yeast breads, so you can use a gluten-free brand of liquid egg substitute (which is made from the whites) for these. If you substitute liquid egg for the whole egg in a recipe, you might want to add an extra ½ tablespoon of oil, butter, or shortening to make up the fat of each yolk called for in a recipe. Substitute ¼ cup of the egg substitute for each large whole egg or 3 tablespoons for each white. You can also use dried egg whites, reconstituting them as suggested on the package.

The egg yolk is used in the batter breads (quick breads) as a binder and also helps improve the texture and flavor. I find that today's liquid egg substitutes often don't work as well as fresh eggs in some of these breads. But if you are counting cholesterol carefully, then by all means try the substitutes listed above.

Q. What do you do with those egg yolks left over?

A. Frankly, I put them down my disposal, but that's because I have to watch my cholesterol. Egg yolks can go into French toast, rich custards, puddings, and other desserts that call for extra egg yolks. Cook them for your potato salads, or if you're a bird lover, cook them and add to the bird feeder tray.

Q. I'm allergic to eggs. Is there any substitute?

A. Yes. If you are allergic to both whites and yolks, then you can't use liquid egg substitute because most are made from egg whites. If you are allergic only to the yolks, then you can use liquid egg substitutes.

There are two egg substitutes that work with our flours. One is the powder sold as Egg Replacer. This is put out by Ener-G Foods and is available in many health food stores. The other is a Canadian product put out by Kingsmill. They have similar ingredients and are basically an extra leavening agent. They do not give the flavor of eggs to a product, so be sure you have enough flavor in your bread to satisfy your taste when using a powdered egg replacer.

The usual formula when baking with wheat is 1½ teaspoons of Egg Replacer stirred into 2 tablespoons of water for each egg called for in a recipe. I find that with our flours we have better success by almost doubling the amount of powder to achieve the correct rise in the breads. Some recipes in this book use this substitution as a leavening.

Another substitute that works in our breads is flaxseed. This can be the seed you have to grind or pulverize or ready-to-use flax meal. To use the pulverized flaxseed or meal, the ratio is 1 tablespoon of ground meal to 2 or 3 tablespoons of water. Use as you would liquid egg substitute: consider 1 egg to be ¼ cup and an egg white to be 3 tablespoons. The problem with flaxseed as a substitute is that it is sold as a laxative and can cause diarrhea, gas, or bloating for some people.

Q. Can I use any brand of bean flour? I found some ground bean flour on the store shelf that is far cheaper than ordering Authentic Foods' Garfava flour.

A. You may be very disappointed because it may not produce good flavor and texture. The two companies I recommend process their beans before grinding. There is no guarantee that your bean flour comes from processed beans (or even the same kind of beans). The Canadian processing is called "micronizing," while Authentic Foods calls their actions "processing." This helps take the bitterness out of the final flour. But do remember that companies change, and perhaps in the future other companies will make processed bean flour, and when even wheat eaters recognize the food value of bean flour, it may be on all grocery shelves.

Q. Can I grind my own dried beans for bread flour?

A. Sure. But read the answer above. You won't end up with the same flavor as the processed bean. Neither the texture nor the taste will be the same.

Q. Our Canadian bean flour is different from the Authentic Foods Garfava flour. Will it work in your recipes?

A. Your bean flour is ground from processed Romano (cranberry) beans and is a single-bean flour. You can dilute the stronger flavor by mixing it with equal parts of garbanzo bean flour. Use it in any of the recipes that call for the Garfava flour in this book. When I tested this, I found the results very similar to the lighter flour.

Q. I am not lactose intolerant, but I cannot stand the taste of the nonfat, non-instant dried milk that you called for in past bread recipes.

A. You are not the only one who has mentioned the strong taste of milk in their baking. Since I have always been lactose intolerant, I realized that I couldn't tolerate the taste but had no idea that this was stronger than any other dried milk until letters arrived from readers. I suggest you get a regular instant milk from the grocery store for your dry milk in the breads. Always remember that a milk product should be used as fresh as possible, and if there is a chance that you have stored it too long, replace your box or carton with a fresh one for the best flavored bread.

Q. Why do you adjust with water rather than flour in your recipes? When I baked with wheat flour, I always adjusted the flour in the recipe.

A. I remember my mother making wheat bread and tossing in a handful or more of flour to get the dough the right texture. Well, we don't bake with a single flour. Ours is composed of several flours, some xanthan gum, maybe some Egg Replacer and gelatin. It would be impossible to create exactly the correct formula by a handful of one and then a pinch of the other and so on. Thus it is easier (and more accurate) to adjust the texture of our doughs by watching the water (which is a single unit).

Q. What if I put in too much water and the dough becomes too thin?

A. You will have to add more flour. I suggest adding the basic flour mix called for in the recipe, 1 tablespoon at a time, using as little as necessary to get the correct texture. This might change the formula a little bit, but unless you have a heavy hand with the water, the bread should still turn out fine. If you have none of the mix, substitute sweet rice flour, adding it 1 tablespoon at a time.

Q. Does the water quality make a difference?

A. Yes. According to several bread books, water quality does affect your bread. Hard water can retard the yeast's formation and extra-soft water makes a sticky dough. The best water would be bottled spring water or tap water with a pH balance of 5.5 to 6.5. You can ask your water company to determine the pH of your tap water.

Never use softened water; it has a very high sodium content.

Q. What is dough enhancer and where can I get it? How does it differ from vinegar?

A. Dough enhancer is a powder containing ascorbic acid (as in vinegar) plus some flavoring, yeast, and other ingredients that improve the texture and shelf life of bread. Vinegar provides ascorbic acid only. Dough enhancer is available in specialty stores that sell grains and products for baking. It has a long shelf life and can be stored with such products as baking powder and baking soda. Dietary Specialties, The Gluten-Free Pantry, and Ener-G Foods carry it. Check other suppliers to see if they stock it.

Q. My bread always takes more time to rise than you state in the recipe Why? What can I do?

A. I assume that you are baking bread by hand. The recipes in this book were created for the average altitude and humidity, so one of several things can create this problem. Those who live in an area of high humidity or lots of rainfall might have to increase the yeast a bit. I live right at the edge of the water and always increase the yeast ¼ to ½ teaspoon to get my bread to rise in the prescribed time. One tester who lives in my area said she had to almost double the time of rising, but I discovered her room temperature was in the 50s, which just wasn't warm enough for usual rising. My testers living at a high altitude often find they have to decrease the yeast a bit or count on a shorter rising time.

Another answer may be a simple one: The ingredients may be too cold or the water too cool. If you have average humidity and live at an altitude of less than two thousand feet, try taking all the ingredients from the refrigerator, bringing them to room temperature, and checking the temperature of your liquid and the room. The room should be at least 68 degrees, but if you can find a warm corner, put your bread there.

Q. You give a wide range of baking time (50 to 60 minutes) for loaf breads. Why? How can I choose the exact time for my bread?

A. The amount of baking time will depend on your altitude, the humidity, the bread ingredients, and slight differences in ovens. I suggest you start with the longer temperature time to be sure the bread is fully baked. If the crust is too thick and hard and the bread seems dry, try shortening the time by about 3 minutes for each baking until you achieve the perfect loaf for your altitude and average humidity.

Q. I heard that celiacs aren't supposed to use quick-rising yeast. Why?

A. I know of no reason not to use quick-rising yeast. I use it for most of my bread baking. It is possible that some "off brands" or yeasts from other countries are made differently from those in the United States, but I was assured by Red Star Yeast that their regular and quick-rising yeasts do not contain gluten. If you think the yeast you are using contains any gluten, contact the company scientist and query him about their methods and ingredients.

Q. Are there any special rules for high-altitude bread baking?

A. The rules are not as complex as they are for baking cakes. My high-altitude testers say they add about 1 to 2 tablespoons more flour to each recipe, and in the sweet doughs (as for cakes at high altitudes) they cut the sugar a bit (1 to 2 teaspoons per recipe). You will have to adjust this to your location. They also find that the rising time is often shorter and the baking time may be shorter by up to 10 minutes for loaves. At higher altitudes (5,000 feet or more), the bread may overflow the pan or pans. If this happens, put a little of the dough into muffin tins to prevent this from happening again.

Q. Can I use any brand of margarine in my bread baking? Is there a difference? Can I replace it with oil?

A. Always use the hard or stick margarines for baking (not the soft or spreadable kind). I prefer the taste and texture of a soy margarine for all my baking; the corn oil–based margarines tend to make a heavier loaf that is not as finely textured. The second question, about vegetable oil, is harder to answer. Yes, you can substitute oil. I suggest you use a very light oil such as Saffola and always remember to decrease the water quantity by the amount of oil. You may sacrifice some of the light texture of the loaf by using oil.

Q. I am trying to use substitutes for sugar and fat whenever possible. How do I substitute?

A. The usual rule for gluten-free flours is not to substitute unless the substitution is written in the recipe—or unless you want to do a lot of experimentation. The way to substitute is to do it with only one ingredient at a time. For example, using fruit puree for oil and some of the sweetening may work with wheat flours, but in gluten-free recipes my testers and I have found that you can only substitute some puree for some of the fat, and then the batter (or dough) is likely to turn out like a pudding. For sugars it's better to stick with a solid substitution such as maple sugar or date sugar instead of trying to use molasses, honey, or a fruit puree. Of course, if you have severe allergies, you will have to work out the changes you make, but don't expect your bread to have the consistency or texture of the original recipe.

You can replace the margarine or butter with oil and reduce the liquid a little, but the texture of the bread will be different. Some recipes in this book use little fat, and you can actually cut the fat in others. The less fat, the drier the bread will be, so you be the judge of just how much you want to cut and how much quality you are willing to sacrifice.

Q. Can I replace xanthan gum with guar gum?

A. Yes. This is a straight volume-for-volume exchange. Guar gum was used before xanthan gum; but remember, guar gum is sold in health food stores as a laxative, and for some celiacs this might not prove a practical replacement.

Q. Is there any way to make mixes from a favorite recipe? I get tired of pulling out all those ingredients every time I make bread.

A. The easiest way is one I learned long ago. When making a recipe, I get out one or more plastic storage bags. As I fill the dry ingredient bowl for the loaf I'm baking, I measure out the same for the extra bags *except for the yeast*. You then have several bags of mixes to store on the cupboard shelf along with a note reminding you to add the yeast or slip the packet of yeast in with the mix. (Be sure to use this before the expiration date on the yeast.) Never add the yeast to the dry ingredients if you are going to store them because the yeast will absorb moisture from the flours and may not be active.

Another way is to use either of the two bread mixes in this book and adapt them to your taste by using the variations. See Bette's Four Flour Bread Mix (page 41) and French Bread/Pizza Mix (page 190).

Q. Is there any way to cut really fresh bread? I am so hungry for the new bread that I try to cut it before it cools.

A. I don't blame you. A friend told me her secret. She sprays her knife with Pam, and presto! It slices the hot bread without crushing the loaf. Be sure to use a serrated knife for all bread slicing.

Q. Which do you prefer, hand mixing or the bread machine? Why?

A. The bread machine can be a useful tool for the novice bread maker. Years ago, as a novice myself, I hailed bread machines as my savior. I was completely ignorant of the science of rising and proofing bread, and expected the machine to think for me. It did, up to a point. The bread was overmixed and often came out with a concave top (a sign of overproofing), but it still tasted better than anything we could buy. Now that food scientists and bread experts in different companies have revealed the whys and wherefores of some of the complications of bread making with gluten-free flours, I find I get better results by using my KitchenAid heavy-duty mixer and baking my breads in the oven. There are several reasons:

First, there are few machines on the market that are as programmable as my old trusty R-2, D-2, Welbilt. Even the new Zojurishi, although still programmable, has taken off the cool-down cycle that allowed me to be away from home when the bread finished baking.

Second, we now know that we don't need the stir down or second beating, so all we have to do is beat the batter (dough) for 3½ minutes with a mixer and then spoon it into the pan. By using rapid-rising yeast (and sometimes adding a bit more) we can have the loaf or loaves ready for the oven in about 40 minutes. Then baking time is 1 hour—not much time out of a day.

Third, baking by hand allows me to have complete control of the rising time, and the bread is neither underproofed (not risen enough) nor overproofed (risen too high). I get a perfect loaf every time—or almost. I live in an area of very changeable humidity, but I can watch the bread and pick the exact moment to pop it into the oven.

Fourth, I can make exactly the size loaf that is perfect for my use. I usually make one 8½" by 4½" loaf for specialty breads and two loaves for basic breads. I can eat one loaf and freeze the other.

BREAD MACHINE QUESTIONS

Q. What machine should I buy to make gluten-free breads?

A. This is almost impossible to answer with all the new machines coming on the market and the old ones changing each year. The best suggestion I can make is to look for certain features:

1. The machine should be programmable so you can eliminate the second (unnecessary) rising. It is even better if you can program as the bread is rising and begin to bake at exactly the time it reaches the point it should be baked. This will prevent overproofing and the inevitable collapse of the loaf.

2. The machine should have a strong motor and a solid or double paddle (not the dough hook–shaped paddle). This will ensure that the dough gets thoroughly mixed and fully beaten.

3. Be sure the paddle is easily removed even when dough is in the pan. This will prevent having huge holes in the bottom of the loaf. I always remove the paddle the minute the first mix is finished in any machine I test. (This will also prevent the stir down in case that can't be deleted from the program.) Do this with a Teflon-coated pair of tongs to prevent scratching the paddle or pan.

4. Other desirable features are a cool-down period at the end of baking so you don't have to be present to take the loaf out as soon as it finishes baking. It is nice to have a machine that warms the liquids before it starts mixing to ensure that your liquid isn't too hot or too cold, but this is not necessary.

The final answer about what machine to buy is that one should ask another celiac owner and see if his or her machine will fit your needs. Only you can judge just how much you want to demand of your machine.

Q. My bread machine leaves big holes in the bottom of the loaf. Is there any way to avoid these?

A. Read number 3 in the answer above. Removing the paddle or paddles will leave only one or two small nail-sized holes in the loaf.

Q. Your ingredient list adds the yeast to the dry ingredients while my machine manual says to put it in on top of the flour. What should I do?

A. The reason for this separation is that the yeast will pick up moisture from the flour if left standing a long time (as some people may do with wheat-flour recipes). Since we use fresh eggs and can't leave our ingredients standing out for long periods, this separation is not necessary. Just put your yeast in with the dry ingredients and save yourself trouble (or the chance of forgetting). But if you are making up mixes as

I suggested above, don't add the yeast until you are ready to put the mix into the machine.

Q. I was given an old Multilogic Welbilt bread machine when my daughter bought herself a new loaf-shaped machine. How can I cut the round loaf?

A. You are lucky. You have one of the best programmable machines ever on the market. The shape of the loaf may have led to its demise, and it is no longer manufactured. To cut the loaf, slice down through the top to the bottom. That leaves two half-round loaves. Turn them on the flat side and slice as you would a regular loaf. So what if you have semicircles for toast and sandwiches. The bread will taste just as good.

Q. My machine has a very tiny viewing window. Can I lift the top to watch the mixing?

A. During mixing it is advisable and necessary to watch, so lift the lid to check that the dough is the correct texture. You'll want to do this to remove the paddle, but never do it during baking or your oven heat will be uneven and the bread may not bake thoroughly.

I realize I have answered only a few questions about bread machines, but that is because of the many differences between machines. For those who have bread machines, please read your manual carefully. Some of your problems will be answered within the manual.

Suggested Reading: *The Bread Machine Magic Book of Helpful Hints* by Linda Rehberg and Lois Conway (New York: St. Martin's Press, 1993).

For Bread Machine Help: Phone Red Star Yeast & Products at (800) 445-4746.

A Beginner's Guide to
Understanding Gluten-free Flours

A diagnosis of celiac disease, gluten intolerance, or wheat allergy is not only a shock to most people but the beginning of a plunge into a whole new world of grains and flours. Many of them will be strange except to patrons of health food stores. Whoever thought one could not only exist but come to enjoy eating bread made from tapioca or a cake whose base was beans? Certainly I never dreamed I would.

I was no scratch cook when I was diagnosed with celiac disease, so I was absolutely floored by the idea of trying to make my bread (which would be muffins, pancakes, and biscuits for some years) without wheat flour or rye, barley, and oats. There were no good cookbooks dealing with gluten-free cooking at the time, and the few recipes available in the first one I found in an English book were measured in grams. The results were absolutely inedible. Back to rice cakes.

It was those utterly boring rice cakes that drove me to experiment. And many of those experiments slipped noisily down the garbage disposal when even my poodle, who loved "people" food, rejected my first attempts using the only flour with which I was familiar—cornmeal. It didn't take me long to start experimenting with potato starch and sweet rice flour in those itsy-bitsy packages on the top shelf in the baking section of the local grocery. I found I never had enough, and it was costing me an arm and a leg. So I discovered a local supplier of these and rice flour, and started carting home twenty-pound bags in my station wagon. With the far less costly bulk buying, I could toss some dismal failures and not weep to think of them as gold pouring down the disposal.

Now when someone hears I can't have flour (meaning wheat) and feels sorry for me, I hasten to say that I probably use more flours than most people have ever heard of, from rice, corn, and potato to tapioca, bean, and sorghum. And I go on to add that I have everything from pancakes and waffles to bread, pizza, and cakes and cookies.

It wasn't always this way. I can remember the early '70s when we thought it impossible to make yeast breads with our flours, so waffles, pancakes, and self-rising breads had to satisfy our longing for something on which to spread butter and jam. And I remember hailing xanthan gum as a miracle because it gave us the chance for "real" bread with yeast.

It is true that our "alternative flours" take a little getting used to. They are not going to act like wheat flour in baking, but once you understand just how they do act, you can turn out food that no one would guess is gluten free.

When I first started using these weird flours, I just dumped and guessed and dumped some more to arrive at formulas that worked satisfactorily. At first I had many failures, but slowly, as I used the flours, I became accustomed to their taste, texture, and disposition. I call it disposition because, like cranky kids, each flour reacts in a different way to the other flours. Some combine as if they were made for each other; others seem to fight. Some are best for bread, others for cookies and cakes; and one unusual combination makes wonderful pasta. On the following pages are charts of the basic baking flours and supplemental flours, showing their uses and keeping qualities.

Flour	Taste	Combines with	Best for	Used alone?	1-cup Weight (grams)	Suggestions
White rice	Bland	Tapioca flour Cornstarch Potato starch	Cakes Cookies	Sometimes	140	Inexpensive Stores on shelf Absorbs moisture from air
Brown rice	Grainy	Tapioca flour Cornstarch Potato starch	Bread Crackers	Not suggested	126	Buy fresh Keep refrigerated or frozen
Garbanzo bean	Strong Bitter Nutty	Cornstarch Tapioca flour Romano bean flour	Bread Chocolate cake	Not suggested	127	Suggest refrigeration because of oils
Garfava*	Nutty Slightly bitter	Cornstarch Tapioca flour Sorghum	Bread Cakes Cookies Pasta	Not suggested	117	Stores on shelf Keeps well
Romano or Canadian bean	Strong Very bitter	Garbanzo Tapioca flour Cornstarch	Bread Cakes	Not suggested	148	Stores on shelf Keeps well High fiber
Soy	Strong Nutty	Rice	Fruited cakes Cookies	Never	82	Goes rancid easily Refrigerate
Sorghum	Heavy Sweet	Tapioca flour Cornstarch Bean flours	Cakes, Cookies Fruited breads	Sometimes	127	Cut sugar slightly in most recipes Stores on shelf

*A combination of garbanzo beans and fava beans from Authentic Foods.

These charts may make more sense if you know whether the flour comes from a grain, tuber, or seed.

ARROWROOT

This white flour is ground from the root of a West Indian plant and can be exchanged measure for measure with cornstarch in recipes and mixes if you are allergic to corn.

SUPPLEMENTAL FLOURS

Flour	Taste	Combines with	Best for	Used alone?	1-cup Weight (grams)	Suggestions
Arrowroot	Bland	Other flours in mixes	Replacing cornstarch in mixes	As thickening	127	Keeps well
Cornstarch	Bland	Other flours in mixes	Combining in mixes	As thickening	140	Store on pantry shelf
Potato flour	Dry, strong potato flavor	Featherlight Mix	Flavor and balance in mixes	No	185	Buy fresh in small quantities
Potato starch	Light potato flavor	Tapioca and rice flours	Balance in mixes	Seldom	187	Keeps well on pantry shelf
Sweet rice	Bland, grainy	Rice flour	Thickening bread dough	As thickening	162	Keeps well on pantry shelf
Tapioca starch	Bland	Rice, bean, or sorghum flours	Fruit dishes Use with other flours	As thickening	125	Keeps well on pantry shelf

GARBANZO BEAN FLOUR

Ground from garbanzo beans (often called chickpea or cici beans), this flour may be used in combination with Romano bean flour or used as called for in several of my bread recipes. This, like all bean products, is high in protein and food value.

GARFAVA FLOUR

This is a combination flour of garbanzo and fava beans produced by Authentic Foods (see suppliers, page 271). This smooth and easily stored flour is a staple in many of the bean recipes. It is the basic flour in my Light Bean Flour Mix and the new Four Flour Bean Mix. The few people sensitive to the fava bean may combine garbanzo and the Romano bean flours in the mixes or recipes calling for Garfava flour.

ROMANO BEAN FLOUR

This dark, strong-tasting bean flour is milled from the Romano (or cranberry) bean. The flour is high in fiber and can be used in many of my recipes but also combines well with garbanzo bean flour to make a lighter-tasting bean flour to be used in the Four Flour Bean Mix or Light Bean Flour Mix. It can be purchased in health food stores in Canada and by mail-order suppliers there. See suppliers, page 271.

BUCKWHEAT FLOUR

In spite of the unfortunate name, this flour is not related to wheat but to rhubarb. Because of its strong taste, it is more easily accepted when used in small amounts to give flavor to bland breads such as rice-based ones.

CORNSTARCH

This refined starch from corn is used in combination with other flours to make my baking mixes. If allergic to corn, replace this with arrowroot in mixes and recipes.

CORNMEAL

This meal, ground from corn, is used mostly in muffins and spoon bread.

CORN FLOUR

A flour milled from corn (maize), this can be blended with cornmeal when making corn breads and corn muffins.

POTATO STARCH FLOUR

Made from potatoes, this fine white flour is used in my Gluten-free Flour Mix. This keeps well and can be bought in quantity.

POTATO FLOUR

Do not confuse this with potato starch flour. This is a heavy flour but is a necessary ingredient in my new Featherlight Rice Flour Mix. Buy it in small quantities because you will need very little of it in the mix. Store this in the refrigerator.

WHITE RICE FLOUR

This very bland (and not very nutritious) flour milled from polished white rice doesn't distort the taste of any flavorings used. It has long been a basic in gluten-free baking, but the more nutritious bean flours are now gaining popularity. I use this in both my original Gluten-free Flour Mix and the new Featherlight Rice Flour Mix.

BROWN RICE FLOUR

Since this flour is milled from unpolished brown rice, it contains the bran and is higher in nutrient value than white rice flour. It can be used in both my Gluten-free Flour Mix and the Featherlight Rice Flour Mix. The slight bran taste will come out in the breads. Always store brown rice flour and any mix that contains it in the refrigerator or freezer because the oils in the bran have a tendency to become rancid rapidly.

SWEET RICE FLOUR

I use very little of this in my breads, but if your dough is too thin, it can be thickened with sweet rice flour. It is handy to have on hand for other thickenings, such as sauces. It can be stored at room temperature for long periods.

SORGHUM FLOUR

This new flour ground from specially bred sorghum grain and available from Jowar (see suppliers, page 273) was the impetus for many of the new bread recipes in this book. By combining the sorghum and beans, both flours proved more tasty and workable. This is stored on the pantry shelf.

SOY FLOUR

This high-protein, high-fat flour has a nutty taste and is most successful when combined with other flours. I use it more for cookies and cakes than for breads. Store in the refrigerator and always check before using to be sure it still tastes fresh.

TAPIOCA FLOUR

Made from the root of the cassava plant, this light, velvety white flour imparts "chew" to our baked goods. I use it in all my mixes. It can be stored at room temperature for a long time.

AMARANTH, QUINOA, MILLET, AND TEFF

These four flours, more exotic and less well known, have been accepted in Canada for years as gluten free. Some of the United States groups are coming to accept them since botanically they are not connected to the gluten-containing grains. As with all flours, there is always the chance that a person will be allergic to one or another. Since these have not been a staple of the diet here, introduction of any of these grains is best made slowly. An understanding of their botanical relatives may help to determine whether you should try these flours, which have nutritive value far surpassing that of rice.

Amaranth flour is ground from the seed of a plant related to pigweed.

Quinoa seeds come from the plant in a family related to spinach and beets. These grow with a bitter coating, so always buy debittered flour.

Millet and *Teff (Tef)* are grains in the same grass family as corn, rice, and sorghum.

SPELT, KAMUT, CLUB, DURUM, BULGUR, EINKORN, AND SEMOLINA

These are all different species of wheat and should be eliminated in any form from the gluten-free diet.

TRITICALE

This is a hybrid of rye and wheat. Not for a gluten-free diet!

All the information above is not going to help when you face that mixing bowl full of flours strange to you. If you don't want to turn out a doorstop or a panful of crumbs, I suggest starting with combinations that have proved to work in recipes already tested. If you keep on hand the four mixes given below, you can make almost every recipe in this book and will soon feel so confident that you can start experimenting on your own.

GLUTEN-FREE FLOUR MIX

This is the original mix I developed, and many suppliers carry it. It is a heavy mix and leaves a slightly grainy taste in the baked product, but the mix exchanges cup for cup with wheat flour in adapting recipes. Because of its low protein count, you must add extra protein and/or leavening (egg whites, dry milk or nondairy substitute, gelatin, Egg Replacer).

	For 9 cups	For 12 cups
Rice flour (white or brown) (2 parts)	6 cups	8 cups
Potato starch (⅔ part)	2 cups	2⅔ cups
Tapioca flour (⅓ part)	1 cup	1⅓ cups

LIGHT BEAN FLOUR MIX

This is my first bean flour mix as used in *The Gluten-free Gourmet Cooks Fast and Healthy*. It makes wonderful bread but will not exchange cup for cup with wheat flour and so is hard to use in adapting recipes—although it does contain more protein than rice flour mixes.

	For 9 cups	For 12 cups
Garfava bean flour (1 part)	3 cups	4 cups
Tapioca flour (1 part)	3 cups	4 cups
Cornstarch (1 part)	3 cups	4 cups

FOUR FLOUR BEAN MIX

This combination may revolutionize gluten-free baking. Not only does this exchange cup for cup with wheat flour, but it has enough protein so that in many cases you can take your regular cake or cookie recipe and not have to make any changes or additions except for some xanthan gum.

	For 9 cups	For 12 cups
Garfava bean flour (⅔ part)	2 cups	2⅔ cups
Sorghum flour (⅓ part)	1 cup	1⅓ cups
Cornstarch (1 part)	3 cups	4 cups
Tapioca flour (1 part)	3 cups	4 cups

FEATHERLIGHT RICE FLOUR MIX

Another new mix. This will turn out a lighter rice product and exchanges cup for cup with wheat flour. It does not contain the protein of the Four Flour Bean Mix and so is more difficult to use in adapting old wheat recipes. It can be substituted in any rice flour recipe to achieve better texture and a lighter baked product.

	For 9 cups	For 12 cups
Rice flour (1 part)	3 cups	4 cups
Tapioca flour (1 part)	3 cups	4 cups
Cornstarch (1 part)	3 cups	4 cups
Potato flour (*not* potato starch) (1 teaspoon per cup)	3 tablespoons	4 tablespoons

Working with these flours in tested recipes should give you the confidence you need, and then when you realize that gluten-free doughs seldom resemble or act like wheat doughs, you can try your own combinations. Start to improvise with additives such as eggs, flavorings, seeds, and nuts. Use those that taste best with the flour combinations.

And how do you tell? When I'm working on a new recipe, I taste the dry ingredients after mixing them by dipping a wet finger into the flours. This will give an idea of your true flour mix taste. If you have added sugar as in bread, it should be appealing to you. If for a cake, make allowance for the sugar, butter, and flavorings. But whatever you do, don't use the flour mix if it is too strong tasting or bitter because that will carry over into the baked product. Sometimes it can be toned down with the addition of a bit more tapioca flour or cornstarch, or sometimes more sugar. With bean flour, changing the white sugar to brown and adding a little molasses may control any bitterness.

Once in a while—and I admit it has happened to me—the flour has become stale or rancid. This happens because of incorrect storage at home or buying old flour; a store that sells very little of it may have stored it too long. No additives can remedy this problem. You'll have to abandon this baking and start with fresh flour.

You may wonder, "Just how much food value do our breads have? How do they compare to wheat breads?" I know the bean breads contain more food value than the rice breads, for I'm able to judge by my own reactions. When my breakfast toast is rice bread, I'm hungry by 11:00 A.M.; when it is bean bread, I have to remember to eat lunch. No chart has to tell me that something is filling me up.

But I know that others aren't satisfied with that explanation, so by checking around I filled out a table of some of the flour values. I secured these from various sources as well as from the U.S. Department of Agriculture. This is not very scientific because some of the percentages had to come from the producers of the product, and in many cases the figures do not add up to 100 percent.

Ordinarily I'm not happy when faced with numbers, but even I can see that they tell a story here. We have flours on our gluten-free list that have more protein and fiber than wheat flours. Isn't that great, even if we do have to lighten them with some that contain little but carbohydrates?

From a bit of calculating I can easily see that my GF Gourmet Mix using white rice flour is going to contain only about 4.14 percent protein and no fiber while the Bean Flour Mix contains 6.4 percent protein and 2.5 percent fiber. Go even further and add some brown rice flour (as I do for bread), and you get 7.2 percent protein and 2.71 percent fiber. This compares well with the wheat flour listed on the chart. And if you've read the back of any sack of all-purpose wheat flour, you'll note in most cases that barley and other enrichments have been added.

So we add the other enrichments to our bread. First we use eggs (protein and fat), and then we use milk or a milk substitute. Look at the chart below and see what these and other ingredients can add up to.

Dried milk gives us a lot of protein; so does the substitute Ener-G's Lacto-Free.

A COMPARISON OF GLUTEN-FREE FLOURS TO WHEAT FLOUR

FLOUR	CARBOHYDRATES %	PROTEIN %	FAT %	FIBER %	ADDITIONAL TRACE ELEMENTS
Amaranth	66	13	6	0	Iron, calcium
Bean (Canadian)	64	18.2	1.27	23.5	Iron rich
Buckwheat	72	11.5	0	1.6	B vitamins
Corn	76	7	1	14	Vitamin A
Cornmeal	77	8	3	10	Vitamin A
Cornstarch	88	Trace	0	Trace	Few trace elements
Garbanzo	60	20	4	12	Potassium
Garfava (Authentic Foods)	59	23	6.5	7.5	Iron rich
Millet	73	10	3	3	Magnesium
Potato	80	8	0.05	3.5	Phosphorus, potassium
Potato starch	77	0.05	0	0	Iron rich
Quinoa	66	12	5	7	Potassium, calcium
Rice (brown)	79	6	1	2	Vitamins, minerals
Rice (sweet)	80	6	0	0	Few trace elements
Rice (white)	76	6	0	0	Few trace elements
Sorghum	75	10	4	2	Iron, B vitamins
Soy	30	36	20	2.5	Amino acids
Tapioca	99	1	0	0	Few trace elements
Teff	71	11	4	3	Iron, some thiamin
Wheat Flour	76	10	1	3	

NutQuik or almond meal (found at health food stores) will add some fat, but this is good fat and helps the bread become tender while also adding protein and some fiber. Even more can be added with molasses, various seeds we use in specialty breads, and the nuts and raisins of sweet breads.

Because I use bean flour for most of my own bread, this doesn't mean that I abandoned using my rice mixes. In some recipes they work best, and for celiacs allergic to

ADDITIVE	CARBOHYDRATE %	PROTEIN %	FAT %	FIBER %	CHOLESTEROL %	SPECIAL
Dairy whey	75	12	0	0	0	Calcium rich
Dried milk (nonfat)	51	43	Trace	7	0	Calcium rich
Dried milk (regular)	38	38	26	7	12	High cholesterol
Ener-G Lacto-Free	31	45	0.9	22	0	Calcium, vitamin D
Flax Meal	20	20	46	23	0	Vitamins, minerals
NutQuik or Almond Meal	16	22	50	2	0	Fat is unsaturated
Rice Bran	28	11	15	27	0	High B vitamins
Ener-G SoyQuik	24	42	15	16	0	High B vitamins
Isomil (baby formula)	46	11	24	NA	0	Niacin
Buttermilk	55	20	Trace	0	Trace	Calcium rich

beans, they are the answer at this time. Also, in many recipes that have little flavor of their own, they don't overpower the delicate flavors such as vanilla, orange, or lemon. With the stronger-flavored bean, lentil, and brown rice flours, you have to complement or cover the flavor of the flour.

This is a lot to think about as you spoon flour and other ingredients into a mixing bowl, and many of you may feel as I do that the most important things are taste and texture. But according to the charts above, we are getting not only those but also good nutrition.

I have listed the more exotic and, to me, basically untested flours of amaranth, millet, quinoa, and teff to this chapter, but I have worked with only two of these flours at this time, quinoa and millet. (See Quinoa Bread, page 70; Quinoa Buns, page 168; and Basic Millet Bread, page 82.) When I find what I consider safe sources, there will still be the question of how they combine with the other flours in baking. Will they fight with the others or blend well? Only testing will tell.

For now I am convinced that we have gluten-free products that rival any wheat-based foods, and I can prove they are just as nutritious. What the future holds for celiacs can only be better health.

REFERENCES

Susan E. Gebhardt and Ruth H. Matthews, *Nutritive Value of Foods* (Washington, D.C.: U.S. Dept. of Agriculture, Home and Garden Bulletin No. 72, 1981 and 1988).

Marjorie Hurt Jones, R.N., *Super Foods: Amaranth, Quinoa, Kamut, Buckwheat, Spelt, Teff* (Coeur d'Alene, ID: Mast Enterprises, Inc., 1998).

Donald Kasarda, Ph.D., "Plant Toxonomy in Relation to Celiac Toxicity." Presentation at International Coeliac Symposium, Dublin, 1992.

Donald Kasarda, Ph.D., "Celiac Disease." Presentation at North American Society for Pediatric Gastroenterology and Nutrition, Toronto, Canada, October 1997.

Gayla J. Kirshman, *Nutrition Almanac, 4th ed.* (New York: McGraw Hill, 1996).

Laurel Robertson, *Laurel's Kitchen* (Berkeley, CA: Ten Speed Press, 1986).

Yeast Breads

Flour Mix Formulas

Bette's Four Flour Bread Mix

Bean-Based Breads

Bette's Four Flour Bread
Poppy Seed Bread
Oregon Bread
Sweet Granola Bread
Sesame Bean Bread
Walnut Bread
Basic Yogurt Bread
   Granola Yogurt Bread
   Cinnamon-Raisin Yogurt Bread
   Cinnamon-Nut Yogurt Bread
   Cranberry Yogurt Bread
   Cranberry-Cashew Yogurt Bread
   Herbed Yogurt Bread
Honey-Sweetened Hawaiian Bread

Basic Garbanzo Bread
   Sesame Garbanzo Bread
   Garbanzo Bread with Lemon and
     Poppy Seeds
Garbanzo Bread with Buttermilk
   Garbanzo-Based Sesame Seed Bread
   Garbanzo-Based Seed and Nut Bread
Orange Garbanzo Bread
   Orange-Walnut Garbanzo Bread
   Fruited Garbanzo Bread
Zucchini Cheese Bread
   Parmesan-Herb Yeast Bread
   Banana-Cheese Yeast Bread
Boston Bean Bread
Basic Carrot Bread
   Carrot and Seed Bread
   Carrot-Nut Bread
   Carrot-Raisin Bread
   Garden Bread
Quinoa Bread

Rice-Based Breads

Basic Featherlight Rice Bread
    Almond Featherlight Bread
    Lemon–Poppy Seed Rice Bread
    Almond-Cherry Rice Bread
    Almond-Apricot Bread
New French Bread
    Rosemary French
Buttermilk Casserole Bread
    Sesame Casserole Bread
    Casserole Seed Bread
    Orange-Nut Casserole Bread
    Spiced Fruit Casserole Bread
    Herbed Casserole Bread
Almond–Wild Rice Bread

Bean and Rice Breads

Touch o' Bean Bread
    Sesame Touch o' Bean
    Lemon–Poppy Seed Touch o' Bean

Breads with Other Grains

Basic Millet Bread
    Almond Millet Bread
    Cinnamon-Raisin Millet Bread
    Three-Seed Millet Bread
Basic Sorghum Bread
    Cinnamon-Nut Sorghum Loaf
    Raisin Filled Sorghum Bread
    Lemon–Poppy Seed Sorghum Bread

Sourdough Breads

Sourdough Starter
Honey Almond Sourdough
Seattle Sourdough
    Lemon–Poppy Seed Sourdough
    Sesame Seed Sourdough
Sourdough Rye

Rye Breads

Applesauce Rye Bread
Hawaiian Rye Bread
Swedish Rye Bread
Caraway Rye Bread

Egg-Free Breads

Egg-Free Bean Bread (Egg and
    Lactose Free)
    Egg-Free Poppy Seed Bread
    Egg-Free Sesame Seed Bread
    Egg-Free Raisin-Nut Bread
    Egg-Free Seed Bread
Flaxseed Bean Bread (Egg and
    Lactose Free)
    Sesame Seed Flaxseed Bread
    Seed and Nut Flaxseed Bread
    Cinnamon and Raisin Flaxseed Bread
New Allergy Rice Bread (Egg, Dairy, and
Soy Free)

Yeast Bread Recipes from Other Books in the Gluten-free Gourmet Series

Gone forever are the days of crumbly rice bread that won't stay together for a sandwich. This chapter of new and springy textured yeast breads using bean, sorghum, and/or rice flours should let you have any bread you can desire. I have used four different flour mixes and even created some breads blending several flours not used frequently. Three of the flour formulas are new, so please turn to page 40 for a full description of these formulas and recipes for making them in several amounts.

You'll find a new easy-to-use format to allow the choice of oven baking with different-sized loaves, making one loaf or two or, if you prefer, using one of the three sizes of bread machines (when the recipe is suitable). An explanation of the heading sizes follows:

> **Small:** One 8½" × 4½" loaf pan or a 1-pound bread machine
> **Medium:** One 9" × 5" loaf pan or a 1½-pound bread machine
> **Large:** Two 8½" × 4½" loaf pans or a 2-pound bread machine

If there is no medium size given, this means the bread is only suitable for loaves, as in French Bread, or for another baking pan (such as a casserole). The one exception is the Boston Bean Bread (page 66), which has an explanation in the Note.

If you want to use a favorite yeast bread recipe from my other books, you will find them listed at the end of this chapter (page 107).

Flour Mix Formulas

	For 9 cups	For 12 cups
Gluten-free Flour Mix (original rice mix)		
Rice flour (2 parts)	6 cups	8 cups
Potato starch (⅔ part)	2 cups	2⅔ cups
Tapioca flour (⅓ part)	1 cup	1⅓ cups
Light Bean Flour Mix		
(from *Fast and Healthy*)		
Garfava bean flour* (1 part)	3 cups	4 cups
Tapioca flour (1 part)	3 cups	4 cups
Cornstarch (1 part)	3 cups	4 cups
Four Flour Bean Mix (new)		
Garfava bean flour* (⅔ part)	2 cups	2⅔ cups
Sorghum flour† (⅓ part)	1 cup	1⅓ cups
Cornstarch (1 part)	3 cups	4 cups
Tapioca flour (1 part)	3 cups	4 cups
Featherlight Rice Flour Mix (new)		
Rice flour (1 part)	3 cups	4 cups
Tapioca flour (1 part)	3 cups	4 cups
Cornstarch (1 part)	3 cups	4 cups
Potato flour‡ (1 teaspoon per cup)	3 tablespoons	4 tablespoons

*Garfava flour is from Authentic Foods.
†Sorghum flour can be obtained from Jowar.
‡This is potato flour, not potato starch.

Bette's Four Flour Bread Mix

Keep a bag of this basic mix on your pantry shelf, and you can make up any number of tasty breads in minutes without the fuss of measuring any dry ingredients.* I've given a few variations, but this mild-flavored bread can take other additions, including cocoa powder, grains, nuts, and a whole variety of fruits. Make it with water, as the original recipe suggests, or use fruit juice, milk (or milk substitute), or a carbonated beverage. Use your imagination or get ideas from the many bread recipes now being published for wheat breads.

Note: *To blend this thoroughly use either a large container and stir well or place in a strong plastic kitchen bag and tumble to mix.*

	12 cups (6 single loaves)	24 cups (12 single loaves)
Garfava bean flour	3 cups	6 cups
Sorghum flour	1 cup	2 cups
Tapioca flour	4 cups	8 cups
Cornstarch	4 cups	8 cups
Xanthan gum	3 tablespoons	6 tablespoons
Salt	1 tablespoon	2 tablespoons
Egg Replacer	1 tablespoon	2 tablespoons
Unflavored gelatin (optional)	3 (7-gram) envelopes	6 (7-gram) envelopes
Sugar	¾ cup	1½ cups

*Dry yeast granules must be added at the time of making up the bread recipes.

Bette's Four Flour Bread

A mild-flavored, wonderfully springy bread that has become my basic bread. Use it plain as shown here or vary it in a dozen different ways. The bread mix recipe given below enables you to make tasty breads in minutes without the fuss of measuring any dry ingredients. Keep a bag of it on your pantry shelf.

DRY INGREDIENTS	SMALL	MEDIUM	LARGE
Bette's Four Flour Bread Mix (page 41)	2¼ cups	3⅓ cups	4½ cups
Dry yeast granules	2¼ teaspoons	2¼ teaspoons	2¼ teaspoons
WET INGREDIENTS			
Eggs	1 plus 1 white	1 plus 2 whites	1 plus 3 whites
Margarine or butter	3 tablespoons	4½ tablespoons	⅓ cup
Dough enhancer or vinegar	½ teaspoon	¾ teaspoon	1 teaspoon
Warm water, milk, or nondairy substitute (more or less)	1 cup	1½ cups	2 cups

Grease your chosen pan(s) and dust with rice flour.

The liquid temperature will be different for hand mixing and bread machines. For hand mixing have it about 110° to 115°; for your bread machine, read the directions in the manual.

For both hand mixing and machine mixing, combine the dry ingredients in a medium bowl. Set aside.

In another bowl (or the bowl of your heavy-duty mixer), whisk the egg and white(s), margarine, and dough enhancer. Add most of the water. The remaining water should be added as needed after the bread has started mixing, either in the bowl of your mixer or in the pan of the bread machine.

For hand mixing: With the mixer turned to low, add the dry ingredients (including the yeast) a little at a time. Check to be sure the dough is the right consistency (should be like cake batter). Add more of the reserved water as necessary. Turn the mixer to high and beat for 3½ minutes. Spoon the dough into the prepared pan(s), cover, and let rise in a warm place about 35–45 minutes for rapid-rising yeast, 60 or more minutes for regular yeast or until the dough reaches the top of the pan. Bake in a preheated 400° oven for 50–60 minutes, covering after 10 minutes with aluminum foil.

For bread machine: Place the ingredients in the bread machine in the order suggested by your machine manual. Use the setting for white bread with medium crust.

VARIATIONS:

LEMON–POPPY SEED: For each cup of mix used, add 1 teaspoon dried lemon peel and 1 teaspoon poppy seeds to the dry ingredients.

QUINOA BREAD: For each cup of mix used, add 1 tablespoon quinoa flour to the dry ingredients and 1 teaspoon honey to the wet ingredients.

ALMOND BREAD: For each cup of mix used, add 1½ tablespoons almond meal to the dry ingredients and ½ teaspoon almond flavor to the wet ingredients.

CINNAMON-NUT: For each cup of mix used, add ½ teaspoon cinnamon to the dry ingredients and stir in 2 tablespoons chopped nuts after the dough is mixed when baking by hand; when using a bread machine, add the nuts when the machine manual suggests.

SESAME BEAN BREAD: For each cup of mix used, add 1 tablespoon toasted sesame seeds to the dry ingredients and 1 teaspoon molasses to the wet ingredients.

Nutrients per slice: Calories 90, Fat 3g, Carbohydrate 14g, Cholesterol 0mg, Sodium 90mg, Fiber 1g, Protein 3g.
Dietary exchanges: Bread 1, Fat ½.

Poppy Seed Bread
400°

Another great textured bread. This lemony poppy seed bread is one I make often for sandwiches because the flavor doesn't overpower cheeses or even mild-flavored meats like chicken breast, and it has enough flavor to be eaten plain. This is especially great for morning toast and jam.

DRY INGREDIENTS	SMALL	MEDIUM	LARGE
Four Flour Bean Mix (page 41)	2 cups	3 cups	4 cups
Xanthan gum	1½ teaspoons	2¼ teaspoons	3 teaspoons
Egg Replacer	1 teaspoon	1½ teaspoons	2 teaspoons
Unflavored gelatin	1 teaspoon	1½ teaspoons	2 teaspoons
Salt	½ teaspoon	¾ teaspoon	1 teaspoon
Sugar	3 tablespoons	4½ tablespoons	⅓ cup
NutQuik or almond meal	2 tablespoons	3 tablespoons	4 tablespoons
Lemon zest	2 teaspoons	3 teaspoons	4 teaspoons
Dry yeast granules	2¼ teaspoons	2¼ teaspoons	2¼ teaspoons
Poppy seeds	2 teaspoons	3 teaspoons	4 teaspoons
WET INGREDIENTS			
Instant potato flakes	1 teaspoon	1½ teaspoons	2 teaspoons
Warm water (more or less)	1 cup	1½ cups	2 cups
Eggs	1 plus 1 white	1 plus 2 whites	1 plus 3 whites
Margarine or butter	3 tablespoons	4½ tablespoons	6 tablespoons
Dough enhancer or vinegar	½ teaspoon	¾ teaspoon	1 teaspoon

Grease your chosen pan(s) and dust with rice flour.

In a medium bowl, whisk together the dry ingredients.

Dissolve the potato flakes in the cup of warm water. Set aside.

For hand mixing: In the bowl of your mixer, place the eggs and white, add the margarine (cut into small chunks) and dough enhancer. Beat on low until the eggs are foamy. Add most of the potato water, reserving about 2 tablespoons to add later if needed. With the mixer on low, add the flour (including the yeast) a little at a time. Beat on high and then check to see if you need the reserved water to achieve a cakelike texture. Beat 3 minutes on high. Spoon into the prepared pan(s).

Let rise until the dough reaches the top of the pan (about 35–45 minutes for rapid-rising yeast, and 60–80 minutes for regular). Bake in a preheated 400° oven for 50–60 minutes, covering after 10 minutes with aluminum foil. Turn out of the pan and rub top with margarine or butter for a softer crust. Cool before slicing.

For bread machine: Follow directions in the machine manual for the order in which ingredients are placed in the pan. Use water at the temperature instructed.

Nutrients per slice: Calories 90, Fat 3g, Carbohydrate 15g, Cholesterol 0mg, Sodium 90mg, Fiber 1g.
Dietary exchanges: Bread 1, Fat ½.

Oregon Bread

400°

This wonderful bread filled with seeds and nuts is one of my testers' favorites. Try it when you want a fiber-filled treat.

DRY INGREDIENTS	SMALL	MEDIUM	LARGE
Four Flour Bean Mix (page 40)	2 cups	3 cups	4 cups
Xanthan gum	1½ teaspoons	2¼ teaspoons	3 teaspoons
Salt	½ teaspoon	¾ teaspoon	1 teaspoon
Unflavored gelatin	1 teaspoon	1½ teaspoons	2 teaspoons
Egg Replacer	1 teaspoon	1½ teaspoons	2 teaspoons
Brown sugar	1 tablespoon	2 tablespoons	3 tablespoons
Chopped hazelnuts	¼ cup	⅓ cup	½ cup
Sesame seeds	1 tablespoon	1½ tablespoons	2 tablespoons
Poppy seeds	1 teaspoon	1½ teaspoons	2 teaspoons
Flax seeds	1 teaspoon	1½ teaspoons	2 teaspoons
Dry yeast granules	2½ teaspoons	2½ teaspoons	2½ teaspoons
WET INGREDIENTS			
Eggs	1 plus 1 white	1 plus 2 whites	1 plus 3 whites
Honey	2 tablespoons	3 tablespoons	4 tablespoons
Margarine or butter	2 tablespoons	3 tablespoons	4 tablespoons
Dough enhancer or vinegar	½ teaspoon	¾ teaspoon	1 teaspoon
Warm water (more or less)	1 cup	1½ cups	2 cups

Grease your chosen pan(s) and dust with rice flour.

The water temperature will be different for hand mixing and for bread machines. For hand mixing have it about 110°; for your bread machine, read the directions in the manual.

For both hand mixing and machine mixing, combine the dry ingredients in a medium bowl. Set aside.

In another bowl (or the bowl of your heavy-duty mixer), whisk the eggs slightly and add the honey, margarine (cut in pieces), dough enhancer, and most of the water. The remaining water should be added as needed after the bread has started mixing, either in the bowl of your mixer or in the pan of the bread machine.

For hand mixing: With the mixer turned to low, add the dry ingredients (including the yeast) a little at a time to the liquids. Check to see if more water is necessary. The dough should resemble cake batter. Turn the mixer to high and beat for 3½ minutes. Spoon into the prepared pan(s), cover, and let rise about 35–45 minutes for rapid-rising yeast, 60 or more minutes for regular yeast. Bake in a preheated 400° oven for 50–60 minutes, covering after 10 minutes with aluminum foil.

For bread machine: Place the ingredients in the bread machine in the order suggested in the machine manual. Use the setting for white bread with a medium crust.

Nutrients per slice: Calories 110, Fat 4g, Carbohydrate 16g, Cholesterol 10mg, Sodium 110mg, Fiber 1g, Protein 3g.
Dietary exchanges: Bread 1, Fat 1.

Sweet Granola Bread 400°

Full of fiber, delicious, and easy to make if you have granola on hand, whether it is homemade or some of Ener-G-Food's packaged Trail Mix. Or just toss seeds, nuts, dried fruit, and some GF breakfast cereal in your food processor with some sweet coconut flakes (if desired) and grind out enough for the bread.

DRY INGREDIENTS	SMALL	MEDIUM	LARGE
Granola	½ cup	¾ cup	1 cup
Four Flour Bean Mix (page 40)	2 cups	3 cups	4 cups
Xanthan gum	1½ teaspoons	2¼ teaspoons	3 teaspoons
Egg Replacer	1 teaspoon	1 teaspoon	1 teaspoon
Unflavored gelatin	1 teaspoon	1½ teaspoons	2 teaspoons
Salt	½ teaspoon	¾ teaspoon	1 teaspoon
Sugar	3 tablespoons	4½ tablespoons	6 tablespoons
Almond meal or NutQuik	2 tablespoons	3 tablespoons	4 tablespoons
Yeast	2¼ teaspoons	2¼ teaspoons	2¼ teaspoons
WET INGREDIENTS			
Eggs	1 plus 1 white	1 plus 2 whites	1 plus 3 whites
Margarine or butter	3 tablespoons	4½ tablespoons	6 tablespoons
Dough enhancer or vinegar	½ teaspoon	¾ teaspoon	1 teaspoon
Warm water (more or less)	1 cup	1½ cups	2 cups

Grease your chosen pan(s) and dust with rice flour.

The water temperature will be different for hand mixing and for bread machines. For hand mixing have water at about 110°; for your bread machine, read the directions in the manual.

For both hand mixing and machine mixing, measure the granola and set aside in a small bowl. Combine the other dry ingredients in a medium bowl and set aside.

In another bowl (or the bowl of your heavy-duty mixer) whisk the egg and white(s), margarine (in chunks), dough enhancer, and most of the water. The remaining water should be added as needed after the bread has started mixing, either in the bowl of your mixer or in the pan of the bread machine.

For hand mixing: With the mixer turned to low, add the dry ingredients (including the yeast but with the exception of the granola) a little at a time. Check to be sure the dough is the right consistency (like cake batter). Add more of the reserved water as necessary. Turn the mixer to high and beat for 3½ minutes. Stir in the granola. Spoon the dough into the prepared pan(s), cover, and let rise about 35 minutes for rapid-rising yeast, 60 or more minutes for regular yeast (or until the dough reaches slightly above the top of the pan). Bake in a preheated 400° oven for 50–60 minutes, covering after 10 minutes with aluminum foil.

For bread machine: Place the ingredients in the bread machine in the order suggested in the machine manual. Use the setting for light crust. After the dough has mixed and you have determined that it is the right consistency, add the granola.

Nutrients per slice: Calories 100, Fat 3g, Carbohydrate 16g, Cholesterol 10mg, Sodium 95mg, Fiber 1g, Protein 3g.
Dietary exchanges: Bread 1, Fat ½.

Sesame Bean Bread   400°

This recipe from The Gluten-free Gourmet Cooks Fast and Healthy *is so special I have repeated it in this book. As the basic bread at my house, it means toast for breakfast, a sandwich for lunch, and raves from everyone who tastes it. Not only is the flavor wonderful, but the texture is that of regular wheat breads. No more lapful of crumbs when you take a bite.*

DRY INGREDIENTS	SMALL	MEDIUM	LARGE
Light Bean Flour Mix (page 40)	2 cups	3 cups	4 cups
Xanthan gum	1½ teaspoons	2¼ teaspoons	3 teaspoons
Salt	½ teaspoon	¾ teaspoon	1 teaspoon
Unflavored gelatin	1 teaspoon	1½ teaspoons	2 teaspoons
Brown sugar	2 tablespoons	3 tablespoons	4 tablespoons
Egg Replacer	1 teaspoon	1½ teaspoons	2 teaspoons
Toasted sesame seeds	1 tablespoon	1½ tablespoons	2 tablespoons
Dry yeast granules	2¼ teaspoons	2¼ teaspoons	2¼ teaspoons
WET INGREDIENTS			
Eggs	1 plus 1 white	1 plus 2 whites	1 plus 3 whites
Dough enhancer or vinegar	½ teaspoon	¾ teaspoon	1 teaspoon
Margarine or butter	3 tablespoons	4¼ tablespoons	5½ tablespoons
Molasses	2 teaspoons	3 teaspoons	4 teaspoons
Water (more or less)	1¼ cups	1¾ cups	2½ cups

Grease your chosen pan(s) and dust with rice flour.

The water temperature will be different for hand mixing and for bread machines. For hand mixing have it about 110°; for your bread machine, read the directions in the manual.

For both hand mixing and machine mixing, combine the dry ingredients in a medium bowl. Set aside.

In another bowl or the bowl of your heavy-duty mixer, whisk the egg and white(s) slightly and add the dough enhancer, margarine (cut in chunks), molasses, and most of the water. The remaining water should be added as needed after the bread has started mixing, either in the bowl of your mixer or in the pan of the bread machine.

For hand mixing: Turn the mixer to low and add the dry ingredients (including the yeast) a little at a time. Check to be sure the dough is the right consistency (like cake batter). Add more of the reserved water as necessary. Turn the mixer to high and beat for 3½ minutes. Spoon into the prepared pan(s), cover, and let rise in a warm place about 35 minutes for rapid-rising yeast, 60 or more minutes for regular yeast or until the dough reaches the top of the pan. Bake in a preheated 400° oven for 50–60 minutes, covering after 10 minutes with aluminum foil.

For bread machine: Place the ingredients in the bread machine in the order suggested in the machine manual. Use the setting for white bread with medium crust.

Nutrients per slice: Calories 90, Fat 3g, Carbohydrate 14g, Cholesterol 10mg, Sodium 95mg, Fiber 1g, Protein 2g.
Dietary exchanges: Bread 1, Fat 1.

Walnut Bread   400°

This is another of the springy textured, wonderfully flavored new breads from the new formulas.

DRY INGREDIENTS	SMALL	MEDIUM	LARGE
Four Flour Bean Mix (page 40)	2 cups	3 cups	4 cups
Xanthan gum	1½ teaspoons	2¼ teaspoons	3 teaspoons
Salt	½ teaspoon	¾ teaspoon	1 teaspoon
Unflavored gelatin	1 teaspoon	1½ teaspoons	2 teaspoons
Egg Replacer	1 teaspoon	1½ teaspoons	2 teaspoons
Brown sugar	2 tablespoons	3 tablespoons	4 tablespoons
Dry yeast granules	2¼ teaspoons	2¼ teaspoons	2¼ teaspoons
WET INGREDIENTS			
Eggs	1 plus 1 white	1 plus 2 whites	1 plus 3 whites
Honey	1 tablespoon	1½ tablespoons	2 tablespoons
Walnut or vegetable oil	2 tablespoons	3 tablespoons	4 tablespoons
Dough enhancer or vinegar	½ teaspoon	¾ teaspoon	1 teaspoon
Warm water (more or less)	¾ cup	1⅛ cups	1½ cups
Chopped walnuts	½ cup	¾ cup	1 cup

Grease your chosen pan(s) and dust with rice flour.

For both hand mixing and machine mixing, combine the dry ingredients in a medium bowl. Set aside.

In another bowl (or the bowl of your heavy-duty mixer), whisk the egg and white(s), honey, oil, and dough enhancer. Add most of the water. The remaining water should be added as needed after the bread has started mixing, either in the bowl of your mixer or in the pan of the bread machine.

For hand mixing: With the mixer turned to low, add the dry ingredients (including the yeast) a little at a time. Check to be sure the dough is the right consistency (should be like cake batter). Add more of the reserved water as necessary. Turn the mixer to high and beat for 3½ minutes. Stir in the walnuts. Spoon the dough into the prepared pan(s), cover, and let rise about 35–45 minutes for rapid-rising yeast, 60 or more minutes for regular yeast or until the dough reaches the top of the pan. Bake in a preheated 400° oven for 50–60 minutes, covering after 10 minutes with aluminum foil.

For bread machine: Place the ingredients in the bread machine in the order suggested in the machine manual. Use the setting for white bread with medium crust and add the walnuts as the manual suggests.

Nutrients per slice: Calories 100, Fat 3g, Carbohydrate 5g, Cholesterol 10mg, Sodium 75mg, Fiber 1g, Protein 3g.
Dietary exchanges: Bread 1, Fat 1.

Basic Yogurt Bread

400°

Moist, tender, and delicious, this bread adapts well to many variations in flavor with the addition of fruit, nuts, seeds, or herbs. For the lactose-intolerant celiac this may be a way of adding protein to the bread since yogurt seems to be easier to tolerate than any other form of milk. Note the larger amount of yeast used in this bread.

DRY INGREDIENTS	SMALL	MEDIUM	LARGE
Four Flour Bean Mix (page 40)	2 cups	3 cups	4 cups
Xanthan gum	1½ teaspoons	2¼ teaspoons	3 teaspoons
Salt	½ teaspoon	¾ teaspoon	1 teaspoon
Unflavored gelatin	1 teaspoon	1½ teaspoons	2 teaspoons
Egg Replacer	1 teaspoon	1½ teaspoons	2 teaspoons
Baking soda	½ teaspoon	¾ teaspoon	1 teaspoon
Sugar	3 tablespoons	4½ tablespoons	6 tablespoons
Dried lemon peel	1 teaspoon	1½ teaspoons	2 teaspoons
Dry yeast granules	1 tablespoon	1 tablespoon	1 tablespoon
WET INGREDIENTS			
Eggs	1 plus 1 white	1 plus 2 whites	1 plus 3 whites
Margarine or butter	3 tablespoons	4½ tablespoons	6 tablespoons
Dough enhancer	½ teaspoon	¾ teaspoon	1 teaspoon
Honey	½ tablespoon	¾ tablespoon	1 tablespoon
Yogurt (warmed to 110°)	¾ cup	1⅛ cups	1½ cups
Warm water (more or less)	½ cup	¾ cup	1 cup

Grease your chosen pan(s) and dust with rice flour.

The water temperature will be different for hand mixing and for bread machines. For hand mixing have it about 110°; for your bread machine, read the directions in the manual.

For both hand mixing and machine mixing, combine the dry ingredients in a medium bowl. Set aside.

In another bowl (or the bowl of your heavy-duty mixer), whisk the egg and white(s), margarine (cut in chunks), dough enhancer, and honey. Warm the yogurt in the microwave (40 seconds on high for ¾ cup). Add this plus most of the warm water. The remaining water should be added as needed after the bread has started mixing, either in the bowl of your mixer or in the pan of the bread machine.

For hand mixing: With the mixer turned to low, add the dry ingredients (including the yeast) a little at a time. Check to be sure the dough is the right consistency (should be like cake batter). Add more of the reserved water as necessary. Turn the mixer to high and beat for 3½ minutes. Spoon the dough into the prepared pan(s), cover, and let rise about 35–45 minutes for rapid-rising yeast, 60 or more minutes for regular yeast or until the dough reaches the top of the pan. Bake in a preheated 400° oven for 50–60 minutes, covering after 10 minutes with aluminum foil.

For bread machine: Place ingredients in the bread machine in the order suggested in the machine manual. Use the setting for white bread with medium crust.

VARIATIONS: The amounts given are for the small recipe. Increase proportionately for larger recipes.

GRANOLA YOGURT BREAD: Add ⅓ cup homemade or purchased gluten-free granola to the dry ingredients.

CINNAMON-RAISIN YOGURT BREAD: Substitute cinnamon for the lemon peel and add ⅓ cup raisins to the dough after mixing.

CINNAMON-NUT YOGURT BREAD: Substitute cinnamon for the lemon peel and add ⅓ cup chopped walnuts to the dough after mixing.

CRANBERRY YOGURT BREAD: Stir in ⅓ cup dried cranberries to the dough after mixing.

CRANBERRY-CASHEW YOGURT BREAD: Stir in ¼ cup dried cranberries and ¼ cup chopped cashews to the dough after mixing.

HERBED YOGURT BREAD: Add 1 to 2 teaspoons crushed fresh rosemary, dill, or other herbs to the dry ingredients. If you substitute dried herbs, cut the amount by half.

Nutrients per slice: Calories 100, Fat 3g, Carbohydrate 16g, Cholesterol 15mg, Sodium 135mg, Fiber 1g, Protein 3g.
Dietary exchanges: Bread 1, Fat 1.

Honey-Sweetened Hawaiian Bread

With its springy texture and hint of the tropics, this bread is great either for breakfast toast or a luncheon sandwich.

DRY INGREDIENTS	SMALL	MEDIUM	LARGE
Four Flour Bean Mix (page 40)	2 cups	3 cups	4 cups
Xanthan gum	1½ teaspoons	2¼ teaspoons	3 teaspoons
Baking soda	¼ teaspoon	⅓ teaspoon	½ teaspoon
Salt	½ teaspoon	¾ teaspoon	1 teaspoon
Egg Replacer (optional)	1 teaspoon	1 teaspoon	1 teaspoon
NutQuik or almond meal	3 tablespoons	4½ tablespoons	6 tablespoons
Dried orange peel	¾ teaspoon	1¼ teaspoons	1½ teaspoons
Unflavored gelatin	1 teaspoon	1½ teaspoons	2 teaspoons
Yeast	4 teaspoons	4 teaspoons	4 teaspoons
WET INGREDIENTS			
Eggs	1 plus 1 white	1 plus 2 whites	1 plus 3 whites
Dough enhancer or vinegar	½ teaspoon	¾ teaspoon	1 teaspoon
Honey	2 tablespoons	3 tablespoons	4 tablespoons
Margarine or butter	3 tablespoons	4½ tablespoons	⅓ cup
One (6-ounce) can Pineapple, Orange, Banana Juice		9 ounces	12 ounces
Water	¼ cup	⅓ cup	½ cup

Grease your chosen pan(s) and dust with rice flour.

The combined water and juice temperature will be different for hand mixing and for bread machines. For hand mixing have the liquids about 110°; for your bread machine, read the directions in the manual.

For both hand mixing and machine mixing, combine the dry ingredients in a medium bowl and set aside.

In another bowl (or the bowl of your heavy-duty mixer) whisk the egg and white(s), dough enhancer, honey, and margarine (in chunks) until blended. Combine the water and juice, and warm to the desired temperature. Add most of it to the liquids. The rest should be added as needed after the bread has started mixing, either in the bowl of your mixer or in the pan of the bread machine.

For hand mixing: With the mixer turned to low, add the dry ingredients (including the yeast) a little at a time. Check to be sure the dough is the right consistency (should be like cake batter). Add more of the reserved juice and water blend as necessary. Turn the mixer to high and beat for 3½ minutes. Spoon into the prepared pan(s), cover, and let rise in a warm place for about 35 minutes for rapid-rising yeast, 60 or more minutes for regular yeast or until the dough reaches the top of the pan. Bake in a preheated 375° oven for 50–55 minutes, covering after 10 minutes with aluminum foil.

For bread machine: Place the ingredients in the bread machine pan in the order suggested in the machine manual. Use the setting for light crust.

Nutrients per slice: Calories 110, Fat 3g, Carbohydrate 17g, Cholesterol 10mg, Sodium 115mg, Fiber 1g, Protein 3g.
Dietary exchanges: Bread 1, Fat 1.

Basic Garbanzo Bread 400°

This recipe and its variations were created for those readers who prefer garbanzo bean flour to the mixed bean flour from Authentic Foods. Because garbanzo flour absorbs more water than the Authentic Foods flour, this bread will be slightly heavier but is still lighter and has a more springy texture than any rice bread.

DRY INGREDIENTS	SMALL	MEDIUM	LARGE
Garbanzo bean flour	⅓ cup	½ cup	⅔ cup
Sorghum flour	⅓ cup	½ cup	⅔ cup
Tapioca flour	⅔ cup	1 cup	1⅓ cups
Cornstarch	⅔ cup	1 cup	1⅓ cups
Xanthan gum	1½ teaspoons	2¼ teaspoons	3 teaspoons
Salt	½ teaspoon	¾ teaspoon	1 teaspoon
Unflavored gelatin	1 teaspoon	1 teaspoon	1 teaspoon
Brown sugar	2 tablespoons	3 tablespoons	4 tablespoons
Egg Replacer	1 teaspoon	1 teaspoon	1 teaspoon
Almond meal	2 tablespoons	3 tablespoons	4 tablespoons
Dry yeast granules	2½ teaspoons	2½ teaspoons	2½ teaspoons

WET INGREDIENTS			
Eggs	1 plus 1 white	1 plus 2 whites	1 plus 3 whites
Margarine or butter	3 tablespoons	4½ tablespoons	⅓ cup
Dough enhancer or vinegar	½ teaspoon	¾ teaspoon	1 teaspoon
Honey	2 teaspoons	3 teaspoons	4 teaspoons
Warm water (more or less)	1 cup	1½ cups	2 cups

Grease your chosen pan(s) and dust with rice flour.

The water temperature will be different for hand mixing and bread machines. For hand mixing have it about 110° to 115°; for your bread machine, read the directions in the manual.

For both hand mixing and machine mixing, combine the dry ingredients in a medium bowl. Set aside.

In another bowl (or the bowl of your heavy-duty mixer), whisk the egg and white(s), margarine, dough enhancer, and honey. Add most of the water. The remaining water should be added as needed after the bread has started mixing, either in the bowl of your mixer or in the pan of the bread machine.

For hand mixing: With the mixer turned to low, add the dry ingredients (including the yeast) a little at a time. Check to be sure the dough is the right consistency (should be like cake batter). Add more of the reserved water as necessary. Turn the mixer to high and beat for 3½ minutes. Spoon the dough into the prepared pan(s), cover, and let rise about 35–45 minutes for rapid-rising yeast, 60 or more minutes for regular yeast or until the dough reaches the top of the pan. Bake in a preheated 400° oven for 50–60 minutes, covering after 10 minutes with aluminum foil.

For bread machine: Place the ingredients in the bread machine in the order suggested in the machine manual. Use the setting for white bread with medium crust.

VARIATIONS: Changes are given for the small recipe; increase proportionately for other recipes.

SESAME GARBANZO BREAD: Add 1 tablespoon toasted sesame seeds to the dry ingredients. Change honey to molasses in the wet ingredients.

GARBANZO BREAD WITH LEMON AND POPPY SEEDS: Add 2 teaspoons dried lemon peel and 2 teaspoons poppy seeds to the dry ingredients.

Nutrients per slice: Calories 90, Fat 3g, Carbohydrate 15g, Cholesterol 10mg, Sodium 120mg, Fiber 2g, Protein 2g.
Dietary exchanges: Bread 1, Fat ½.

Garbanzo Bread with Buttermilk   400°

Buttermilk lightens this interesting bread with its mild, nutty taste. Use any filling you wish in sandwiches since the taste will not overpower the filling. This flavor is especially tasty used for French toast and in bread puddings.

DRY INGREDIENTS	SMALL	MEDIUM	LARGE
Garbanzo bean flour	⅓ cup	½ cup	⅔ cup
Sorghum flour	⅓ cup	½ cup	⅔ cup
Tapioca flour	⅔ cup	1 cup	1⅓ cups
Cornstarch	⅔ cup	1 cup	1⅓ cups
Xanthan gum	1½ teaspoons	2¼ teaspoons	3 teaspoons
Egg Replacer	1 teaspoon	1½ teaspoons	2 teaspoons
Salt	½ teaspoon	1 teaspoon	1 rounded teaspoon
Unflavored gelatin	1 teaspoon	1½ teaspoons	2 teaspoons
Sugar	3 tablespoons	4½ tablespoons	6 tablespoons
Buttermilk powder	⅓ cup	½ cup	⅔ cup
Yeast	2¼ teaspoons	2¼ teaspoons	2¼ teaspoons

WET INGREDIENTS			
Eggs	1 plus 1 white	1 plus 2 whites	1 plus 3 whites
Margarine or butter	3 tablespoons	4½ tablespoons	6 tablespoons
Dough enhancer or vinegar	½ teaspoon	¾ teaspoon	1 teaspoon
Warm water (more or less)	1 cup	1½ cups	2 cups

Grease your chosen pan(s) and dust with rice flour.

   The water temperature will be different for hand mixing and for bread machines. For hand mixing have it about 110°; for your bread machine, read the directions in the manual.

   For both hand mixing and machine baking, combine the dry ingredients in a medium bowl. Set aside.

   In another bowl (or the bowl of your heavy-duty mixer), whisk the egg and white(s), margarine, and dough enhancer. Add most of the water. The remaining water should be added as needed after the bread has started mixing, either in the bowl of your mixer or in the pan of the bread machine.

For hand mixing: With the mixer turned to low, add the dry ingredients (including the yeast) a little at a time. Check to be sure the dough is the right consistency (should be like cake batter). Add more of the reserved water as necessary. Turn the mixer to high and beat for 3½ minutes. Spoon the dough into the prepared pan(s), cover, and let rise about 35–45 minutes for rapid-rising yeast, 60 or more minutes for regular yeast or until the dough reaches the top of the pan. Bake in a preheated 400° oven for 50–60 minutes, covering after 10 minutes with aluminum foil.

For bread machine: Place the ingredients in the bread machine in the order suggested in the machine manual. Use the setting for white bread with medium crust.

VARIATIONS: Measurements are given for the small size. Increase proportionately for other sizes.

GARBANZO-BASED SESAME SEED BREAD: Add 1 tablespoon sesame seeds to the dry ingredients.

GARBANZO-BASED SEED AND NUT BREAD: Add 2 teaspoons sesame seeds, 2 teaspoons chopped pumpkin seeds, and ¼ cup chopped hazelnuts to the dry ingredients.

Nutrients per slice: Calories 90, Fat 2.5g, Carbohydrate 16g, Cholesterol 15mg, Sodium 105mg, Fiber 1g, Protein 2g.
Dietary exchanges: Bread 1, Fat ½.

Orange Garbanzo Bread 400°

Some basic changes turn the garbanzo bread into a fruit-flavored treat. This takes well to the addition of nuts, raisins, or dried fruit. See variations below.

DRY INGREDIENTS	SMALL	MEDIUM	LARGE
Garbanzo bean flour	⅓ cup	½ cup	⅔ cup
Sorghum flour	⅓ cup	½ cup	⅔ cup
Tapioca flour	⅔ cup	1 cup	1⅓ cups
Cornstarch	⅔ cup	1 cup	1⅓ cups
Xanthan gum	1½ teaspoons	2¼ teaspoons	3 teaspoons
Salt	¾ teaspoon	1 teaspoon	1 rounded teaspoon
Baking soda	¼ teaspoon	⅓ teaspoon	½ teaspoon
Unflavored gelatin	1 teaspoon	1½ teaspoons	2 teaspoons
Sugar	2 tablespoons	3 tablespoons	4 tablespoons
Egg Replacer	1 teaspoon	1½ teaspoons	2 teaspoons
Dried orange peel	1 teaspoon	1½ teaspoons	2 teaspoons
Almond meal	3 tablespoons	4½ tablespoons	6 tablespoons
Dry yeast granules	2¼ teaspoons	2¼ teaspoons	2¼ teaspoons
WET INGREDIENTS			
Eggs	1 plus 2 whites	1 plus 2 whites	1 plus 3 whites
Margarine or butter	3 tablespoons	4½ tablespoons	6 tablespoons
Dough enhancer or vinegar	½ teaspoon	¾ teaspoon	1 teaspoon
Honey	2 teaspoons	3 teaspoons	4 teaspoons
Warm orange juice (more or less)	1 cup	1½ cups	2 cups

Grease your chosen pan(s) and dust with rice flour.

The orange juice temperature will be different for hand mixing and for bread machines. For hand mixing, heat it to about 110°; for your bread machine, read the directions in the manual.

For both hand mixing and machine mixing, combine the dry ingredients in a medium bowl. Set aside.

In another bowl (or the bowl of your heavy-duty mixer), whisk the eggs, margarine, dough enhancer, and honey. Add most of the orange juice. The remaining should be added as needed, after the bread has started mixing either in the bowl of your mixer or in the pan of the bread machine.

For hand mixing: With the mixer turned to low, add the dry ingredients (including the yeast) a little at a time. Check to be sure the dough is the consistency of cake batter. Add more of the reserved orange juice as necessary. Turn the mixer to high and beat for 3½ minutes. Spoon the dough into the prepared pan(s), cover, and let rise about 35–45 minutes for rapid-rising yeast, 60 or more minutes for regular yeast or until the dough reaches the top of the pan. Bake in a preheated 400° oven for 50–60 minutes, covering after 10 minutes with aluminum foil.

For bread machine: Place the ingredients in the bread machine in the order suggested in the machine manual. Use the setting for white bread with medium crust the first time. If too dark, try a lighter crust because this has more sugar in the dough and might darken faster.

VARIATIONS: The amounts given are for a small recipe; increase proportionately for other size recipes.

ORANGE-WALNUT GARBANZO BREAD: Add ¼ cup walnuts to the dough after beating. For a pecan taste, add pecans.

FRUITED GARBANZO BREAD: Add ⅓ cup raisins, dried cranberries, or mixed dried fruit to the dough after beating.

Nutrients per slice: Calories 100, Fat 3g, Carbohydrate 17g, Cholesterol 10mg, Sodium 140mg, Fiber 2g, Protein 2g.
Dietary exchanges: Bread 1, Fat ½.

Zucchini Cheese Bread 400°

I created this originally as a yeast-free bread for a friend who can't have yeast, but it is so delicious, I transposed the recipe to a yeast base. Note that in this recipe the yeast is listed with the wet ingredients.

DRY INGREDIENTS	SMALL	MEDIUM	LARGE
Four Flour Bean Mix (page 40)	2 cups	3 cups	4 cups
Xanthan gum	1½ teaspoons	2¼ teaspoons	3 teaspoons
Egg Replacer	1 teaspoon	1½ teaspoons	2 teaspoons
Unflavored gelatin	1 teaspoon	1½ teaspoons	2 teaspoons
Sugar	⅓ cup	½ cup	⅔ cup
Grated Parmesan cheese	2 tablespoons	3 tablespoons	4 tablespoons
Salt	½ teaspoon	¾ teaspoon	1 teaspoon
Dry buttermilk powder	2½ tablespoons	3¾ tablespoons	5 tablespoons
Shredded zucchini, squeezed or patted dry	⅔ cup	1 cup	1⅓ cups

WET INGREDIENTS			
Eggs	1 plus 1 white	1 plus 2 whites	1 plus 3 whites
Margarine or butter	⅓ cup	½ cup	⅔ cup
Dough enhancer	½ teaspoon	¾ teaspoon	1 teaspoon
Grated onion	1¼ tablespoons	1¾ tablespoons	2½ tablespoons
Warm water (more or less)	⅔ cup	1 cup	1⅓ cups
Dry yeast granules	2¼ teaspoons	2¼ teaspoons	2¼ teaspoons

Prepare loaf pan(s) by greasing and dusting with rice flour.

The water temperature will be different for hand mixing and for bread machines. For hand mixing have it about 110°; for your bread machine, read the directions in the manual.

For both hand mixing and machine mixing combine the dry ingredients. In another bowl, whisk the egg and white(s) slightly and add the margarine (cut in pieces), dough enhancer, and grated onion.

For hand mixing: Dissolve the yeast in the warm water. Place the dry ingredients in the bowl of your heavy-duty mixer. Add the wet ingredients and most of the yeast water. Blend on low. Check to be sure the dough is the right texture (should be like cake batter). Add more yeast water if too thick. With the mixer on high, beat for 3½ minutes. Spoon the dough into the prepared pan(s), cover, and let rise about 35–45 minutes for rapid-rising yeast, 60 or more minutes for regular yeast or until the bread has almost doubled in bulk. Bake in a preheated 400° oven for 50–60 minutes, covering after 10 minutes with aluminum foil.

For bread machine: Place the ingredients in the bread machine in the order suggested in the machine manual. Use the setting for a light crust. If this isn't brown enough or doesn't bake thoroughly, try the medium crust.

VARIATIONS: The amounts given are for the small recipe. Increase proportionately for other sizes.

PARMESAN-HERB YEAST BREAD: Add 2 teaspoons Italian seasoning to the dry ingredients.

BANANA-CHEESE YEAST BREAD: Replace the zucchini with ripe mashed bananas; replace the Parmesan and onion with 3¼ tablespoons grated Jack cheese. Add 2 tablespoons finely chopped nuts.

Nutrients per slice: Calories 120, Fat 4g, Carbohydrate 17g, Cholesterol 15mg, Sodium 130mg, Fiber 1g, Protein 3g.
Dietary exchanges: Bread 1, Fat 1.

Boston Bean Bread

400°

With a change of flours my original Boston Brown Bread (More from the Gluten-free Gourmet) becomes more tender and tasty, much like the brown bread you ate before giving up wheat. Popcorn flour can be ordered from Authentic Foods; red corn flour, from The Gluten Free Pantry. The amount of water needed may change if you use cornmeal.

Note: *The large recipe will fit both 1½-pound and 2-pound bread machines. No need for a medium recipe.*

DRY INGREDIENTS	SMALL	LARGE
Four Flour Bean Mix (page 40)	1½ cups	3 cups
Popcorn flour or cornmeal	6 tablespoons	¾ cup
Xanthan gum	1½ teaspoons	3 teaspoons
Buttermilk powder	¼ cup	½ cup
Baking soda	½ teaspoon	1 teaspoon
Egg Replacer	1 teaspoon	2 teaspoons
Unflavored gelatin	1 teaspoon	2 teaspoons
Salt	¾ teaspoon	1½ teaspoons
Brown sugar	1 tablespoon	2 tablespoons
Dry yeast granules	1 tablespoon	1 tablespoon

WET INGREDIENTS		
Eggs (beaten with fork)	2 small	3 large
Dough enhancer or vinegar	½ teaspoon	1 teaspoon
Molasses	⅓ cup	⅔ cup
Vegetable oil	2 tablespoons	¼ cup
Water (more or less)	½ cup	1 cup
Raisins or dried cranberries	⅓ cup	⅔ cup

Grease the pan(s) if making loaves and dust with rice flour.

The water temperature will be different for hand mixing and for bread machines.

For hand mixing have it about 110°; for your bread machine read the directions in the manual.

For both hand mixing and machine mixing, combine the dry ingredients in a medium bowl. Set aside.

In another bowl (or the bowl of your heavy-duty mixer), whisk the eggs slightly and add the dough enhancer, molasses, oil, and most of the water. The remaining water should be added as needed after the bread has started mixing, either in the bowl of your mixer or in the pan of the bread machine.

For hand mixing: With the mixer on low, add the dry ingredients (including the yeast) to the liquids in the mixing bowl, a little at a time. Turn the mixer on high and beat for 3½ minutes. Stir in the raisins or cranberries. Spoon into the prepared pan(s), cover, and let rise about 35–45 minutes for rapid-rising yeast, 60 or more minutes for regular yeast. Bake in a preheated 400° oven for 50–60 minutes, covering after 10 minutes with aluminum foil.

For bread machine: Place the ingredients in the bread machine in the order suggested in the machine manual. Use the setting for white bread with medium crust. Drop in the raisins or cranberries near the end of the first kneading or when the machine manual suggests.

Nutrients per slice: Calories 120, Fat 2.5g, Carbohydrate 22g, Cholesterol 25mg, Sodium 150mg, Fiber 1g, Protein 3g.
Dietary exchanges: Bread 1½, Fat ½.

Basic Carrot Bread

400°

For a healthy as well as a tasty treat, try this high-fiber bread in all its variations. The carrots and almond meal add texture and flavor but do not overpower the other ingredients. All in all, a perfect bread for a mild-tasting sandwich filling such as turkey or chicken breast. Wonderful as toast.

DRY INGREDIENTS	SMALL	MEDIUM	LARGE
Four Flour Bean Mix (page 40)	2 cups	3 cups	4 cups
Xanthan gum	1½ teaspoons	2¼ teaspoons	3 teaspoons
Brown sugar	2 tablespoons	3 tablespoons	4 tablespoons
Egg Replacer	1 teaspoon	1½ teaspoons	2 teaspoons
Unflavored gelatin	1 teaspoon	1½ teaspoons	2 teaspoons
Almond meal	2 tablespoons	3 tablespoons	4 tablespoons
Dry milk powder or nondairy substitute	3 tablespoons	4½ tablespoons	⅓ cup
Salt	½ teaspoon	¾ teaspoon	1 teaspoon
Cinnamon	½ teaspoon	¾ teaspoon	1 teaspoon
Dried orange peel	1 teaspoon	1½ teaspoons	2 teaspoons
Carrot, finely grated and patted dry	⅔ cup	1 cup	1⅓ cups
Dry yeast granules	2¼ teaspoons	2¼ teaspoons	2¼ teaspoons
WET INGREDIENTS			
Eggs	1 plus 1 white	1 plus 2 whites	1 plus 3 whites
Margarine or butter	3 tablespoons	4½ tablespoons	6 tablespoons
Dough enhancer	½ teaspoon	¾ teaspoon	1 teaspoon
Warm water (more or less)	¾ cup	1⅛ cups	1½ cups

Grease your chosen pan(s) and dust with rice flour.

The water temperature will be different for hand mixing and for bread machines.

For hand mixing have it about 110°; for your bread machine, read the directions in the manual.

For both hand mixing and machine mixing, combine the dry ingredients in a medium bowl. Set aside.

In another bowl (or the bowl of your heavy-duty mixer), whisk the egg and white(s), margarine, and dough enhancer. Add most of the water. The remaining water should be added as needed after the bread has started mixing, either in the bowl of your mixer or in the pan of the bread machine.

For hand mixing: With the mixer turned to low, add the dry ingredients (including the yeast) a little at a time. Check to be sure the dough is the right consistency (should be like cake batter). Add more of the reserved water as necessary. Turn the mixer to high and beat for 3½ minutes. Spoon the dough into the prepared pan(s), cover, and let rise about 35–45 minutes for rapid-rising yeast, 60 or more minutes for regular yeast or until the dough reaches the top of the pan. Bake in a preheated 400° oven for 50–60 minutes, covering after 10 minutes with aluminum foil.

For bread machine: Place the ingredients in the bread machine in the order suggested in the machine manual. Use the setting for white bread with medium crust. If this browns too much, lower the setting to light crust.

VARIATIONS: The amounts given are for 1 loaf. Increase proportionately for larger recipes.

CARROT AND SEED BREAD: Eliminate the cinnamon. Stir in about ⅓ cup chopped sunflower seeds after the final beating.

CARROT-NUT BREAD: Stir in ⅓ cup chopped walnuts or pecans after the final beating.

CARROT-RAISIN BREAD: Stir in about ⅓ cup golden raisins after the final beating.

GARDEN BREAD: Eliminate the cinnamon. Stir in 2 finely sliced green onions and 2 teaspoons chopped fresh parsley after the final beating.

Nutrients per slice: Calories 100, Fat 3g, Carbohydrate 15g, Cholesterol 10mg, Sodium 100mg, Fiber 1g, Protein 3g.
Dietary exchanges: Bread 1, Fat ½.

Quinoa Bread

400°

This high-protein grain, just now being accepted as gluten free by some of the United States celiac organizations, adds not only a more nutty flavor but higher nutrient value to any loaf. Always be sure your grain is free of contamination by buying from a reputable source.

DRY INGREDIENTS	SMALL	MEDIUM	LARGE
Four Flour Bean Mix (page 40)	2 cups	3 cups	4 cups
Quinoa flour	2 tablespoons	3 tablespoons	¼ cup
Xanthan gum	1½ teaspoons	2¼ teaspoons	3 teaspoons
Salt	½ teaspoon	¾ teaspoon	1 teaspoon
Unflavored gelatin	1 teaspoon	1½ teaspoons	2 teaspoons
Egg Replacer	1 teaspoon	1½ teaspoons	2 teaspoons
Brown sugar	2 tablespoons	3 tablespoons	4 tablespoons
Dry yeast granules	2¼ teaspoons	2¼ teaspoons	2¼ teaspoons
WET INGREDIENTS			
Eggs	1 plus 1 white	1 plus 2 whites	1 plus 3 whites
Margarine or butter	3 tablespoons	4¼ tablespoons	5½ tablespoons
Dough enhancer or vinegar	½ teaspoon	¾ teaspoon	1 teaspoon
Warm water (more or less)	1 cup	1½ cups	2 cups

Grease your chosen pan(s) and dust with rice flour.

The water temperature will be different for hand mixing and bread machines. For hand mixing have it about 110° to 115°; for your bread machine, read the directions in the manual.

For both hand mixing and machine mixing, combine the dry ingredients in a medium bowl. Set aside.

In another bowl (or the bowl of your heavy-duty mixer), whisk the egg and white(s), margarine, and dough enhancer. Add most of the water. The remaining water should be added as needed after the bread has started mixing, either in the bowl of your mixer or in the pan of the bread machine.

For hand mixing: With the mixer turned to low, add the dry ingredients (including the yeast) a little at a time. Check to be sure the dough is the right consistency (should be like cake batter). Add more of the reserved water as necessary. Turn the mixer to high and beat for 3½ minutes. Spoon the dough into the prepared pan(s), cover, and let rise about 35–45 minutes for rapid-rising yeast, 60 or more minutes for regular yeast or until the dough reaches the top of the pan. Bake in a preheated 400° oven for 50–60 minutes, covering after 10 minutes with aluminum foil.

For bread machine: Place the ingredients in the bread machine in the order suggested in the machine manual. Use the setting for white bread with medium crust.

Nutrients per slice: Calories 100, Fat 3g, Carbohydrate 14g, Cholesterol 10mg, Sodium 95mg, Fiber 1g, Protein 2g.
Dietary exchanges: Bread 1, Fat 1.

Basic Featherlight Rice Bread
(With 4 Variations)

400°

Finally, a rice bread that feels like a wheat bread in texture! This bread will not crumble in a sandwich or have to be toasted to be palatable. And the taste is wonderful!

DRY INGREDIENTS	SMALL	MEDIUM	LARGE
Featherlight Rice Flour Mix (page 40)	2 cups	3 cups	4 cups
Xanthan gum	1½ teaspoons	2¼ teaspoons	3 teaspoons
Unflavored gelatin	1 teaspoon	1½ teaspoons	2 teaspoons
Egg Replacer	1 teaspoon	1½ teaspoons	2 teaspoons
Salt	½ teaspoon	¾ teaspoon	1 teaspoon
Sugar	2 tablespoons	3 tablespoons	¼ cup
Dry milk powder or nondairy substitute	¼ cup	⅓ cup	½ cup
Dry yeast granules	2¼ teaspoons	2¼ teaspoons	2¼ teaspoons
WET INGREDIENTS			
Eggs	1 plus 1 white	1 plus 2 whites	1 plus 3 whites
Margarine or butter	3 tablespoons	4½ tablespoons	⅓ cup
Dough enhancer or vinegar	½ teaspoon	¾ teaspoon	1 teaspoon
Honey or molasses	2 teaspoons	3 teaspoons	4 teaspoons
Water (more or less)	1 cup	1½ cups	2 cups

Grease your chosen pan(s) and dust with rice flour.

The water temperature will be different for hand mixing and for bread machines. For hand mixing have it about 110°; for your bread machine, read the directions in the manual.

For both hand mixing and machine mixing, combine the dry ingredients in a medium bowl and set aside.

In another bowl (or the bowl of your heavy-duty mixer) whisk the egg and white(s), margarine (cut in chunks), dough enhancer, and honey until blended. Add most of the water to the egg mixture. The remaining water should be added as needed after the bread has started mixing, either in the bowl of your mixer or in the pan of the bread machine.

For hand mixing: With the mixer turned to low, add the dry ingredients (including the yeast) a little at a time. Check to be sure the dough is the right consistency (should be like cake batter). Add more of the water as necessary. Turn the mixer to high and beat for 3½ minutes. Spoon into the prepared pan(s), cover, and let rise in a warm place for about 35 minutes for rapid-rising yeast, 60 or more minutes for regular yeast or until the dough reaches the top of the pan. Bake in a preheated 400° oven for 50–60 minutes, covering after 10 minutes with aluminum foil.

For bread machine: Place the ingredients in the machine pan in the order suggested in the manual. Use the setting for medium crust.

VARIATIONS: Amounts given are for a small loaf. Increase proportionately for other sizes.

ALMOND FEATHERLIGHT BREAD: Use almond meal in place of the powdered milk or nondairy substitute. Use the amount shown in the recipe.

LEMON–POPPY SEED RICE BREAD: Add 1 teaspoon dried lemon peel and 2 teaspoons poppy seeds to the dry ingredients.

ALMOND-CHERRY RICE BREAD: Increase the sugar to 4 tablespoons. Use almond meal in place of the milk powder or nondairy substitute, increasing to ⅓ cup. Add 1 teaspoon almond flavor to the wet ingredients, and after the mixing, stir in ⅓ cup chopped dried cherries.

ALMOND-APRICOT BREAD: Follow the directions for the Almond-Cherry Rice Bread but replace the cherries with chopped dried apricots.

Nutrients per slice: Calories 100, Fat 3g, Carbohydrate 16g, Cholesterol 15mg, Sodium 100mg, Fiber 0g, Protein 2g.
Dietary exchanges: Bread 1, Fat 1.

New French Bread

A full-flavored loaf that surpasses any other French bread I've created. Using the new French Bread/Pizza Mix and rapid-rising yeast, this is so easy to stir up, you can have it in a little over one hour. The formula works best with dry milk powder or a nut milk substitute rather than a soy-based substitute. This recipe is not formulated for bread machines.

DRY INGREDIENTS	SMALL	LARGE
French Bread/Pizza Mix (page 190)	1¾ cups	3½ cups
Dry milk powder or nondairy substitute	3 tablespoons	6 tablespoons
Salt	½ teaspoon	1 teaspoon
Baking powder	½ teaspoon	1 teaspoon
Yeast	1 tablespoon	1 tablespoon

WET INGREDIENTS		
Egg whites	2 small	3 large
Dough enhancer or vinegar	½ teaspoon	1 teaspoon
Vegetable oil	1½ tablespoons	3 tablespoons
Warm water	⅔ cup	1⅓ cups

Prepare a French bread pan or cookie sheet by greasing and dusting with cornmeal (if desired).

In the bowl of a heavy-duty mixer, combine the dry ingredients (including the yeast). In a small bowl, beat the egg whites, dough enhancer, and oil slightly with a fork. Add most of the warm water. Add these to the dry ingredients and beat on high for 3 minutes. Check after the first few seconds of mixing to see if more water is needed. The dough should be thick but not dry or forming a ball.

Spoon into the French bread pan or onto the cookie sheet in the shape of a French loaf. If necessary, smooth the top with greased fingers. Cover and let rise about 35 minutes for rapid-rising yeast, 60–75 minutes for regular yeast. Bake in a preheated 425° oven for 25 to 30 minutes, or until nicely browned and the loaf sounds hollow when thumped.

VARIATION:

ROSEMARY FRENCH: To the dry ingredients add 1 teaspoon chopped fresh rosemary per cup of flour.

Nutrients per slice: Calories 70, Fat 1g, Carbohydrate 13g, Cholesterol 0mg, Sodium 90mg, Fiber 0g, Protein 1g.
Dietary exchanges: Bread 1.

Buttermilk Casserole Bread
(With 5 Variations)

A new flavor with great texture! Like most of the breads in this book, this is an entirely new formula that turns out a bread with no hint of the rice base. It is smooth textured, springy, and holds together wonderfully in a sandwich. The interesting shape of the casserole makes this an exciting "guest" bread while the flavors can be anything from the basic bread to sesame, mixed seeds, herbs, fruit, spice, or fruit-nut. This dough will be thicker than your usual rice breads. If you prefer loaf shapes, use one 9" × 5" pan or two 7¼" × 3¼" pans.

DRY INGREDIENTS	ROUND 1½-QUART CASSEROLE
Brown or white rice flour	1½ cups
Cornstarch	½ cup
Tapioca flour	¼ cup
Xanthan gum	2 teaspoons
Baking soda	¾ teaspoon
Salt	1 teaspoon
Egg Replacer (optional)	1 teaspoon
Unflavored gelatin	1 teaspoon
NutQuik or almond meal	¼ cup
Dry yeast granules	1 tablespoon

WET INGREDIENTS	
Margarine or butter	3 tablespoons
Buttermilk	1½ cups
Sugar	¼ cup
Instant potato flakes	¼ cup
Eggs	2 plus 1 white
Dough enhancer or vinegar	1 teaspoon

Grease your chosen pan(s). Set aside.

In a medium bowl, combine the dry ingredients (including the yeast). Set aside.

In a small saucepan, melt the margarine. Add the buttermilk and sugar, and heat until just warm (120° to 130°). Remove from the stove and stir in the potato flakes.

Break the eggs into the bowl of your heavy-duty mixer. Add the dough enhancer and beat until blended. Add the buttermilk mixture. With the mixer on low, slowly spoon in the flour mix. Turn the mixer to high and beat for several seconds. Check to see that the dough is of a consistency between cake batter and soft bread dough, and not as thin as most of the rice flour doughs. Add warm water if necessary, a spoonful at a time. Turn the mixer to high and beat for 3½ minutes.

Spoon the dough into the prepared pan, cover, and let rise about 35–45 minutes for rapid-rising yeast, 65–90 minutes for regular yeast or until the dough has almost doubled in bulk. Bake in a preheated 425° oven for 10 minutes. Cover with aluminum foil and lower the oven temperature to 400°. Bake 55 minutes longer for a casserole or large pan. Bake about 40–45 minutes longer for small loaf pans. Turn bread out of the pan(s) while still hot, and cool before slicing.

VARIATIONS:

SESAME CASSEROLE BREAD: Add 1½ tablespoons sesame seeds to the dry ingredients.

CASSEROLE SEED BREAD: Add to the dry ingredients 2 tablespoons chopped sunflower seeds, 2 tablespoons poppy seeds, 1 tablespoon caraway seeds, and 2 tablespoons crushed sliced almonds.

ORANGE-NUT CASSEROLE BREAD: Add 1 teaspoon dried orange peel or 2 teaspoons fresh orange zest to the dry ingredients. Just before spooning the dough into the pan, stir in ½ cup chopped walnuts or pecans.

SPICED FRUIT CASSEROLE BREAD: Add 1 teaspoon apple pie spice to the dry ingredients. Just before spooning into the pan, stir in ½ cup Dried Fruit Bites (found at your local grocery store) or your choice of finely chopped dried fruit.

HERBED CASSEROLE BREAD: Add 1 to 2 teaspoons dried herbs to the dry ingredients. Pick your favorites from dillweed, rosemary, or basil, or combine others you enjoy. Or use Italian Pizza Seasoning, available in the spice section of most large grocery stores.

Nutrients per slice: Calories 130, Fat 4g, Carbohydrate 21g, Cholesterol 25mg, Sodium 230mg, Fiber 1g, Protein 3g.
Dietary exchanges: Bread 1½, Fat 1.

Almond–Wild Rice Bread

400°

Try this new and exciting taste in a rice bread. Using Featherlight Rice Flour Mix makes this lighter and springier than most of the old rice recipe breads. Wild rice flour is available in some health food stores and from The Gluten Free Pantry. This recipe calls for potato flour, not potato starch.

DRY INGREDIENTS	SMALL	MEDIUM	LARGE
Featherlight Rice Flour Mix (page 40)	2 cups	3 cups	4 cups
Potato flour	2 teaspoons	3 teaspoons	4 teaspoons
Wild rice flour	2 tablespoons	3 tablespoons	4 tablespoons
Xanthan gum	1½ teaspoons	2¼ teaspoons	3 teaspoons
Salt	½ teaspoon	¾ teaspoon	1 teaspoon
Egg Replacer	1 teaspoon	1½ teaspoons	2 teaspoons
Unflavored gelatin	1 teaspoon	1½ teaspoons	2 teaspoons
Dry milk powder or nondairy substitute	¼ cup	⅓ cup	½ cup
NutQuik or almond meal	2 tablespoons	3 tablespoons	¼ cup
Dried lemon peel	½ teaspoon	¾ teaspoon	1 teaspoon
Brown sugar	2 tablespoons	3 tablespoons	¼ cup
Dry yeast granules	2¼ teaspoons	2¼ teaspoons	2¼ teaspoons

WET INGREDIENTS			
Eggs	1 plus 1 white	1 plus 2 whites	1 plus 3 whites
Dough enhancer or vinegar	½ teaspoon	¾ teaspoon	1 teaspoon
Margarine or butter	3 tablespoons	4½ tablespoons	6 tablespoons
Almond flavoring	1 teaspoon	1½ teaspoons	2 teaspoons
Warm water (more or less)	1 cup	1½ cups	2 cups
Chopped blanched almonds	¼ cup	⅓ cup	½ cup

Grease your chosen pan(s) and dust lightly with rice flour.

    The water temperature will be different for hand mixing and bread machines. For hand mixing have it about 110°; for your bread machine, read the directions in the manual.

For both hand mixing and machine mixing, combine the dry ingredients in a medium bowl. Set aside.

In another bowl (or the bowl of your heavy-duty mixer), whisk the egg and white(s) slightly and add the dough enhancer, margarine (cut in pieces), almond flavoring, and most of the water. The remaining water should be added as needed after the bread has started mixing, either in the bowl of your mixer or in the pan of the bread machine.

For hand mixing: With the mixer turned to low, add the dry ingredients (including the yeast) a little at a time. Check to be sure the dough is the right texture (should be like cake batter). Add the reserved water if necessary. Turn the mixer to high and beat for 3½ minutes. Spoon the dough into the prepared pan(s), cover, and let rise about 35–45 minutes for rapid-rising yeast, 60 or more minutes for regular yeast or until the bread reaches the top of the pan. Bake in a preheated 400° oven for 50–60 minutes, covering after 10 minutes with aluminum foil.

For bread machine: Place the ingredients in the bread machine in the order suggested in the machine manual. Use the setting for white bread with medium crust.

Nutrients per slice: Calories 120, Fat 4g, Carbohydrate 17g, Cholesterol 15mg, Sodium 100mg, Fiber 1g, Protein 3g.
Dietary exchanges: Bread 1, Fat 1.

Touch o' Bean Bread

400°

This rice-based bread relies on a small amount of Authentic Foods bean flour for part of the protein, and brown sugar for some of the flavor. For those just starting to use the flour from Authentic Foods, this may be just what you need to introduce you to the taste. For best flavor use brown rice in the Featherlight mix.

DRY INGREDIENTS	SMALL	MEDIUM	LARGE
Featherlight Rice Flour Mix (page 40)	2 cups	3 cups	4 cups
Authentic Foods bean flour	3 tablespoons	4½ tablespoons	6 tablespoons
Xanthan gum	1½ teaspoons	2¼ teaspoons	3 teaspoons
Egg Replacer	1 teaspoon	1½ teaspoons	2 teaspoons
Unflavored gelatin	1 teaspoon	1½ teaspoons	2 teaspoons
Salt	½ teaspoon	¾ teaspoon	1 teaspoon
Dry milk powder or nondairy substitute	3 tablespoons	4½ tablespoons	6 tablespoons
Brown sugar	2 tablespoons	3 tablespoons	4 tablespoons
Dry yeast granules	2¼ teaspoons	2¼ teaspoons	2¼ teaspoons

WET INGREDIENTS			
Eggs	1 plus 1 white	1 plus 2 whites	1 plus 3 whites
Margarine or butter	2 tablespoons	3 tablespoons	4 tablespoons
Dough enhancer or vinegar	½ teaspoon	¾ teaspoon	1 teaspoon
Molasses	2 teaspoons	3 teaspoons	4 teaspoons
Warm water (more or less)	1 cup	1½ cups	2 cups

Grease your chosen pan(s) and dust with rice flour.

The water temperature will be different for hand mixing and for bread machines. For hand mixing have it about 110°; for your bread machine, read the directions in the manual.

For both hand mixing and machine mixing, combine the dry ingredients in a medium bowl. Set aside.

In another bowl (or the bowl of your heavy-duty mixer), whisk the egg and white(s) slightly and add the margarine (cut in pieces), dough enhancer, molasses, and most of the water. The remaining water should be added as needed after the bread has started mixing, either in the bowl of your mixer or in the pan of the bread machine.

For hand mixing: With the mixer turned to low, add the dry ingredients (including the yeast) a little at a time. Check to see if more water is necessary. The dough should resemble cake batter. Turn the mixer to high and beat for 3½ minutes. Spoon into the prepared pan(s), cover, and let rise about 35–45 minutes for rapid-rising yeast, 60 or more minutes for regular yeast. Bake in a preheated 400° oven for 50–60 minutes, covering after 10 minutes with aluminum foil.

For bread machine: Place the ingredients in the bread machine in the order suggested in the machine manual. Use the setting for white bread with a medium crust.

VARIATIONS: Measurements are for the small recipe. Increase proportionately for medium and large.

SESAME TOUCH O' BEAN: Add 2 teaspoons sesame seeds to the dry ingredients.

LEMON–POPPY SEED TOUCH O' BEAN: Add 1 teaspoon lemon zest and 2 teaspoons poppy seeds to the dry ingredients. Substitute honey for the molasses in the wet ingredients.

Nutrients per slice: Calories 100, Fat 3g, Carbohydrate 17g, Cholesterol 15mg, Sodium 100mg, Fiber 1g, Protein 2g.
Dietary exchanges: Bread 1, Fat 1.

Basic Millet Bread 400°

This is a mild-tasting, slightly sweet bread that takes well to many variations. Millet has just begun to be accepted as gluten free by most of the celiac organizations, so always check to be sure the seller can guarantee no contamination.

DRY INGREDIENTS	SMALL	MEDIUM	LARGE
Millet flour	⅔ cup	1 cup	1⅓ cups
Cornstarch	⅔ cup	1 cup	1⅓ cups
Tapioca flour	⅔ cup	1 cup	1⅓ cups
Xanthan gum	1½ teaspoons	2¼ teaspoons	3 teaspoons
Salt	½ teaspoon	¾ teaspoon	1 teaspoon
Unflavored gelatin	1 teaspoon	1½ teaspoons	2 teaspoons
Egg Replacer	1 teaspoon	1½ teaspoons	2 teaspoons
Sugar	2 tablespoons	3 tablespoons	4 tablespoons
Dry milk powder or nondairy substitute	¼ cup	⅓ cup	½ cup
Dry yeast granules	2¼ teaspoons	2¼ teaspoons	2¼ teaspoons
WET INGREDIENTS			
Eggs	1 plus 1 white	1 plus 2 whites	1 plus 3 whites
Dough enhancer or vinegar	½ teaspoon	¾ teaspoon	1 teaspoon
Margarine or butter	3 tablespoons	4¼ tablespoons	5½ tablespoons
Water (more or less)	1 cup	1½ cups	2 cups

Grease your chosen pan(s) and dust with rice flour.

The water temperature will be different for hand mixing and for bread machines. For hand mixing have it about 110°; for your bread machine, read the directions in the manual.

For both hand mixing and machine mixing, combine the dry ingredients in a medium bowl. Set aside.

In another bowl or the bowl of your heavy-duty mixer, whisk the egg and white(s) slightly, and add the dough enhancer, margarine (cut in chunks), and most of the water. The remaining water should be added as needed after the bread has started mixing, either in the mixer or in the pan of your bread machine.

For hand mixing: Turn the mixer to low and add the dry ingredients (including the yeast) a little at a time. Check to be sure the dough is the right consistency (like cake batter). Add more of the reserved water as necessary. Turn the mixer to high and beat for 3½ minutes. Spoon into the prepared pan(s), cover, and let rise in a warm place about 35 minutes for rapid-rising yeast, 60 or more minutes for regular yeast or until the dough reaches the top of the pan. Bake in a preheated 400° oven for 50–60 minutes, covering after 10 minutes with aluminum foil.

For bread machine: Place the ingredients in the bread machine in the order suggested in the machine manual. Use the setting for white bread with medium crust.

VARIATIONS: Changes are for the small size; increase proportionately for larger sizes.

ALMOND MILLET BREAD: Add 2 tablespoons almond meal to the dry ingredients. Add 1 teaspoon almond flavoring to the wet ingredients.

CINNAMON-RAISIN MILLET BREAD: Add 1 teaspoon cinnamon to the dry ingredients and ¼ cup raisins after the dough has been mixed and before putting into the pan.

THREE-SEED MILLET BREAD: Add 1 tablespoon each of any three of these seeds or nuts: sunflower seeds, pumpkin seeds, soy nuts (chopped), sesame seeds, almond meal, or crushed sliced almonds.

Nutrients per slice: Calories 100, Fat 3g, Carbohydrate 16g, Cholesterol 20mg, Sodium 95mg, Fiber 1g, Protein 2g.
Dietary exchanges: Bread 1, Fat 1.

Basic Sorghum Bread 400°

This bread was specially formulated for those who want to use the sorghum flour without bean flour. It is not as light as the combination in the Four Flour Bean Mix, but it works very well in bread and can be made with several variations. Almond meal is a great nondairy substitute in the basic bread.

DRY INGREDIENTS	SMALL	MEDIUM	LARGE
Sorghum flour (Jowar)	1 cup	1½ cups	2 cups
Tapioca flour	½ cup	¾ cup	1 cup
Cornstarch	½ cup	¾ cup	1 cup
Xanthan gum	1½ teaspoons	2¼ teaspoons	3 teaspoons
Dry milk powder or nondairy substitute	⅓ cup	½ cup	⅔ cup
Salt	½ teaspoon	¾ teaspoon	1 teaspoon
Unflavored gelatin	1 teaspoon	1½ teaspoons	2 teaspoons
Egg Replacer	1 teaspoon	1½ teaspoons	2 teaspoons
Sugar	2 tablespoons	3 tablespoons	4 tablespoons
Dry yeast granules	2¼ teaspoons	2¼ teaspoons	2¼ teaspoons
WET INGREDIENTS			
Eggs	1 plus 1 white	1 plus 2 whites	1 plus 3 whites
Margarine or butter	2½ tablespoons	3¾ tablespoons	5 tablespoons
Dough enhancer	½ teaspoon	¾ teaspoon	1 teaspoon
Water (more or less)	1¼ cups	2 cups	2½ cups

Grease your chosen pan(s) and dust with rice flour.

The water temperature will be different for hand mixing and for bread machines. For hand mixing have it about 110°; for your bread machine, read the directions in the manual.

For both hand mixing and machine mixing, combine the dry ingredients in a medium bowl. Set aside.

In another bowl (or the bowl of your heavy-duty mixer), whisk the egg and white(s) slightly; add the margarine, dough enhancer, and most of the water. The remaining water should be added as needed after the bread has started mixing, either in your mixer or in the pan of the bread machine.

For hand mixing: Turn the mixer to low and add the dry ingredients (including the yeast) a little at a time. Check to be sure the dough is the right consistency (like cake batter). Add more of the reserved water as necessary. Turn the mixer to high and beat for 3½ minutes. Spoon into the prepared pan(s), cover, and let rise in a warm place about 35–45 minutes for rapid-rising yeast, 60 or more minutes for regular yeast or until the dough reaches the top of the pan. Bake in a preheated 400° oven for 50–60 minutes, covering after 10 minutes with aluminum foil.

For bread machine: Place the ingredients in the bread machine in the order suggested in the machine manual. Use the setting for white bread at medium crust.

VARIATIONS: Measurements are given for the small recipe. Increase proportionately for medium and large.

CINNAMON-NUT SORGHUM LOAF: Add 1 teaspoon cinnamon to the dry ingredients. At the end of beating stir in ¼ cup chopped walnuts or pecans.

RAISIN-FILLED SORGHUM BREAD: Add 1 teaspoon cinnamon or cardamom to the dry ingredients. At end of beating stir in ¼ cup raisins.

LEMON–POPPY SEED SORGHUM BREAD: Use NutQuik or almond meal for the milk substitute. Add 2 teaspoons lemon zest and 2 teaspoons poppy seeds to the dry ingredients.

Nutrients per slice: Calories 110, Fat 3g, Carbohydrate 17g, Cholesterol 15mg, Sodium 100mg, Fiber 2g, Protein 3g.
Dietary exchanges: Bread 1, Fat ½.

Sourdough Breads

If you miss those sourdough breads you ate before diagnosis, try one of the new recipes below. These are hearty, smell of the sourdough, and make wonderful sandwiches. But since sourdough begins with a starter, as a celiac you can't go out and buy one. You'll have to make your own. This is made, fermented, and then replenished each time you use it or once a week if you haven't baked in that time. If the crock is too full, just discard all but about ¾ cup of the old starter and add ½ cup lukewarm water and ¾ cup rice flour to what is left. The older the starter, the more taste the bread will have.

If you are making new starter, it should be made at least one day before you plan to bake. Three days is better. Mix it in a crock or glass jar (never metal or plastic) and set aside or place in the refrigerator. If refrigerated, take out at least ten hours before baking or the night before. If you use it often, as I do, let it stand on the kitchen counter between bakings. Refrigerate or freeze it only when you leave on vacation.

Rice flour works well for a starter for both rice and bean breads.

SOURDOUGH STARTER

Dry yeast granules	2¼ teaspoons (1 packet)
Lukewarm potato water	1 cup
left over after boiling potatoes (or water with 1 teaspoon instant potato flakes)	
Sugar	1 teaspoon
White rice flour	1½ cups

In a 1- or 1½-quart glass jar or pottery crock, dissolve the yeast in the potato water. Add the sugar and rice flour. Cover and let the jar sit until fermented (1 to 3 days), stirring every few hours at first. This will bubble up and ferment and then die down with a skim of liquid on the top. Be sure to stir well before using. The consistency should be like pancake batter.

Replenish by feeding the remaining starter with ½ cup (or 1 cup) lukewarm water and ¾ cup (or 1½ cups) rice flour as needed each time you bake.

Honey Almond Sourdough

This wonderful new sourdough is perfect for sandwiches because the flavor is mild and the texture springy. Note that less yeast is necessary when a sourdough starter is used.

DRY INGREDIENTS	SMALL	MEDIUM	LARGE
Four Flour Bean Mix (page 40)	2 cups	3 cups	4 cups
Xanthan gum	1½ teaspoons	2¼ teaspoons	3 teaspoons
Salt	½ teaspoon	¾ teaspoon	1 teaspoon
Egg Replacer	1 teaspoon	1 teaspoon	1 teaspoon
Unflavored gelatin	1 teaspoon	1 teaspoon	1 teaspoon
Almond meal or NutQuik	3 tablespoons	4½ tablespoons	6 tablespoons
Dry yeast granules	1½ teaspoons	1½ teaspoons	1½ teaspoons

WET INGREDIENTS			
Eggs	1 plus 1 white	1 plus 2 whites	1 plus 3 whites
Dough enhancer or vinegar	½ teaspoon	¾ teaspoon	1 teaspoon
Sourdough starter	½ cup	¾ cup	1 cup
Vegetable oil	3 tablespoons	4½ tablespoons	6 tablespoons
Honey	3 tablespoons	4½ tablespoons	6 tablespoons
Warm water (more or less)	1 cup	1½ cups	2 cups

Grease your chosen pan(s) and dust with rice flour.

The water temperature will be different for hand mixing and for bread machines. For hand mixing have it about 110° to 115°; for your bread machine, read the directions in the manual.

For both hand mixing and machine mixing, combine the dry ingredients in a medium bowl. Set aside.

In another bowl (or the bowl of your heavy-duty mixer), whisk the egg and white(s), dough enhancer, sourdough starter, vegetable oil, and honey. Add most of the water. The remaining water should be added as needed after the bread has started mixing, either in the bowl of your mixer or in the pan of the bread machine.

For hand mixing: With the mixer turned to low, add the dry ingredients (including the yeast) a little at a time. Check to be sure the dough is the right consistency (like cake batter). Add more of the reserved water as necessary. Turn the mixer to high and beat for 3½ minutes. Spoon the dough into the prepared pan(s), cover, and let rise about 35–45 minutes for rapid-rising yeast, 60 or more minutes for regular yeast or until the bread has risen about 50 percent more than its original size. *Note: This is not the same as most doughs, which double in bulk.* Bake in a preheated 400° oven for 50–60 minutes, covering after 10 minutes with aluminum foil.

For bread machine: Place the ingredients in the bread machine in the order suggested in the machine manual. Use the setting for white bread with medium crust.

Nutrients per slice: Calories 130, Fat 4g, Carbohydrate 22g, Cholesterol 10mg, Sodium 75mg, Fiber 1g, Protein 3g.
Dietary exchanges: Bread 1½, Fat 1.

Seattle Sourdough

This loaf comes out lighter and more flavorful than any former rice-based sourdoughs. Although it doesn't rise as high as the breads made with bean flour, it still makes a springy, fine-textured loaf with no crumbling. Try some of the variations listed below for variety.

Note that less yeast is necessary when sourdough starter is used.

DRY INGREDIENTS	SMALL	MEDIUM	LARGE
Featherlight Rice Flour Mix (page 40)	2 cups	3 cups	4 cups
Xanthan gum	1½ teaspoons	2¼ teaspoons	3 teaspoons
Salt	½ teaspoon	¾ teaspoon	1 teaspoon
Egg Replacer	1 teaspoon	1½ teaspoons	2 teaspoons
Unflavored gelatin	1 teaspoon	1½ teaspoons	2 teaspoons
Buttermilk powder	⅓ cup	½ cup	⅔ cup
Dried lemon peel	1 teaspoon	1½ teaspoons	2 teaspoons
Sugar	3 tablespoons	4½ tablespoons	⅓ cup
Dry yeast granules	1½ teaspoons	1½ teaspoons	1½ teaspoons
WET INGREDIENTS			
Eggs	1 plus 1 white	1 plus 2 whites	1 plus 3 whites
Dough enhancer	½ teaspoon	¾ teaspoon	1 teaspoon
Sourdough starter	½ cup	¾ cup	1 cup
Vegetable oil	3 tablespoons	4½ tablespoons	⅓ cup
Warm water (more or less)	1 cup	1½ cups	2 cups

Grease your chosen pan(s) and dust with rice flour.

The water temperature will be different for hand mixing and for bread machines. For hand mixing have it about 110°; for your bread machine, read the directions in the manual.

For both hand mixing and machine mixing, combine the dry ingredients in a medium bowl. Set aside.

In another bowl (or the bowl of your heavy-duty mixer), whisk the egg and white(s), dough enhancer, sourdough starter, and vegetable oil. Add most of the water. The remaining water should be added as needed after the bread has started mixing, either in the bowl of your mixer or in the pan of the bread machine.

For hand mixing: With the mixer turned to low, add the dry ingredients (including the yeast) a little at a time. Check to be sure the dough is like a thick cake batter (thicker than the bean-based bread doughs). Add more of the reserved water as necessary. Turn the mixer to high and beat for 3½ minutes. Spoon the dough into the prepared pan(s), cover, and let rise about 35–45 minutes for rapid-rising yeast, 60 or more minutes for regular yeast or until the bread has risen about 50 percent more than its original size. (Note: This is not the same as most doughs, which almost double in bulk.) Bake in a preheated 400° oven for 50–60 minutes, covering after 10 minutes with aluminum foil.

For bread machine: Place the ingredients in the bread machine in the order suggested in the machine manual. Use the setting for white bread with medium crust.

VARIATIONS: Amounts are given for the small recipe; increase proportionately for other recipes.

LEMON–POPPY SEED SOURDOUGH: Increase the lemon peel to 2 teaspoons and add 2 teaspoons poppy seeds to the dry ingredients.

SESAME SEED SOURDOUGH: Use brown rice flour in the Featherlight mix, change the regular sugar to brown sugar, and add 1 tablespoon sesame seeds to the dry ingredients.

Nutrients per slice: Calories 130, Fat 3g, Carbohydrate 22g, Cholesterol 15mg, Sodium 80mg, Fiber 1g, Protein 3g.
Dietary exchanges: Bread 1½, Fat ½.

Sourdough Rye

A basic bread for anyone who likes a taste of sourdough and rye. The rye flavor is so subtle that this can be used with any topping and filling. Rye flavor powder may be ordered from Authentic Foods (see page 271).

DRY INGREDIENTS	SMALL	MEDIUM	LARGE
Four Flour Bean Mix (page 40)	2 cups	3 cups	4 cups
Xanthan gum	1½ teaspoons	2¼ teaspoons	3 teaspoons
Salt	½ teaspoon	¾ teaspoon	1 teaspoon
Egg Replacer	1 teaspoon	1½ teaspoons	2 teaspoons
Unflavored gelatin	1 teaspoon	1½ teaspoons	2 teaspoons
Buttermilk powder or nondairy substitute	⅓ cup	½ cup	⅔ cup
Caraway seeds	1 teaspoon	1½ teaspoons	2 teaspoons
Cardamom	1 teaspoon	1½ teaspoons	2 teaspoons
Dried lemon peel	1 teaspoon	1½ teaspoons	2 teaspoons
Rye flavor powder	⅛ teaspoon	3/16 teaspoon	¼ teaspoon
Brown sugar	3 tablespoons	4½ tablespoons	6 tablespoons
Yeast	1½ teaspoons	1½ teaspoons	1½ teaspoons
WET INGREDIENTS			
Eggs	1 plus 1 white	1 plus 2 whites	1 plus 3 whites
Dough enhancer	½ teaspoon	¾ teaspoon	1 teaspoon
Sourdough starter	½ cup	¾ cup	1 cup
Vegetable oil	3 tablespoons	4½ tablespoons	6 tablespoons
Warm water (more or less)	1 cup	1½ cups	2 cups

Grease your chosen pan(s) and dust with rice flour.

The water temperature will be different for hand mixing and for bread machines. For hand mixing have it about 110°; for your bread machine, read the directions in the manual.

For both hand mixing and machine mixing, combine the dry ingredients in a medium bowl. Set aside.

In another bowl (or the bowl of your heavy-duty mixer), whisk the egg and white(s), dough enhancer, sourdough starter, and vegetable oil. Add most of the water. The remaining water should be added as needed after the bread has started mixing, either in the bowl of your mixer or in the pan of the bread machine.

For hand mixing: With the mixer turned to low, add the dry ingredients (including the yeast) a little at a time. Check to be sure the dough is the right consistency (like cake batter). Add more of the reserved water as necessary. Turn the mixer to high and beat for 3½ minutes. Spoon the dough into the prepared pan(s), cover, and let rise about 35–45 minutes for rapid-rising yeast, 60 or more minutes for regular yeast or until the bread has risen about 50 percent more than its original size. (Note: This is not the same as most doughs, which almost double in bulk.) Bake in a preheated 400° oven for 50–60 minutes, covering after 10 minutes with aluminum foil.

For bread machine: Place the ingredients in the bread machine in the order suggested in the machine manual. Use the setting for white bread with medium crust.

Nutrients per slice: Calories 130, Fat 3g, Carbohydrate 22g, Cholesterol 15mg, Sodium 85mg, Fiber 1g, Protein 4g.
Dietary exchanges: Bread 1½, Fat ½.

Applesauce Rye Bread

400°

Slightly rye tasting, slightly sweet, this bread can be a tasty variation to your basic breads. Note that the yeast is increased slightly. Rye powder is available from Authentic Foods.

DRY INGREDIENTS	SMALL	MEDIUM	LARGE
Four Flour Bean Mix (page 40) or Light Bean Flour Mix (page 40)	2 cups	3 cups	4 cups
Xanthan gum	1½ teaspoons	2¼ teaspoons	3 teaspoons
Egg Replacer	1 teaspoon	1 teaspoon	1 teaspoon
Salt	½ teaspoon	¾ teaspoon	1 teaspoon
Unflavored gelatin	1 teaspoon	1½ teaspoons	2 teaspoons
Brown sugar	2 tablespoons	3 tablespoons	4 tablespoons
Caraway seeds	2 teaspoons	3 teaspoons	4 teaspoons
Rye flavor powder (optional)	¼ teaspoon	⅓ teaspoon	½ teaspoon
Dry milk powder or nondairy substitute	3 tablespoons	4½ tablespoons	6 tablespoons
Baking soda	¼ teaspoon	⅓ teaspoon	½ teaspoon
Instant espresso powder	1 teaspoon	1½ teaspoons	2 teaspoons
Dry yeast granules	1 tablespoon	1 tablespoon	1 tablespoon

WET INGREDIENTS			
Eggs	1 plus 1 white	1 plus 2 whites	1 plus 3 whites
Dough enhancer or vinegar	½ teaspoon	¾ teaspoon	1 teaspoon
Molasses	1½ tablespoons	2¼ tablespoons	3 tablespoons
Margarine or butter	2 tablespoons	3 tablespoons	4 tablespoons
Applesauce	½ cup	¾ cup	1 cup
Water, to thin applesauce	½ cup	¾ cup	1 cup
Extra water	1–3 tablespoons	2–4 tablespoons	3–5 tablespoons

Grease your chosen pan(s) and dust with rice flour.

The applesauce and water temperature will be different for hand mixing and for bread machines. For hand mixing have the water and applesauce combined heated to about 110°; for your bread machine, read the directions in the manual.

For both hand mixing and machine mixing, combine the dry ingredients in a medium bowl. Set aside.

In another bowl (or the bowl of your heavy-duty mixer) whisk the egg and white(s), dough enhancer, molasses, and margarine. Add the heated applesauce and water, reserving 2 to 4 tablespoons. This should be added as needed after the bread has started mixing, either in the bowl of your mixer or in the pan of the bread machine.

For hand mixing: With the mixer turned to low, add the dry ingredients (including the yeast) a little at a time. Check to be sure the dough is the right consistency (like cake batter). Add more of the reserved applesauce and water as necessary. Turn the mixer to high and beat for 3½ minutes. Spoon the dough into the prepared pan(s), cover, and let rise about 35 minutes for rapid-rising yeast, 60 or more minutes for regular yeast or until the dough reaches the top of the pan. Bake in a preheated 400° oven for 50–60 minutes, covering after 10 minutes with aluminum foil.

For bread machine: Place the ingredients in the bread machine in the order suggested in the machine manual. Use the setting for light crust.

Nutrients per slice: Calories 100, Fat 2.5g, Carbohydrate 16g, Cholesterol 15mg, Sodium 110mg, Fiber 1g, Protein 3g.
Dietary exchanges: Bread 1, Fat ½.

Hawaiian Rye

This sweet rye has a tropical flavor and wonderfully light texture. Use it for sandwiches and toast or for spreading with creamy cheese or meat fillings. Rye powder can be obtained from Authentic Foods. (See suppliers, page 271)

DRY INGREDIENTS	SMALL	MEDIUM	LARGE
Four Flour Bean Mix (page 40)	2 cups	3 cups	4 cups
Xanthan gum	1½ teaspoons	2¼ teaspoons	3 teaspoons
Baking soda	¼ teaspoon	⅓ teaspoon	½ teaspoon
Salt	½ teaspoon	¾ teaspoon	1 teaspoon
Egg Replacer	1 teaspoon	1½ teaspoons	2 teaspoons
NutQuik or almond meal	3 tablespoons	4½ tablespoons	6 tablespoons
Cocoa powder	2 teaspoons	1 tablespoon	4 teaspoons
Caraway seeds	2 teaspoons	1 tablespoon	4 teaspoons
Rye flavor powder (optional)	¼ teaspoon	⅓ teaspoon	½ teaspoon
Unflavored gelatin (optional)	1 teaspoon	1½ teaspoons	2 teaspoons
Yeast	4 teaspoons	4 teaspoons	4 teaspoons

WET INGREDIENTS			
Eggs	1 plus 1 white	1 plus 2 whites	1 plus 3 whites
Dough enhancer or vinegar	½ teaspoon	¾ teaspoon	1 teaspoon
Honey	2 tablespoons	3 tablespoons	4 tablespoons
Margarine or butter	3 tablespoons	4½ tablespoons	⅓ cup
One (6-ounce) can Pineapple, Orange, Banana juice	6 ounces	9 ounces	12 ounces
Water	¼ cup	⅓ cup	½ cup

Grease your chosen pan(s) and dust with rice flour.

The combined juice and water temperature will be different for hand mixing and for bread machines. For hand mixing have the liquids about 110°; for your bread machine, read the directions in the manual.

For both hand mixing and machine mixing, combine the dry ingredients in a medium bowl and set aside.

In another bowl (or the bowl of your heavy-duty mixer), whisk the egg and white(s), dough enhancer, honey, and margarine (in chunks) until blended. Add most of the heated juice and water to the egg mixture. The rest should be held back to be added as needed after the bread has started mixing, either in the bowl of your mixer or in the pan of the bread machine.

For hand mixing: With the mixer turned to low, add the dry ingredients (including the yeast) a little at a time. Check to be sure the dough is the right consistency (like cake batter). Add more of the reserved juice and water blend as necessary. Turn the mixer to high and beat for 3½ minutes. Spoon into the prepared pan(s), cover, and let rise in a warm place for about 35 minutes for rapid-rising yeast, 60 or more minutes for regular yeast or until the dough reaches the top of the pan. Bake in a preheated 375° oven for 50–55 minutes, covering after the first 10 minutes with aluminum foil.

For bread machine: Place the ingredients in the bread machine in the order suggested in the machine manual. Use the setting for light crust.

Nutrients per slice: Calories 110, Fat 3g, Carbohydrate 17g, Cholesterol 10mg, Sodium 115mg, Fiber 1g, Protein 3g.
Dietary exchanges: Bread 1, Fat 1.

Swedish Rye Bread 400°

This light, slightly sweet, rye-flavored bread might become one of your basic breads because it goes with everything from jams to meats, cheese to peanut butter. See Authentic Foods for rye powder.

DRY INGREDIENTS	SMALL	MEDIUM	LARGE
Four Flour Bean Mix (page 40)	1¾ cups	2⅔ cups	3½ cups
Brown rice flour	¼ cup	⅓ cup	½ cup
Xanthan gum	1½ teaspoons	2¼ teaspoons	3 teaspoons
Salt	½ teaspoon	¾ teaspoon	1 teaspoon
Unflavored gelatin	1 teaspoon	1½ teaspoons	2 teaspoons
Almond meal or NutQuik	¼ cup	⅓ cup	½ cup
Caraway seeds	1 teaspoon	1½ teaspoons	2 teaspoons
Cardamom	1 teaspoon	1½ teaspoons	2 teaspoons
Dried lemon peel	1 teaspoon	1½ teaspoons	2 teaspoons
Brown sugar	⅓ cup	½ cup	⅔ cup
Rye flavor powder (optional)	¼ teaspoon	⅓ teaspoon	½ teaspoon
Dry yeast granules	2¼ teaspoons	2¼ teaspoons	2¼ teaspoons
WET INGREDIENTS			
Eggs	1 plus 1 white	1 plus 2 whites	1 plus 3 whites
Dough enhancer or vinegar	½ teaspoon	¾ teaspoon	1 teaspoon
Margarine or butter	3 tablespoons	4½ tablespoons	6 tablespoons
Molasses	1 teaspoon	1½ teaspoons	2 teaspoons
Almond flavoring	½ teaspoon	¾ teaspoon	1 teaspoon
Warm water (more or less)	1 cup	1½ cups	2 cups

Grease your chosen pan(s) and dust with rice flour.

The water temperature will be different for hand mixing and for bread machines. For hand mixing have it about 110°; for your bread machine, read the directions in the manual.

For both hand mixing and machine mixing, combine the dry ingredients in a medium bowl. Set aside.

In another bowl (or the bowl of your heavy-duty mixer), whisk the egg and white(s) slightly; add the dough enhancer, margarine (cut in pieces), molasses, almond flavoring, and most of the water. The remaining water should be added as needed after the bread has started mixing, either in the bowl of your mixer or in the pan of the bread machine.

For hand mixing: With the mixer turned to low, add the dry ingredients (including the yeast) a little at a time. Check to be sure the dough is the right consistency (like cake batter). Add more water if necessary. Turn the mixer to high and beat for 3½ minutes. Spoon into the prepared pan(s), cover, and let rise about 35–45 minutes for rapid-rising yeast, 60 or more minutes for regular yeast. Bake in a preheated 400° oven for 50–60 minutes, covering after 10 minutes with aluminum foil.

For bread machine: Place the ingredients in the bread machine in the order suggested in the machine manual. Use the setting for white bread with medium crust. Because this bread has more sugar than most, you might find you have to lower the bake setting to light.

Nutrients per slice: Calories 110, Fat 4g, Carbohydrate 18g, Cholesterol 10mg, Sodium 100mg, Fiber 1g, Protein 3g.
Dietary exchanges: Bread 1, Fat 1.

Caraway Rye Bread

400°

You won't believe this isn't a true rye bread since the texture and taste rivals any wheat-based rye. If allergic to nuts, replace the almond meal with dry milk powder or nondairy substitute. The rye powder is not necessary for this bread but does add more rye flavor.

DRY INGREDIENTS	SMALL	MEDIUM	LARGE
Four Flour Bean Mix (page 40)	1¾ cups	2⅔ cups	3½ cups
Brown rice flour	¼ cup	⅓ cup	½ cup
Xanthan gum	1½ teaspoons	2¼ teaspoons	3 teaspoons
Salt	½ teaspoon	¾ teaspoon	1 teaspoon
Unflavored gelatin	1 teaspoon	1½ teaspoons	2 teaspoons
Almond meal or NutQuik	¼ cup	⅓ cup	½ cup
Caraway seeds	2 teaspoons	3 teaspoons	4 teaspoons
Cocoa powder	1 teaspoon	1½ teaspoons	2 teaspoons
Rye flavor powder	¼ teaspoon	⅓ teaspoon	½ teaspoon
Freeze-dried coffee crystals	1½ teaspoons	2¼ teaspoons	3 teaspoons
Dried orange peel	1 teaspoon	1½ teaspoons	2 teaspoons
Brown sugar	2 tablespoons	3 tablespoons	4 tablespoons
Dry yeast granules	2¼ teaspoons	2¼ teaspoons	2¼ teaspoons

WET INGREDIENTS			
Eggs	1 plus 1 white	1 plus 2 whites	1 plus 3 whites
Dough enhancer	½ teaspoon	¾ teaspoon	1 teaspoon
Margarine or butter	3 tablespoons	4½ tablespoons	6 tablespoons
Molasses	1 teaspoon	1½ teaspoons	2 teaspoons
Warm water (more or less)	1 cup	1½ cups	2 cups

Grease your chosen pan(s) and dust lightly with rice flour.

The water temperature will be different for hand mixing and for bread machines.

For hand mixing have it about 110°; for your bread machine, read the directions in the manual.

For both hand mixing and machine mixing, combine the dry ingredients in a medium bowl. Set aside.

In another bowl (or the bowl of your heavy-duty mixer), whisk the egg and white(s) slightly; add the dough enhancer, margarine (cut in pieces), molasses, and most of the water. The remaining water should be added as needed after the bread has started mixing, either in the bowl of your mixer or in the pan of the bread machine.

For hand mixing: With the mixer turned to low, add the dry ingredients (including the yeast) a little at a time. Check to be sure the dough is the right consistency (like cake batter). Add more water if necessary. Turn the mixer to high and beat for 3½ minutes. Spoon the dough into the prepared pan(s), cover, and let rise about 35–45 minutes for rapid-rising yeast, 60 or more minutes for regular yeast or until the dough has reached the top of the pan. Bake in a preheated 400° oven for 50–60 minutes, covering after 10 minutes with aluminum foil.

For bread machine: Place the ingredients in the bread machine in the order suggested in the machine manual. Use the setting for white bread with medium crust.

Nutrients per slice: Calories 100, Fat 4g, Carbohydrate 15g, Cholesterol 10mg, Sodium 95mg, Fiber 1g, Protein 3g.
Dietary exchanges: Bread 1, Fat 1.

Egg-free Bean Bread, using Egg Replacer (Egg and Lactose Free)

400°

Double the size of your egg-free loaf by using the new bean/sorghum mix. With more protein in the flours, the egg substitute makes a well-rounded, light, springy loaf. Using this recipe as a base you can turn out many different breads. See below for variations. If allergic to nuts, substitute dry milk powder or nondairy equivalent.

DRY INGREDIENTS	SMALL	MEDIUM	LARGE
Four Flour Bean Mix (page 40)	2 cups	3 cups	4 cups
Xanthan gum	1½ teaspoons	2¼ teaspoons	3 teaspoons
Salt	½ teaspoon	¾ teaspoon	1 teaspoon
Unflavored gelatin	1 teaspoon	1½ teaspoons	2 teaspoons
NutQuik or almond meal	2 tablespoons	3 tablespoons	¼ cup
Brown sugar	2 tablespoons	3 tablespoons	¼ cup
Dried lemon peel	1 teaspoon	1½ teaspoons	2 teaspoons
Dry yeast granules	2¼ teaspoons	2¼ teaspoons	2¼ teaspoons

WET INGREDIENTS			
Egg Replacer	4 teaspoons	6 teaspoons	8 teaspoons
Cool water	⅓ cup	½ cup	⅔ cup
Honey	1 tablespoon	1½ tablespoons	2 tablespoons
Dough enhancer or vinegar	½ teaspoon	¾ teaspoon	1 teaspoon
Margarine or butter	2 tablespoons	3 tablespoons	4 tablespoons
Warm water (more or less)	1 cup	1½ cups	2 cups

If using loaf pan(s), grease and dust with rice flour.

The water temperature will be different for hand mixing and for bread machines. For hand mixing have it about 110°; for your bread machine, read the directions in the manual.

For both hand mixing and machine mixing, combine the dry ingredients in a medium bowl. Set aside.

In another bowl (or the bowl of your mixer), whisk the Egg Replacer and the cool water until it resembles egg whites. Add the honey, dough enhancer, margarine, and most of the warm water. The remaining water should be added as needed after the dough has started mixing, either in the bowl of your mixer or in the pan of the bread machine.

For hand mixing: With the mixer turned to low, add the dry ingredients (including the yeast) a little at a time. Check to be sure the dough is the right consistency (like cake batter). Add more of the reserved water as necessary. Turn the mixer to high and beat for 3½ minutes. Spoon the dough into the prepared pan(s), cover, and let rise about 35–45 minutes for rapid-rising yeast, 60 or more minutes for regular yeast or until the bread reaches the top of the pan. Bake in a preheated 400° oven for 50–60 minutes, covering after 10 minutes with aluminum foil.

For bread machine: Place the ingredients in the bread machine in the order suggested in the machine manual. Use the setting for white bread with medium crust the first time. If necessary, lower to light crust if overbaked.

VARIATIONS: Measurements given are for a small recipe. Increase as needed for other sizes.

EGG-FREE POPPY SEED BREAD: Add 2 teaspoons poppy seeds and increase the lemon peel to 2 teaspoons.

EGG-FREE SESAME SEED BREAD: Change the honey to molasses and add 4 teaspoons sesame seeds.

EGG-FREE RAISIN-NUT BREAD: After beating with the mixer, stir in ¼ cup raisins and ¼ cup nuts to the dough. For bread machines add when the manual directs.

EGG-FREE SEED BREAD: Add 2 teaspoons each of the following: poppy seeds, sesame seeds, chopped pumpkin seeds, chopped sunflower kernels.

Nutrients per slice: Calories 90, Fat 2g, Carbohydrate 16g, Cholesterol 0mg, Sodium 80mg, Fiber 1g, Protein 2g.
Dietary exchanges: Bread 1, Fat ½.

Flaxseed Bean Bread
(Egg and Lactose Free)

400°

This flavorful egg substitute may be the answer to your egg allergy. The loaf comes out high and the texture is springy. The flax flavor combines well with other seeds, strong-flavored nuts like walnuts and pecans, and with raisins. Using this one basic recipe you can turn out many variations so you never tire of your bread.

Note: Flax seeds are often used as a laxative, so some celiacs cannot tolerate this substitute, but if you are one who can, this bread will add excellent fiber to your diet.

DRY INGREDIENTS	SMALL	MEDIUM	LARGE
Four Flour Bean Mix (page 40)	2 cups	3 cups	4 cups
Xanthan gum	1½ teaspoons	2¼ teaspoons	3 teaspoons
Salt	½ teaspoon	¾ teaspoon	1 teaspoon
Unflavored gelatin	1 teaspoon	1½ teaspoons	2 teaspoons
NutQuik or almond meal	2 tablespoons	3 tablespoons	4 tablespoons
Brown sugar	2 tablespoons	3 tablespoons	4 tablespoons
Dried orange peel	1 teaspoon	1½ teaspoons	2 teaspoons
Egg Replacer (optional)	1 teaspoon	1½ teaspoons	2 teaspoons
Dry yeast granules	2¼ teaspoons	2¼ teaspoons	2¼ teaspoons

WET INGREDIENTS			
Flaxmeal	4 teaspoons	2 tablespoons	8 teaspoons
Cool water	⅓ cup	½ cup	⅔ cup
Honey	1 tablespoon	1½ tablespoons	2 tablespoons
Dough enhancer or vinegar	½ teaspoon	¾ teaspoon	1 teaspoon
Margarine or butter	2 tablespoons	3 tablespoons	4 tablespoons
Warm water (more or less)	1 cup	1½ cups	2 cups

Grease your chosen pan(s) and dust with rice flour.

The water temperature will be different for hand mixing and for bread machines.

For hand mixing have it about 110°; for your bread machine, read the directions in the manual.

For both hand mixing and machine mixing, combine the dry ingredients in a medium bowl. Set aside.

In another bowl (or the bowl of your heavy-duty mixer), dissolve the flaxmeal in the cool water and whip with a fork. Add the honey, dough enhancer, margarine (cut in chunks), and most of the water. The remaining water should be added as needed after the bread has started mixing, either in the bowl of your mixer or in the pan of the bread machine.

For hand mixing: With the mixer turned to low, add the dry ingredients (including the yeast) a little at a time. Check to be sure the dough is the right consistency (like cake batter). Add more of the reserved water as necessary. Turn the mixer to high and beat for 3½ minutes. Spoon the dough into the prepared pan(s), cover, and let rise about 35–45 minutes for rapid-rising yeast, 60 or more minutes for regular yeast or until the bread has reached the top of the pan. Bake in a preheated 400° oven for 50–60 minutes, covering after 10 minutes with aluminum foil.

For bread machine: Place the ingredients in the bread machine in the order suggested in the machine manual. Use the setting for white bread with medium crust the first time. If necessary, lower to light crust if overbaked.

VARIATIONS: Amounts given are for a small recipe. Adjust amounts for the other sizes.

SESAME SEED FLAXSEED BREAD: Add about 2 teaspoons per cup of flour to the dry ingredients. Substitute molasses for the honey in the wet ingredients.

SEED AND NUT FLAXSEED BREAD: Add to the dry ingredients a bit less than 1 teaspoon each per cup of flour of the following seeds: sesame seeds, chopped pumpkin seeds, chopped sunflower kernels. Add ¼ cup of finely chopped walnuts.

CINNAMON AND RAISIN FLAXSEED BREAD: Add 1 to 2 teaspoons cinnamon to the dry ingredients and stir in ¼ cup raisins to the dough before pouring it into the pan. Check your bread machine directions for adding raisins to the baking pan.

Nutrients per slice: Calories 90, Fat 2.5g, Carbohydrate 16g, Cholesterol 0mg, Sodium 80mg, Fiber 1g, Protein 2g.
Dietary exchanges: Bread 1, Fat ½.

New Allergy Rice Bread
(Egg, Dairy, and Soy Free)

400°

With the new Featherlight Rice Flour Mix, your egg-free breads become lighter than ever. And this one can be soy and dairy free also if you wish. This is specially formatted for those who can't have bean flours. If you can't have the cornstarch in the mix, substitute arrowroot. If you can't find a margarine to suit you, use vegetable oil, but your bread might be heavier.

DRY INGREDIENTS	SMALL	MEDIUM	LARGE
Featherlight Rice Flour Mix (page 40)	2 cups	3 cups	4 cups
Xanthan gum	1½ teaspoons	2¼ teaspoons	3 teaspoons
Salt	½ teaspoon	¾ teaspoon	1 teaspoon
Unflavored gelatin	1 teaspoon	1½ teaspoons	2 teaspoons
Almond meal or sweet rice flour	¼ cup	⅓ cup	½ cup
Sugar	¼ cup	6 tablespoons	½ cup
Baking powder	1 teaspoon	1½ teaspoons	2 teaspoons
Dry yeast granules	2¼ teaspoons	2¼ teaspoons	2¼ teaspoons

WET INGREDIENTS			
Egg Replacer	5½ teaspoons	8 teaspoons	11 teaspoons
Water	⅓ cup	½ cup	⅔ cup
Vinegar	½ teaspoon	¾ teaspoon	1 teaspoon
Margarine (dairy and soy free)	2 tablespoons	3 tablespoons	4 tablespoons
Molasses	1 tablespoon	2 tablespoons	3 tablespoons
Warm water (more or less)	1 cup	1½ cups	2 cups

If using loaf pan(s), grease and dust with rice flour.

The water temperature will be different for hand mixing and for the bread machines. For hand mixing have it about 110°; for your bread machine, read the directions in the manual.

For both hand mixing and machine mixing, combine the dry ingredients in a medium bowl. Set aside.

In another bowl (or the bowl of your mixer), whisk the Egg Replacer and water until it resembles egg whites. Add the vinegar, margarine (in chunks), molasses, and most of the warm water. The remaining water should be added as needed after the bread has started mixing, either in the bowl of your mixer or in the pan of the bread machine.

For hand mixing: With the mixer turned to low, add the dry ingredients (including the yeast) a little at a time. Check to be sure the dough is the right consistency (like cake batter). Add more of the reserved water as necessary. Turn the mixer to high and beat for 3½ minutes. Spoon the dough into the prepared pan(s), cover, and let rise about 35–45 minutes for rapid-rising yeast, 60 or more minutes for regular yeast or until the bread reaches the top of the pan. Bake in a preheated 400° oven for 50–60 minutes, covering after 10 minutes with aluminum foil.

For bread machine: Place the ingredients in the bread machine in the order suggested in the machine manual. Use the setting for white bread with medium crust the first time. If necessary, lower to light crust if overbaked.

Nutrients per slice: Calories 100, Fat 2.5g, Carbohydrate 17g, Cholesterol 0mg, Sodium 75mg, Fiber 1g, Protein 2g.
Dietary exchanges: Bread 1, Fat ½.

YEAST BREAD RECIPES FROM OTHER BOOKS IN THE GLUTEN-FREE GOURMET SERIES

In my first three books I gave recipes for fifty nonsweet yeast breads. I repeated only one in this volume, so to save you time, here is a list of all the breads and sources for these recipes. The books' abbreviations are *The Gluten-free Gourmet* (GFG), *More from the Gluten-free Gourmet* (More), and *The Gluten-free Gourmet Cooks Fast and Healthy* (F&H).

YEAST BREADS	BASE	BOOK	PAGE
Arrowroot (or Cornflour) Bread	Arrowroot	F&H	91
Banana Nut Bread	Rice	F&H	71
Bette's Best Rice Bread	Rice	F&H	72
Buckwheat Bread	Rice	More	68
Butter-Basted Brown and White Bread	Rice	More	40
Butter-Basted White Bread	Rice	More	38
Carrot-Bran Bread	Rice	More	60
Celiac Sourdough Bread	Rice	GFG	27
Cornstarch Bread	Cornstarch	F&H	92
Cranberry-Pecan Bread	Rice	F&H	76
Dark Mock Rye Bread	Rice	F&H	89
Dilly Casserole Bread	Rice	GFG	33
Donna Jo's French Bread	Rice	GFG	30
Egg Replacer Bread	Rice	More	56
Egg Sesame Bread	Rice	GFG	31
Fat-free French Bread	Rice	F&H	75
Fruit Bread with Cardamom	Rice	F&H	78
Heavenly Honey Sourdough	Rice	F&H	94
Honey-Orange Bread with Sesame Seeds	Bean	F&H	88
Italian Herb Sourdough	Rice	More	71
Lemon-Buttermilk Bread	Rice	F&H	80
Mock Graham Bread	Bean	F&H	82
Mock Oatmeal Bread	Rice	More	64
New Formula Yeast Bread	Rice	F&H	70
Nut Butter Bread	Bean	F&H	84

Sweet Yeast Breads

Bean-Based Breads

Sweet Potato–Cranberry Bread
Apricot Bread
Cinnamon Swirl Bread
   Cranberry Swirl Bread
Cinnamon-Nut Bread
Chocolate Challah

Rice-Based Breads

Basic Featherlight Sweet Bread
   Raisin-Nut Bread
   Pannettone
   Julekaka

New Challah
   Raisin Challah
   Chocolate Chip Challah

Sorghum/Rice-Based Bread

Fruited Sorghum Bread

Sweet Yeast Bread Recipes
   from Other Books in the
   Gluten-free Gourmet Series

For holidays, special occasions, and just for a treat, it's satisfying to know that celiacs and those allergic to wheat can still indulge their sweet tooth. It wasn't so long ago when jam on rice crackers was the closest I could come to a sweet bread treat.

Use these breads for breakfast or luncheons, and don't be afraid to feed them to anyone, for they are springy-textured and won't embarrass you by crumbling into your guests' laps.

I've included new challahs using the bean flour mix, and although they can't be braided (since our dough is so soft), any one of the recipes will make an impressive loaf for the holiday.

For many of these breads I've used new mixes of either bean and sorghum flours or a lighter rice mix. You'll find these mixes on page 40.

Sweet Potato–Cranberry Bread

400°

Absolutely delicious. No one will suspect this flavorful and delicious bread is gluten-free. And by using the new bean formula plus mashed sweet potato, the bread is even more tender and springy. Use either fresh or frozen cranberries.

DRY INGREDIENTS	SMALL	MEDIUM	LARGE
Four Flour Bean Mix (page 40)	1¾ cups	2⅔ cups	3½ cups
Xanthan gum	1½ teaspoons	2¼ teaspoons	3 teaspoons
Egg Replacer	1 teaspoon	1½ teaspoons	2 teaspoons
Unflavored gelatin	1 teaspoon	1½ teaspoons	2 teaspoons
Salt	½ teaspoon	¾ teaspoon	1 teaspoon
Sugar	⅓ cup	½ cup	⅔ cup
Dried orange peel	1 teaspoon	1½ teaspoons	2 teaspoons
Almond meal (optional)	2 tablespoons	3 tablespoons	4 tablespoons
Dry yeast granules	2¼ teaspoons	2¼ teaspoons	2¼ teaspoons

WET INGREDIENTS			
Eggs	1 plus 1 white	1 plus 2 whites	1 plus 3 whites
Margarine or butter	3 tablespoons	4½ tablespoons	6 tablespoons
Dough enhancer or vinegar	½ teaspoon	¾ teaspoon	1 teaspoon
Sweet potato, cooked and mashed	¼ cup	⅓ cup	½ cup
Warm water (more or less)	¾ cup	1⅛ cups	1½ cups
Raw cranberries, chopped	1 cup	1½ cups	2 cups

Grease your chosen pan(s) and dust with rice flour.

The water temperature will be different for hand mixing and for bread machines. For hand mixing have the liquid about 110°; for your bread machine, read the directions in the manual.

For both hand mixing and machine mixing, combine the dry ingredients in a medium bowl. Set aside.

In another bowl (or the bowl of your heavy-duty mixer), whisk the egg and white(s), margarine (cut in chunks), dough enhancer, sweet potato, and most of the water. The remaining water should be added as needed after the dough has started mixing, either in the bowl of your mixer or in the pan of the bread machine.

For hand mixing: With the mixer turned to low, add the dry ingredients (including the yeast) a little at a time. Check to be sure the dough is the right consistency (like cake batter). Add more of the reserved liquid as necessary. Turn the mixer to high and beat for 3½ minutes. Stir in the chopped cranberries and spoon into the prepared pan(s), cover, and let rise about 35 minutes for rapid-rising yeast, 60 or more minutes for regular yeast or until the dough reaches the top of the pan or very slightly above. Bake in a preheated 400° oven for 50–60 minutes, covering after 10 minutes with aluminum foil.

For bread machine: Place the ingredients in the bread machine in the order suggested in the machine manual. Add the chopped cranberries at the time the manual suggests for raisins, other fruits, or nuts. Use the setting for medium crust. If this is too dark, try the light crust setting next time.

If desired, while still hot glaze with a thin icing made with powdered sugar and milk.

Nutrients per slice: Calories 100, Fat 3g, Carbohydrate 17g, Cholesterol 10mg, Sodium
    95mg, Fiber 1g, Protein 2g.
Dietary exchanges: Bread 1, Fat 1.

Apricot Bread

400°

I first made this fruited bread as an experiment and found it so delicious that I just had to add it to this collection. Serve this for a breakfast bread in place of coffee cake, at a luncheon with a salad, or, as I do, with cream cheese in place of dessert. Not suitable for bread machines.

DRY INGREDIENTS	SMALL	LARGE
Four Flour Bean Mix (page 40)	2 cups	4 cups
Xanthan gum	1½ teaspoons	3 teaspoons
Salt	½ teaspoon	1 teaspoon
Baking soda	¼ teaspoon	½ teaspoon
Egg Replacer	1 teaspoon	2 teaspoons
Unflavored gelatin	1 teaspoon	2 teaspoons
Pecan or almond meal	2 tablespoons	¼ cup
Dried orange peel	1 teaspoon	2 teaspoons
Brown sugar	3 tablespoons	6 tablespoons
Dry yeast granules	2¼ teaspoons	2¼ teaspoons
Dried apricots, finely cut	¼ cup	½ cup
WET INGREDIENTS		
Eggs	1 plus 1 white	1 plus 3 whites
Dough enhancer or vinegar	½ teaspoon	1 teaspoon
Margarine or butter	3 tablespoons	6 tablespoons
Apricot nectar	One (5½-ounce) can	Two (5½-ounce) cans
Water	2½ tablespoons	5 tablespoons

Grease your pan(s) and dust with rice flour.

Combine the dry ingredients (except apricots) in a medium bowl. Set aside. Cut apricots and set aside.

In the bowl of your heavy-duty mixer, beat the egg and white(s), dough enhancer, and margarine (cut in chunks). Combine the apricot nectar with the water and warm to 110°. Add most of it to the liquids. The remaining liquid should be added as needed after the bread has started mixing.

With the mixer turned to low, add the dry ingredients (except the apricots), including the yeast, a little at a time. Check to be sure the dough is the right consistency (like cake batter). Add more of the reserved liquid as necessary. Turn the mixer to high and beat for 3½ minutes. Stir in the apricots and spoon the dough into the pan(s), cover, and let rise about 35–45 minutes for rapid-rising yeast, 60 or more minutes for regular yeast or until the dough reaches the top of the pan. Bake in a preheated 400° oven for 50–60 minutes, covering after 10 minutes with aluminum foil.

For a tender, shiny crust, rub with butter or margarine as soon as you turn the loaf out to cool.

Nutrients per slice: Calories 100, Fat 3g, Carbohydrate 17g, Cholesterol 10mg, Sodium 120mg, Fiber 1g, Protein 2g.
Dietary exchanges: Bread 1, Fat ½.

Cinnamon Swirl Bread   400°

When another celiac mentioned how hungry she was for a bread like this, just the name made my mouth water. That sent me to the kitchen to see if I couldn't come up with something. This is the happy result. Not suitable for bread machines.

DRY INGREDIENTS	SMALL	LARGE
Four Flour Bean Mix (page 40)	2 cups	4 cups
Xanthan gum	1½ teaspoons	3 teaspoons
Egg Replacer	1 teaspoon	2 teaspoons
Unflavored gelatin	1 teaspoon	2 teaspoons
Salt	½ teaspoon	1 teaspoon
Sugar	3 tablespoons	6 tablespoons
Almond meal or NutQuik	2 tablespoons	¼ cup
Dry yeast granules	2½ teaspoons	2½ teaspoons
STREUSEL		
Brown sugar	2 tablespoons	¼ cup
Cinnamon	1 teaspoon	2 teaspoons
Margarine or butter	1 tablespoon	2 tablespoons
WET INGREDIENTS		
Instant potato flakes	1 teaspoon	2 teaspoons
Warm water (more or less)	1 cup	2 cups
Eggs	1 plus 1 white	1 plus 3 whites
Margarine or butter	3 tablespoons	6 tablespoons
Dough enhancer or vinegar	½ teaspoon	1 teaspoon
Vanilla flavoring	1 teaspoon	2 teaspoons

Grease your 8½" × 4½" bread pan(s) and dust with rice flour.

In a bowl, whisk together the dry ingredients, including the yeast. Set aside.

Make the streusel by combining the brown sugar, cinnamon, and margarine. Set aside.

Dissolve the potato flakes in the warm water. In the bowl of your mixer, blend the egg and white(s), margarine (cut in small chunks), dough enhancer, and vanilla. Add most of the potato water, reserving about ¼ cup to add later if needed. With the mixer on low, add the dry ingredients a little at a time. Check to see if you need the reserved water to achieve the texture of cake batter. Beat on high for 3 minutes. Spoon about one-third into the prepared pan(s). Sprinkle on one-third of the streusel. Spoon on half of the remaining dough and half of the remaining streusel. Finish with the remaining dough and the last of the streusel on top. Take a knife and swirl through the dough in the pan(s).

Cover the pan(s) and let the dough rise about 35 minutes for rapid-rising yeast, 60 minutes for regular yeast or until the dough reaches the top of the pan. Bake in a preheated 400° oven for 50–60 minutes, covering after 10 minutes with aluminum foil. Turn out of the pan and rub the top with margarine or butter for a more tender crust. Cool before slicing.

VARIATION: Amounts given are for a large recipe; cut about one-third for small.

CRANBERRY SWIRL BREAD: Change the streusel to ⅓ cup chopped raw cranberries, 3 tablespoons brown sugar, 2 tablespoons chopped pecans, ½ teaspoon apple pie spice, and ½ teaspoon dried orange peel.

Nutrients per slice: Calories 100, Fat 4g, Carbohydrate 17g, Cholesterol 10mg, Sodium 115mg, Fiber 1g, Protein 2g.
Dietary exchanges: Bread 1, Fat 1.

Cinnamon-Nut Bread

400°

When my husband toasts his wheat-based cinnamon nut bread every morning, the kitchen smells so wonderful that I decided to try to create a bread that smelled as heavenly. I think this does! Try this wonderfully light-textured new bread and see if I'm right.

Note: *The yeast is listed with the wet ingredients in this recipe.*

DRY INGREDIENTS	SMALL	MEDIUM	LARGE
Four Flour Bean Mix (page 40)	2 cups	3 cups	4 cups
Xanthan gum	1½ teaspoons	2¼ teaspoons	3 teaspoons
Egg Replacer	1 teaspoon	1½ teaspoons	2 teaspoons
Unflavored gelatin	1 teaspoon	1½ teaspoons	2 teaspoons
Salt	½ teaspoon	¾ teaspoon	1 teaspoon
Brown sugar	3 tablespoons	4½ tablespoons	6 tablespoons
NutQuik or almond meal	2 tablespoons	3 tablespoons	4 tablespoons
Cinnamon	1 teaspoon	1½ teaspoons	2 teaspoons
Chopped nuts (pecan or walnut)	⅓ cup	½ cup	⅔ cup

WET INGREDIENTS			
Instant potato flakes	1 teaspoon	1½ teaspoons	2 teaspoons
Warm water (more or less)	1 cup	1½ cups	2 cups
Dry yeast granules	1 tablespoon	1 tablespoon	1 tablespoon
Eggs	1 plus 1 white	1 plus 2 whites	1 plus 3 whites
Margarine or butter	3 tablespoons	4½ tablespoons	6 tablespoons
Dough enhancer or vinegar	½ teaspoon	¾ teaspoon	1 teaspoon

Grease your chosen pan(s) and dust lightly with rice flour.

The water temperature will be different for hand mixing and bread machines. For hand mixing have it about 110° to 115°; for your bread machine, read the directions in the manual.

For both hand and machine mixing, combine the dry ingredients (except the nuts) in a medium bowl. Set aside. Measure the nuts and set aside.

Dissolve the potato flakes in the water.

For hand mixing: Dissolve the yeast in the potato water. Set aside. In the bowl of your heavy-duty mixer, place the egg and white(s), margarine (cut in chunks), and dough enhancer. When the yeast foams, add most of the yeast water to the liquids in the mixer. The remaining yeast water should be added as needed after the bread has started mixing. With the mixer on low, add the dry ingredients 1 spoonful at a time. Check to be sure the dough is the right consistency (like cake batter). Add more yeast water as necessary. Turn the mixer to high and beat 3½ minutes. Stir in the nuts and spoon into the prepared pan(s). Cover and let rise about 35 minutes for rapid-rising yeast, 60 minutes for regular yeast or until the dough reaches the top of the pan. Bake in a preheated 400° oven for 50–60 minutes, covering after 10 minutes with aluminum foil. Turn out of the pan and let cool before slicing.

For bread machine: Place the ingredients in the bread machine in the order suggested in the machine manual. The yeast may be incorporated into the dry ingredients, or it may be either on the top or bottom of the machine pan. Add the nuts when suggested by the manual.

Nutrients per slice: Calories 120, Fat 4g, Carbohydrate 17g, Cholesterol 10mg, Sodium 105mg, Fiber 1g, Protein 3g.
Dietary exchanges: Bread 1, Fat 1.

Chocolate Challah 400°

Challah is a braided sweet bread often served on Jewish holidays, but since our doughs are too soft to be braided, I make this in a loaf pan. With the nuts and fruit, this could be a celiac treat for chocolate lovers anytime.

DRY INGREDIENTS	SMALL	MEDIUM	LARGE
Four Flour Bean Mix (page 40)	2 cups	3 cups	4 cups
Xanthan gum	1½ teaspoons	2¼ teaspoons	3 teaspoons
Unsweetened cocoa powder	2 tablespoons	3 tablespoons	5 tablespoons
Egg Replacer	1 teaspoon	1½ teaspoons	2 teaspoons
Dry milk powder or nondairy substitute	⅓ cup	½ cup	1 cup
Sugar	½ cup	¾ cup	1 cup
Salt	½ teaspoon	¾ teaspoon	1 teaspoon
Orange zest	2 teaspoons	3 teaspoons	4 teaspoons
Dry yeast granules	2¼ teaspoons	2¼ teaspoons	2¼ teaspoons
Pecans, chopped	⅓ cup	½ cup	⅔ cup
Chopped pitted dates or raisins	2 tablespoons	3 tablespoons	4 tablespoons

WET INGREDIENTS			
Eggs	2	3	4
Dough enhancer	½ teaspoon	¾ teaspoon	1 teaspoon
Butter or margarine	3 tablespoons	4¼ tablespoons	5½ tablespoons
Water (more or less)	¾ cup	1⅛ cups	1½ cups

Grease your chosen pan(s) and dust with rice flour.

The water temperature will be different for hand mixing and for bread machines. For hand mixing have it about 110°; for your bread machine, read the directions in the manual.

For both hand mixing and machine mixing, combine the dry ingredients except for the nuts and dates. Set aside. Measure the nuts and dates to have handy.

In another bowl (or the bowl of your heavy-duty mixer), whisk the eggs, dough enhancer, butter (cut in chunks), and most of the water. The remaining water should be added as needed after the dough has started mixing, either in the bowl of your mixer or in the pan of the bread machine.

For hand mixing: With the mixer turned low, add the dry ingredients, except the nuts and dates (including the yeast), a little at a time. Check to be sure the dough is the right consistency (like cake batter). Add more of the reserved water as necessary. Turn the mixer to high and beat for 3½ minutes. Stir in the nuts and dates. Spoon into the prepared pan(s), cover, and let rise about 35 minutes for rapid-rising yeast, 60 or more minutes for regular yeast or until the dough reaches the top of the pan. Bake in a preheated 400° oven for 50–60 minutes, covering after 10 minutes with aluminum foil.

For bread machines: Place the ingredients in the bread machine in the order suggested in the machine manual. Use the setting for medium crust. Add the dates and nuts when suggested by the manual.

If desired, while still hot, glaze with a thin icing made with powdered sugar and milk.

Nutrients per slice: Calories 130, Fat 5g, Carbohydrate 20g, Cholesterol 30mg, Sodium 100mg, Fiber 1g, Protein 3g.
Dietary exchanges: Bread 1½, Fat 1.

Basic Featherlight Sweet Bread

400°

New and better! This basic sweet bread dough can be changed easily to make many variations, from raisin-nut to the Scandinavian julekaka. With the new Featherlight Rice Flour Mix, the bread is springy, tender, and stays fresh-tasting for days.

Note: *The baking soda is necessary only when using orange juice.*

DRY INGREDIENTS	SMALL	MEDIUM	LARGE
Featherlight Rice Flour Mix (page 40)	2 cups	3 cups	4 cups
Xanthan gum	1½ teaspoons	2¼ teaspoons	3 teaspoons
Salt	½ teaspoon	¾ teaspoon	1 teaspoon
Unflavored gelatin	1 teaspoon	1½ teaspoons	2 teaspoons
Egg Replacer	1 teaspoon	1½ teaspoons	2 teaspoons
Almond meal or NutQuik	3 tablespoons	4½ tablespoons	⅓ cup
Sugar	⅓ cup	½ cup	⅔ cup
Baking soda (see Note)	¼ teaspoon	⅓ teaspoon	½ teaspoon
Dry yeast granules	2¼ teaspoons	2¼ teaspoons	2¼ teaspoons
WET INGREDIENTS			
Eggs	3	4 plus 1 white	6
Honey	2 teaspoons	1 tablespoon	4 teaspoons
Dough enhancer or vinegar	½ teaspoon	¾ teaspoon	1 teaspoon
Margarine or butter	⅓ cup	½ cup	⅔ cup
Instant potato flakes	2 teaspoons	1 tablespoon	4 teaspoons
Orange juice or water	1 cup	1½ cups	2 cups

Grease your chosen pan(s) and dust with rice flour.

The orange juice (or water) temperature will be different for hand mixing and for bread machines. For hand mixing have the liquid about 110°; for your bread machine, read the directions in the manual.

For both hand mixing and machine mixing, combine the dry ingredients in a medium bowl. Set aside.

In another bowl (or the bowl of your heavy-duty mixer), whisk the eggs, honey, dough enhancer, and margarine (cut in chunks). Dissolve the potato flakes in the orange juice (or water) and add most of it. The remaining liquid should be added as needed after the dough has started mixing, either in the bowl of your mixer or in the pan of the bread machine.

For hand mixing: With the mixer turned to low, add the dry ingredients (including the yeast) a little at a time. Check to be sure the dough is the right consistency (like cake batter). Add more of the reserved liquid as necessary. Turn the mixer to high and beat for 3½ minutes. Spoon into the prepared pan(s), cover, and let rise about 35 minutes for rapid-rising yeast, 60 or more minutes for regular yeast or until the dough reaches the top of the pan. Bake in a preheated 400° oven for 50–60 minutes, covering after 10 minutes with aluminum foil.

For bread machine: Place the ingredients in the bread machine in the order suggested in the machine manual. Use the setting for light crust. If this doesn't cook thoroughly the first time, increase the setting to medium crust. Add the variation ingredients (if using) according to the manual's suggestions for raisins or other fruit.

If desired, while still hot glaze any of the sweet bread variations with a thin icing made with powdered sugar and milk.

VARIATIONS: Amounts given are for a small recipe. Increase proportionately for a larger size. I usually measure these and tumble them in the bowl of the dry ingredients with the small amount of flour remaining. This way they don't clump together while stirring into the dough.

RAISIN-NUT BREAD: Add 1 teaspoon cardamom to the dry ingredients. After beating, stir in ⅓ cup each raisins and chopped nuts.

PANETTONE: After beating, add about ¼ cup each chopped nuts, chopped citron, and raisins.

JULEKAKA: After beating, add ⅓ cup chopped citron or dried fruitcake mix.

Nutrients per slice: Calories 130, Fat 5g, Carbohydrate 18g, Cholesterol 35mg, Sodium 135mg, Fiber 1g, Protein 2g.
Dietary exchanges: Bread 1, Fat 1.

New Challah

400°

A lighter challah with a more springy texture! The new Featherlight Rice Flour Mix keeps the bread from being so dense.

Note: *The baking soda is necessary only when using orange juice as the liquid.*

DRY INGREDIENTS	SMALL	MEDIUM	LARGE
Featherlight Rice Flour Mix (page 40)	2 cups	3 cups	4 cups
Xanthan gum	1½ teaspoons	2¼ teaspoons	3 teaspoons
Salt	½ teaspoon	¾ teaspoon	1 teaspoon
Egg Replacer	1 teaspoon	1½ teaspoons	2 teaspoons
Dry milk powder or almond meal	¼ cup	⅓ cup	½ cup
Brown sugar	⅓ cup	½ cup	⅔ cup
Baking soda (see Note)	¼ teaspoon	⅓ teaspoon	½ teaspoon
Dry yeast granules	2¼ teaspoons	2¼ teaspoons	2¼ teaspoons
WET INGREDIENTS			
Eggs	3	4 plus 1 white	6
Honey	1 tablespoon	1½ tablespoons	2 tablespoons
Dough enhancer or vinegar	½ teaspoon	¾ teaspoon	1 teaspoon
Butter or margarine	⅓ cup	½ cup	⅔ cup
Instant potato flakes	2 teaspoons	1 tablespoon	4 teaspoons
Orange juice or water	1 cup	1½ cups	2 cups

Grease your chosen pan(s) and dust with rice flour.

The orange juice (or water) temperature will be different for hand mixing and for bread machines. For hand mixing have the liquid about 110°; for your bread machine, read the directions in the manual.

For both hand mixing and machine mixing, combine the dry ingredients in a medium bowl. Set aside.

In another bowl (or the bowl of your heavy-duty mixer), whisk the eggs, honey, dough enhancer, and butter (cut in chunks). Dissolve the potato flakes in the orange juice (or water) and add most of it. The remaining liquid should be added as needed after the dough has started mixing, either in the bowl of your mixer or in the pan of the bread machine.

For hand mixing: With the mixer turned to low, add the flour mix (including the yeast) a little at a time. Check to be sure the dough is the right consistency (like cake batter). Add more of the reserved liquid as necessary. Turn the mixer to high and beat for 3½ minutes. Spoon into the prepared pan(s), cover, and let rise about 35 minutes for rapid-rising yeast, 60 or more minutes for regular yeast or until the dough reaches the top of the pan. Bake in a preheated 400° oven for 50–60 minutes, covering after 10 minutes with aluminum foil.

For bread machines: Place the ingredients in the bread machine in the order suggested in the machine manual. Use the setting for light crust. If this doesn't cook thoroughly the first time, increase the setting to medium crust.

VARIATIONS: After spooning into the loaf pans, you may gently brush the top of the dough with egg wash (beaten egg) and sprinkle on poppy seeds or sesame seeds before letting the dough rise.

RAISIN CHALLAH: After mixing, stir in ⅓ to ½ cup raisins before spooning the dough into a loaf pan. For a bread machine, add when the manual suggests.

CHOCOLATE CHIP CHALLAH: Stir in ⅓ to ½ cup chocolate chips before spooning the dough into a loaf pan. For a bread machine, add when the manual suggests.

Nutrients per slice: Calories 120, Fat 5g, Carbohydrate 18g, Cholesterol 45mg, Sodium 135mg, Fiber 0g, Protein 2g.
Dietary exchanges: Bread 1, Fat 1.

Fruited Sorghum Bread

This sweet bread uses sorghum in place of a lot of the sugar. It's a bit more solid than the Featherlight or bean breads but is still springy, stays fresh-tasting a long time, and doesn't crumble in the hand. The flavor is delightful.

DRY INGREDIENTS	SMALL	MEDIUM	LARGE
Sorghum flour	½ cup	¾ cup	1 cup
Brown rice flour	½ cup	¾ cup	1 cup
Cornstarch	½ cup	¾ cup	1 cup
Tapioca flour	½ cup	¾ cup	1 cup
Xanthan gum	1½ teaspoons	2¼ teaspoons	3 teaspoons
Egg Replacer	1 teaspoon	1½ teaspoons	2 teaspoons
Unflavored gelatin	1 teaspoon	1½ teaspoons	2 teaspoons
Salt	½ teaspoon	¾ teaspoon	1 teaspoon
Sugar	2 tablespoons	3 tablespoons	¼ cup
Cardamom	¾ teaspoon	1 rounded teaspoon	1½ teaspoons
Almond meal, dry milk powder, or nondairy substitute	2 tablespoons	3 tablespoons	¼ cup
Raisins, dried cranberries, or citron (or a combination)	⅓ cup	½ cup	⅔ cup

WET INGREDIENTS			
Eggs	1 plus 1 white	1 plus 2 whites	1 plus 3 whites
Butter or margarine	2½ tablespoons	3¾ tablespoons	5 tablespoons
Dough enhancer or vinegar	½ teaspoon	¾ teaspoon	1 teaspoon
Instant potato flakes	1 teaspoon	1½ teaspoons	2 teaspoons
Warm water (more or less)	1¼ cups	2 cups (scant)	2½ cups
Dry yeast granules	4 teaspoons	4 teaspoons	4 teaspoons

Grease your chosen pan(s) and dust with rice flour.

In a small bowl, whisk together all the ingredients except the fruit. Measure the raisins, cranberries, or citron, and set aside.

For hand mixing: In the bowl of your mixer place the egg and white(s), butter (cut in small chunks), and dough enhancer. With the mixer on low, beat until the eggs are slightly foamy. Dissolve the potato flakes in the water and add the yeast. When it foams, pour into the mixer, reserving some. With the mixer on low, add the flour mixture 1 spoonful at a time. Beat on high for 3 minutes. Stir in the dried fruit and spoon into the prepared pan(s). Cover and let rise about 35 minutes for rapid-rising yeast, 60 or more minutes for regular yeast or until the dough rises to the top of the pan. Bake in a preheated 400° oven for 50–60 minutes, covering after 10 minutes with aluminum foil. Turn out of the pan and let cool before slicing.

For bread machine: Follow the directions above for mixing the dry ingredients and measuring the dried fruit. Blend the wet ingredients except for the yeast. Follow the instructions in the machine manual for adding the yeast. Some manuals suggest combining it with the dry ingredients, and some suggest putting it on top.

Nutrients per slice: Calories 100, Fat 2.5g, Carbohydrate 18g, Cholesterol 15mg, Sodium 90mg, Fiber 1g, Protein 2g.
Dietary exchanges: Bread 1, Fat ½.

SWEET YEAST BREAD RECIPES FROM OTHER BOOKS IN THE GLUTEN-FREE GOURMET SERIES

In previous books I gave very few sweet yeast breads except as variations; to save you the time of searching three indexes for those that are truly sweet breads, I've listed them here (see page 107 for book title abbreviations):

YEAST BREADS	BASE	BOOK	PAGE
Apple-Spice Bread	Rice	More	61
Apricot-Almond Bread	Rice	More	52
Boston Brown Bread	Rice	More	65
Challah	Rice	More	54
Cinnamon-Raisin Nut Bread	Bean	F&H	85
Hawaiian Medley	Rice	More	63
Russian Kulich	Rice	More	50
Single Rising Coffee Bread	Rice	GFG	32

Yeast-free Loaf Breads

Bean-Based Breads

Basic Yeast-free Bean Bread
　Poppy Seed Loaf
　Nut and Raisin Loaf
　Cinnamon-Raisin Loaf
　Sesame Seed Loaf
Bette's Special Three-Vegetable Bread
Yeast-free Garbanzo Bean Bread
　Nut and Raisin Garbanzo Loaf
　Cinnamon-Raisin Garbanzo Loaf
　Sesame Garbanzo Loaf
　Seed and Nut Garbanzo Loaf
Yeast-free Zucchini Cheese Bread
　Parmesan-Herb Loaf
　Banana-Cheese Loaf
Basic Almond Bread
　Seed and Nut Loaf
　Almond-Raisin Loaf

Ballard Bread
High-Fiber Carrot Bread
　Carrot and Seed Loaf
　Carrot-Nut Loaf
　Carrot-Raisin Loaf
　Garden Loaf
Yogurt and Honey Quickbread
　Raisin-Cinnamon Yogurt Loaf
　Cinnamon-Nut Yogurt Loaf
　Cranberry Yogurt Loaf
　Cranberry-Cashew Yogurt Loaf

Rice-Based Breads

Basic Yeast-free Rice Bread
　Poppy Seed Rice Loaf
　Nut and Raisin Rice Loaf
　Cinnamon-Raisin Rice Loaf

Rye Breads

Limpa Bread
   Yeast-free Caraway Rye
   Yeast-free Pumpernickel

Soda Bread

Egg-free Soda Bread

Corn Breads

Springy Corn Bread
Cheesy Vegetable Corn Bread

Sweet Breads

Date Nut Loaf
Elizabeth's Favorite Banana Bread
Four Flour Banana Nut Bread
Pumpkin Tea Bread
Chocolate-Cherry Loaf
   Chocolate-Raspberry Loaf
Pineapple Walnut Loaf

Yeast-free Loaf Bread Recipes from Other Books in the Gluten-free Gourmet Series

Whether you're allergic to yeast or just want a change, you'll find many of the breads in this section as suitable for sandwiches as the yeast-rising loaves. And unlike most of the yeast-free breads of the past, these won't fall apart in your hands, nor will they fill your lap with crumbs.

Although my previous books considered yeast-free synonomous with tea or sweet breads, many of these taste like their yeast-rising counterparts. But if you still crave the sweet taste, you'll find some new sweet yeast-free breads in the last half of the section—and they are better than ever.

In many cases the new format allows you to make one loaf or two using the following headings (unless otherwise directed):

Small: One 8½" × 4½" loaf pan
Large: Two 8½" × 4½" loaf pans

I've used four different flour mixes in these breads. If you are not familiar with them, please turn to page 40 for the formulas.

If you want to use a favorite yeast-free bread recipe from my other books, you will find them listed at the end of this chapter.

Basic Yeast-free Bean Bread 350°

"A winner!" my testers exclaimed. You won't believe this isn't a yeast bread. The texture is springy, the taste is super. For those who can't have yeast, this is a bread to live with. Use it plain or make one of the variations listed below, adding your own seeds, dried fruit, or nuts. My favorite is the Poppy Seed Loaf. Not suitable for bread machines.

For the lactose intolerant, *replace the buttermilk with a nondairy substitute plus 1 tablespoon vinegar per cup of substitute.*

DRY INGREDIENTS	SMALL	LARGE
Four Flour Bean Mix (page 40)	2 cups	4 cups
Xanthan gum	1½ teaspoons	3 teaspoons
Brown sugar	3 tablespoons	⅓ cup
Baking soda	½ teaspoon	1 teaspoon
Baking powder	2 teaspoons	1 rounded tablespoon
Egg Replacer	1 teaspoon	2 teaspoons
Salt	½ teaspoon	1 teaspoon
WET INGREDIENTS		
Eggs	2 plus 1 white	3 plus 2 whites
Margarine or butter, melted	3 tablespoons	6 tablespoons
Honey	1 tablespoon	2 tablespoons
Dough enhancer (optional)	½ teaspoon	1 teaspoon
Buttermilk	¾ cup	1½ cups
Water (more or less)	⅓ cup	½ cup

Preheat oven to 350°. Grease your loaf pan(s) and dust lightly with rice flour.

In a bowl, whisk together the dry ingredients. Set aside.

In the bowl of your mixer, beat the eggs and white(s). Add the melted margarine, honey, dough enhancer (if using), and buttermilk. Turn the mixer to low and blend.

Add the dry ingredients while on low. Add sufficient water to make the dough the consistency of cake batter. Beat 1 minute on high. Spoon into the prepared pan(s) and bake for 55 to 60 minutes, covering after 30 minutes with aluminum foil.

VARIATIONS: The amounts given are for a small recipe; double for large.

POPPY SEED LOAF: Eliminate the honey from the wet ingredients and add 2 teaspoons poppy seeds and 1 teaspoon dried lemon peel to the dry ingredients.

NUT AND RAISIN LOAF: Add 1 teaspoon dried orange peel to the dry ingredients, and after beating, stir in 3 tablespoons each chopped nuts and raisins.

CINNAMON-RAISIN LOAF: Add 1 teaspoon cinnamon to the dry ingredients, and after beating, stir in ¼ cup raisins.

SESAME SEED LOAF: Add 2 teaspoons sesame seeds to the dry ingredients and substitute molasses for the honey in the wet ingredients.

Nutrients per slice: Calories 100, Fat 3g, Carbohydrate 16g, Cholesterol 25mg, Sodium 310mg, Fiber 1g, Protein 2g.
Dietary exchanges: Bread 1, Fat ½.

Bette's Special Three-Vegetable Bread 350°

Don't miss this! With beans, carrots, and zucchini in the batter, this bread is healthy as well as delicious. Only 2 tablespoonfuls of sugar per loaf keep it from being a sweet bread so this can be used with fillings or eaten plain with butter.

DRY INGREDIENTS	SMALL	LARGE
Four Flour Bean Mix (page 40)	1½ cups	3 cups
Xanthan gum	1 teaspoon	2 teaspoons
Baking powder	2 teaspoons	4 teaspoons
Baking soda	1 teaspoon	2 teaspoons
Egg Replacer	1 teaspoon	2 teaspoons
Dried lemon peel	1 teaspoon	2 teaspoons
Brown sugar	2 tablespoons	¼ cup
Salt	¼ teaspoon	½ teaspoon

WET INGREDIENTS		
Eggs	1 plus 1 white	2 plus 2 whites
Vanilla	1 teaspoon	2 teaspoons
Shredded carrot	½ cup	1 cup
Shredded zucchini	½ cup	1 cup
Orange juice	⅓ cup	⅔ cup
Honey	1 tablespoon	2 tablespoons
Vegetable oil	2 tablespoons	¼ cup
Walnuts, chopped	¼ cup	½ cup

Preheat oven to 350°. For a small recipe, grease one 8½" × 4½" loaf pan; for large, grease 2 pans.

In a mixing bowl, whisk together all the dry ingredients.

In a bowl, beat the eggs and vanilla. Add the carrot, zucchini, orange juice, honey, and vegetable oil. Stir this into the flour mixture and beat until moistened. Stir in the walnuts. Spoon the dough into the prepared pan(s) and bake at 350° for approximately 40 minutes, or until a tester inserted in the center comes out clean. Remove from the pan and cool before slicing.

Nutrients per slice: Calories 80, Fat 3g, Carbohydrate 12g, Cholesterol 10mg, Sodium 110mg, Fiber 1g, Protein 2g.
Dietary exchanges: Bread 1, Fat ½.

Yeast-free Garbanzo Bean Bread   350°

Although I prefer using Authentic Foods' Garfava flour (a combination of garbanzo and broad beans) because of the mild taste and smooth texture, some readers may wish to use only garbanzo bean flour. This bread comes out less springy but still finely textured, with a nutty flavor. Use this basic recipe or make any of the variations, or add your own extra ingredients such as seeds, dried fruit, or nuts.

DRY INGREDIENTS	SMALL	LARGE
Garbanzo bean flour	½ cup	1 cup
Sorghum flour	2½ tablespoons	5 tablespoons
Cornstarch	⅔ cup	1⅓ cups
Tapioca flour	⅔ cup	1⅓ cups
Xanthan gum	1 teaspoon	2 teaspoons
Brown sugar	3 tablespoons	⅓ cup
Baking soda	½ teaspoon	1 teaspoon
Baking powder	2 teaspoons	4 teaspoons
Dried orange peel	1 teaspoon	2 teaspoons
Egg Replacer	1 teaspoon	2 teaspoons
Salt	½ teaspoon	1 teaspoon

WET INGREDIENTS

Eggs	2 plus 1 white	4 plus 2 whites
Margarine or butter, melted	3 tablespoons	6 tablespoons
Honey	1 tablespoon	2 tablespoons
Dough enhancer	1 teaspoon	2 teaspoons
Buttermilk or nondairy substitute	¾ cup	1½ cups
Water (more or less)	¼ cup	½ cup

Preheat oven to 350°. For a small loaf grease one 8½" by 4½" loaf pan; for large, prepare 2 pans.

In a medium bowl, whisk together the dry ingredients. Set aside.

In the bowl of your mixer, beat the eggs and white(s). Add the melted margarine, honey, dough enhancer, and buttermilk. Turn the mixer to low and blend. Add the dry ingredients while on low. Add sufficient water to make the dough the consistency of cake batter. Beat 1 minute on high. Spoon the dough into the prepared pan(s) and bake for 55–60 minutes, covering after 30 minutes with aluminum foil.

VARIATIONS: Measurements are given for one loaf; double for two.

NUT AND RAISIN GARBANZO LOAF: Add 1 teaspoon dried orange peel to the dry ingredients, and after beating, stir in 3 tablespoons each raisins and chopped nuts.

CINNAMON-RAISIN GARBANZO LOAF: Add 1 teaspoon cinnamon to the dry ingredients and ¼ cup raisins before spooning into loaf pan.

SESAME GARBANZO LOAF: Add 2 teaspoons sesame seeds to the dry ingredients.

SEED AND NUT GARBANZO LOAF: Add ¼ cup chopped walnuts plus 1 teaspoon each sesame seeds, chopped pumpkin seeds, and chopped sunflower seeds (or to taste).

Nutrients per slice: Calories 90, Fat 3g, Carbohydrate 16g, Cholesterol 25mg, Sodium 200mg, Fiber 1g, Protein 2g.
Dietary exchanges: Bread 1, Fat ½.

Yeast-free Zucchini Cheese Bread   350°

Use this rich, cheese-and-onion-flavored bread with any meat or cheese filling for sandwiches, or serve it with stews or casseroles. It is slightly less springy than one with much the same ingredients using yeast, but if you can't have yeast, this is a great bread. This is very easy to mix and, like muffins, it requires no heavy-duty mixer.

DRY INGREDIENTS	SMALL	LARGE
Four Flour Bean Mix (page 40)	2 cups	4 cups
Xanthan gum	1½ teaspoons	3 teaspoons
Sugar	⅓ cup	⅔ cup
Grated Parmesan cheese	2 tablespoons	¼ cup
Baking powder	2 teaspoons	4 teaspoons
Salt	½ teaspoon	1 teaspoon
Baking soda	1 teaspoon	2 teaspoons
Shredded zucchini, squeezed or patted dry	⅔ cup	1⅓ cups

WET INGREDIENTS		
Eggs	2	4
Margarine or butter, melted	3 tablespoons	6 tablespoons
Buttermilk	⅔ cup	1⅓ cups
Grated fresh onion	1¼ tablespoons	2½ tablespoons

Preheat oven to 350°. Grease your chosen pan(s).

In a mixing bowl, whisk together the dry ingredients except the zucchini. Add the shredded zucchini and blend well.

In a bowl, combine the wet ingredients. Beat until well combined, using a whisk or eggbeater.

Pour the liquids into the dry ingredients and mix thoroughly. Spoon into the pan(s) and bake for 50–60 minutes. Leave in the pan to cool for 15 minutes and then remove to cool completely before slicing.

VARIATIONS: Amounts given are for one loaf; double for two.

PARMESAN-HERB LOAF: Add 2 teaspoons Italian seasoning to the dry ingredients.

BANANA-CHEESE LOAF: Substitute mashed bananas for the zucchini. Substitute 3¼ tablespoons Jack cheese for the Parmesan and onion. Add 2 tablespoons ground nuts.

Nutrients per slice: Calories 110, Fat 5g, Carbohydrate 15g, Cholesterol 25mg, Sodium 200mg, Fiber 1g, Protein 3g.
Dietary exchanges: Bread 1, Fat 1.

Basic Almond Bread
(Yeast and Cholesterol Free)

350°

A nutty-flavored basic bread for those who can't tolerate yeast. This is springy textured and makes great sandwiches. It can be varied with the addition of seeds, nuts, or fruit. See the variations below.

DRY INGREDIENTS	SMALL	LARGE
Four Flour Bean Mix (page 40)	2 cups	4 cups
Xanthan gum	1½ teaspoons	3 teaspoons
Brown sugar	2 tablespoons	¼ cup
Baking soda	½ teaspoon	1 teaspoon
Baking powder	2 teaspoons	4 teaspoons
Egg Replacer	1 teaspoon	2 teaspoons
Almond meal	¼ cup	½ cup
Salt	½ teaspoon	1 teaspoon

WET INGREDIENTS

Liquid egg substitute	⅔ cup	1⅓ cups
Margarine, melted	3 tablespoons	6 tablespoons
Honey	1 tablespoon	2 tablespoons
Dough enhancer	½ teaspoon	1 teaspoon
Nondairy liquid	¾ cup	1½ cups
Vinegar	¾ tablespoon	1½ tablespoons

Preheat oven to 350°. Grease your loaf pan(s) and dust with rice flour.

In a mixing bowl, whisk together the dry ingredients.

In a medium bowl, combine the egg substitute, margarine, honey, dough enhancer, and nondairy liquid with the vinegar in it.

Pour the liquids into the dry ingredients and mix thoroughly, beating with a mixing spoon for a few beats but not an electric beater. Spoon into the prepared pan(s) and bake for 50–60 minutes. Leave in the pan to cool for about 10 minutes and then remove to cool completely before slicing.

VARIATIONS: Amounts given are for a single loaf; double for two.

SEED AND NUT LOAF: Add ¼ cup nuts plus 1 teaspoon each of the following seeds for every cup of flour: sesame, chopped pumpkin, chopped sunflower.

ALMOND-RAISIN LOAF: Add ¼ cup golden raisins.

Nutrients per slice: Calories 120, Fat 5g, Carbohydrate 17g, Cholesterol 0mg, Sodium 190mg, Fiber 1g, Protein 3g.
Dietary exchanges: Bread 1, Fat 1.

Ballard Bread

350°

The name for this anise-flavored, fruit-and-nut-filled bread came from my Ballard neighborhood because this is the type of bread served by Scandinavians for potlucks and church suppers, especially at the holidays.

DRY INGREDIENTS	SMALL	LARGE
Four Flour Bean Mix (page 40)	2 cups	4 cups
Xanthan gum	1½ teaspoons	3 teaspoons
Brown sugar	2 tablespoons	¼ cup
Baking soda	½ teaspoon	1 teaspoon
Baking powder	2 teaspoons	4 teaspoons
Egg Replacer	1 teaspoon	2 teaspoons
Almond meal	1 tablespoon	2 tablespoons
Salt	½ teaspoon	1 teaspoon
Dried orange peel	1 teaspoon	2 teaspoons
Anise seeds	½ teaspoon	1 teaspoon
WET INGREDIENTS		
Eggs	2	4
Butter or margarine, melted	3 tablespoons	6 tablespoons
Honey	1 tablespoon	2 tablespoons
Dough enhancer or vinegar	½ teaspoon	1 teaspoon
Buttermilk or nondairy substitute	¾ cup	1½ cups
FRUIT AND NUTS		
Chopped walnuts	⅓ cup	⅔ cup
Mixed candied fruit, chopped	⅓ cup	⅔ cup

Preheat oven to 350°. Grease your loaf pan(s) and dust with rice flour.

In a mixing bowl, whisk together the dry ingredients.

In a medium bowl, combine the wet ingredients. Beat until well combined using a whisk or eggbeater.

Pour the liquids into the dry ingredients and mix thoroughly. Beat with a mixing spoon for a few beats but not an electric beater. Stir in the nuts and dried fruit. Spoon into the prepared pan(s) and bake for 55–60 minutes. Leave in the pan to cool for about 10 minutes and then remove to cool completely before slicing.

Nutrients per slice: Calories 120, Fat 4g, Carbohydrate 18g, Cholesterol 25mg, Sodium 570mg, Fiber 1g, Protein 3g.
Dietary exchanges: Bread 1, Fat ½.

High-Fiber Carrot Bread 350°

This is a basic bread, not sweet, that can be changed many ways by the addition of nuts, raisins, or chopped sunflower seeds. See the variations below or dream up your own.

For a nondairy substitute, use 1 tablespoon vinegar per 2 cups nondairy milk.

DRY INGREDIENTS	SMALL	LARGE
Four Flour Bean Mix (page 40)	2 cups	4 cups
Xanthan gum	1½ teaspoons	3 teaspoons
Brown sugar	2 tablespoons	4 tablespoons
Baking soda	¾ teaspoon	1½ teaspoons
Baking powder	2 teaspoons	4 teaspoons
Egg Replacer	1 teaspoon	2 teaspoons
Almond meal	2 tablespoons	¼ cup
Salt	½ teaspoon	1 teaspoon
Cinnamon	1 teaspoon	2 teaspoons
Dried orange peel	1 teaspoon	2 teaspoons
Finely grated carrots, squeezed or patted dry	⅔ cup	1⅓ cups

WET INGREDIENTS	SMALL	LARGE
Eggs	2 plus 1 white	4 plus 2 whites
Melted margarine or butter	3 tablespoons	6 tablespoons
Dough enhancer	½ teaspoon	1 teaspoon
Buttermilk or nondairy substitute	½ cup plus 2 tablespoons	1¼ cups

Preheat oven to 350°. Grease your loaf pan(s) and dust with rice flour.

In a mixing bowl, whisk together all the dry ingredients except the carrots. Blend them in after the other ingredients are well mixed.

In a medium bowl, combine the wet ingredients. Beat until well combined, using a whisk or eggbeater.

Pour the liquids into the dry ingredients and mix thoroughly. Beat with a mixing spoon for a few beats but not an electric beater. The batter should have the consistency of cake batter. If too thick, thin with water, 1 tablespoon at a time.

Spoon into the prepared pan(s) and bake for 55–60 minutes. Leave in the pan to cool for about 10 minutes; remove to cool completely before slicing.

VARIATIONS: The amounts given are for one loaf; double for two.

CARROT AND SEED LOAF: Eliminate the cinnamon. Stir in about ⅓ cup chopped sunflower seeds after the final beating.

CARROT-NUT LOAF: Stir in ⅓ cup chopped walnuts or pecans after the final beating.

CARROT-RAISIN LOAF: Stir in about ⅓ cup golden raisins after the final beating.

GARDEN LOAF: Eliminate the cinnamon. Stir in 2 finely sliced green onions and 2 teaspoons chopped parsley after the final beating.

Nutrients per slice: Calories 80, Fat 1.5g, Carbohydrate 170g, Cholesterol 25mg, Sodium 170mg, Fiber 1g, Protein 2g.
Dietary exchanges: Bread 1.

Yogurt and Honey Quickbread

Tender and moist, this bread owes a lot of its flavor and keeping qualities to the yogurt used as the liquid. For lactose-intolerant celiacs, this may be a way of getting calcium without the gas and bloating, for yogurt seems to be easier to digest than milk or buttermilk.

DRY INGREDIENTS	SMALL	LARGE
Four Flour Bean Mix (page 40)	2 cups	4 cups
Xanthan gum	1½ teaspoons	3 teaspoons
Salt	½ teaspoon	1 teaspoon
Egg Replacer	1 teaspoon	2 teaspoons
Baking powder	2 teaspoons	4 teaspoons
Baking soda	½ teaspoon	1 teaspoon
Dried lemon peel (optional)	1 teaspoon	2 teaspoons
Sugar	3 tablespoons	⅓ cup

WET INGREDIENTS		
Eggs	2 plus 1 white	4 plus 2 whites
Margarine or butter, melted	3 tablespoons	6 tablespoons
Honey	1 tablespoon	2 tablespoons
Dough enhancer or vinegar	½ teaspoon	1 teaspoon
Yogurt	¾ cup	1½ cups
Water (more or less)	⅓ cup	⅔ cup

Preheat oven to 350°. Grease your loaf pan(s) and dust with rice flour.

In a mixing bowl, whisk together the dry ingredients.

In a medium bowl, combine the eggs, margarine, honey, and dough enhancer, and whisk until blended. Add the yogurt and half of the water. Whisk again or beat slightly with an eggbeater until smooth.

Pour the liquids into the dry ingredients and mix thoroughly, beating with a spoon until blended. Add enough of the reserved water as necessary to form a cakelike batter. Spoon into the prepared pan(s) and bake for 55–60 minutes. Let cool in the pan for 10 minutes before removing to cool completely before slicing.

VARIATIONS: Amounts given are for a single loaf; double for two loaves.

RAISIN-CINNAMON YOGURT LOAF: Substitute cinnamon for the lemon peel. Add ⅓ cup raisins at the end of mixing.

CINNAMON-NUT YOGURT LOAF: Substitute cinnamon for the lemon peel and add ⅓ cup chopped walnuts or pecans at the end of mixing.

CRANBERRY YOGURT LOAF: Add ⅓ cup dried cranberries at the end of mixing.

CRANBERRY-CASHEW YOGURT LOAF: Add ¼ cup dried cranberries and ¼ cup chopped cashews at the end of mixing.

Nutrients per slice: Calories 100, Fat 3g, Carbohydrate 16g, Cholesterol 25mg, Sodium 180mg, Fiber 1g, Protein 3g.
Dietary exchanges: Bread 1, Fat 1.

Basic Yeast-free Rice Bread (Yeast and Cholesterol Free)

350°

This rice-based bread is not as springy as the yeast-free breads made with bean flours, but it still far surpasses any we had before. This holds together well for sandwiches and has a wonderful flavor achieved by the combination of brown rice, brown sugar, honey, and orange peel.

Note: *Liquid egg substitute may replace the eggs and whites.*

DRY INGREDIENTS	SMALL	LARGE
Featherlight Rice Flour Mix (page 40) using brown rice flour	2 cups	4 cups
Xanthan gum	1 teaspoon	2 teaspoons
Brown sugar	3 tablespoons	⅓ cup
Baking soda	½ teaspoon	1 teaspoon
Baking powder	2 teaspoons	4 teaspoons
Dried orange peel	1 teaspoon	2 teaspoons
Egg Replacer	1 teaspoon	2 teaspoons
Salt	½ teaspoon	1 teaspoon
WET INGREDIENTS		
Eggs	2 plus 1 white	4 plus 2 whites
Margarine or butter, melted	3 tablespoons	6 tablespoons
Honey	1 tablespoon	2 tablespoons
Dough enhancer (optional)	1 teaspoon	2 teaspoons
Buttermilk	¾ cup	1½ cups
Water (more or less)	¼ cup	½ cup

Preheat oven to 350°. Grease an 8½" × 4½" loaf pan for a small recipe; two for large. Dust with rice flour.

In a medium bowl, whisk together the dry ingredients. Set aside.

In the bowl of your mixer, beat the eggs and white(s) until light. Add the melted margarine, honey, dough enhancer, and buttermilk. Turn the mixer to low and blend. Add the dry ingredients while on low. Add sufficient water to make the dough the consistency of cake batter. Beat for 1 minute on high. Spoon into the prepared pan(s) and bake for 55–60 minutes. Cool before slicing.

VARIATIONS: Amounts given are for a single loaf; double for two loaves.

POPPY SEED RICE LOAF: Eliminate the honey from the wet ingredients and the orange peel from the dry ingredients. Add 2 teaspoons poppy seeds and 1 teaspoon dried lemon peel to the dry ingredients.

NUT AND RAISIN RICE LOAF: After beating, stir in 3 tablespoons each chopped nuts and raisins.

CINNAMON-RAISIN RICE LOAF: Add 1 teaspoon cinnamon to the dry ingredients and ¼ cup raisins before spooning into a loaf pan.

Nutrients per slice: Calories 120, Fat 3g, Carbohydrate 16g, Cholesterol 15mg, Sodium 100mg, Protein 2g.
Dietary exchanges: Bread 1, Fat 1.

Limpa Bread
(Swedish Rye)

350°

This is a sweet, mild, rye-flavored bread suitable for sandwiches with any filling. See the variations below for other yeast-free, rye-flavored breads that can be made using the gluten-free rye powder from Authentic Foods.

DRY INGREDIENTS	SMALL	LARGE
Four Flour Bean Mix (page 40)	2 cups	4 cups
Xanthan gum	1½ teaspoons	3 teaspoons
Sugar	2 tablespoons	¼ cup
Baking soda	½ teaspoon	1 teaspoon
Baking powder	2 teaspoons	4 teaspoons
Rye-flavored powder	¼ teaspoon	½ teaspoon
Egg Replacer	1 teaspoon	2 teaspoons
Anise or fennel seed	1 teaspoon	2 teaspoons
Dried orange peel	1 teaspoon	2 teaspoons
Salt	½ teaspoon	1 teaspoon

WET INGREDIENTS		
Eggs	2	4
Vegetable oil	2 tablespoons	4 tablespoons
Molasses	1 tablespoon	2 tablespoons
Dough enhancer or vinegar	½ teaspoon	1 teaspoon
Buttermilk or nondairy substitute	¾ cup	1½ cups

Preheat oven to 350°. Grease your loaf pan(s) and dust with rice flour.

In a mixing bowl, whisk together the dry ingredients.

In a medium bowl, combine the wet ingredients. Beat until well combined using a whisk or eggbeater.

Pour the liquids into the dry ingredients and mix thoroughly. Spoon into the prepared pan(s) and bake for 55–60 minutes. Leave in the pan to cool for 15 minutes; remove to cool completely before slicing.

VARIATIONS: Amounts given are for a single loaf; double for two loaves.

YEAST-FREE CARAWAY RYE: Substitute caraway seeds for the anise or fennel. Add 2 teaspoons freeze-dried coffee crystals to the dry ingredients.

YEAST-FREE PUMPERNICKEL: Eliminate the orange peel. Substitute 1 teaspoon caraway seeds for the anise or fennel and add 1 tablespoon cocoa powder and 2 teaspoons coffee crystals to the dry ingredients.

Nutrients per slice: Calories 90, Fat 2.5g, Carbohydrate 16g, Cholesterol 25mg, Sodium 550mg, Fiber 1g, Protein 2g.
Dietary exchanges: Bread 1, Fat ½.

Egg-free Soda Bread 350°

Finally a soda bread that has the springy texture of the wheat ones! This Irish bread made with no fat and no eggs has not been very successful with rice flour, but now with the new bean flour mix (and some flax meal), it turns out to look, feel, and taste like the soda breads I remember. This makes one or two 7¼" round casseroles.

DRY INGREDIENTS	ONE CASSEROLE	TWO CASSEROLES
Four Flour Bean Mix (page 40)	2 cups	4 cups
Xanthan gum	1 teaspoon	2 teaspoons
Baking powder	2 teaspoons	4 teaspoons
Baking soda	½ teaspoon	1 teaspoon
Salt	½ teaspoon	1 teaspoon
Egg Replacer	1 teaspoon	2 teaspoons

DRY INGREDIENTS	ONE CASEROLE	TWO CASSEROLES
Sugar (brown preferred)	2 tablespoons	¼ cup
Caraway seeds	1½ teaspoons	3 teaspoons
or cardamom	⅛ teaspoon	¼ teaspoon

WET INGREDIENTS		
Buttermilk	1 cup	2 cups
Flax meal	1 tablespoon	2 tablespoons
Water	½ cup	1 cup
Molasses (optional)	2 teaspoons	4 teaspoons

Preheat oven to 350°. Grease your casserole(s) well and dust with rice flour.

In a medium bowl, whisk together the dry ingredients using either caraway seeds or cardamom. Set aside.

In the bowl of your mixer, blend most of the buttermilk, the flax meal stirred into the water, and molasses. Add the dry ingredients and beat on medium until blended. The remaining buttermilk should be added as necessary to get a batter that is slightly thicker than cake batter. Spoon into the prepared pan(s) and bake for about 50 minutes, or until the loaf seems done. Let cool about 5 minutes before turning out to cool completely.

VARIATIONS: The bread can be varied by using the cardamom and ¼ cup raisins, currants, and/or a handful of chopped nuts. The sugar quantity may be increased for a sweeter bread.

Nutrients per slice: Calories 70, Fat .5g, Carbohydrate 15g, Cholesterol 0mg, Sodium 150mg, Fiber 1g, Protein 2g.
Dietary exchanges: Bread 1.

Springy Corn Bread

400°

From childhood I remember corn bread as a crumbly, flat-tasting filler for days when my mother ran out of regular bread. This new corn bread, made with our sorghum and bean flours, doesn't resemble those from my childhood in the least. It's springy, tasty, and definitely not crumbly—not even as next-day leftovers.

DRY INGREDIENTS	8" SQUARE PAN	9" × 12" OBLONG PAN
Four Flour Bean Mix (page 40)	1 cup	2 cups
Yellow cornmeal	1 cup	2 cups
Xanthan gum	½ teaspoon	1 teaspoon
Egg Replacer	1 teaspoon	2 teaspoons
Sugar	¼ cup	½ cup
Baking soda	1 teaspoon	1¾ teaspoons
Baking powder	1 teaspoon	2 teaspoons
Salt	¾ teaspoon	1½ teaspoons
WET INGREDIENTS		
Plain yogurt	1 cup	2 cups
Eggs, slightly beaten	2	4
Margarine, melted	2 tablespoons	4 tablespoons
Orange juice or water	¼ cup	½ cup

Preheat oven to 400°. Grease your chosen pan.

In a mixing bowl, whisk together the dry ingredients. Set aside.

In a smaller bowl, blend the yogurt, beaten eggs, melted margarine, and orange juice. Add to the dry ingredients and stir until just blended. Spoon the dough into the prepared pan and bake for 20–25 minutes for the small pan, 25–35 minutes for the larger pan or until the bread springs back when gently pressed. Cut into squares and serve warm or at room temperature.

Makes 9 (or 20) servings.

Nutrients per serving: Calories 100, Fat 3g, Carbohydrate 16g, Cholesterol 25mg, Sodium 190mg, Fiber 1g, Protein 2g.
Dietary exchanges: Bread 1, Fat ½.

Cheesy Vegetable Corn Bread 400°

Make this flavorful bread to accompany soups or chili. It keeps well and tastes as good the next day or after weeks in the freezer.

INGREDIENTS	9" × 13" OBLONG PAN
Four Flour Bean Mix (page 40)	1 cup
Yellow cornmeal	1 cup
Xanthan gum	½ teaspoon
Egg Replacer	1 teaspoon
Sugar	¼ cup
Baking soda	1 teaspoon
Baking powder	1 teaspoon
Salt	¾ teaspoon
Plain yogurt	1 cup
Eggs, slightly beaten	2
Margarine, melted	2 tablespoons
Orange juice or water	¼ cup
Corn kernels, canned or frozen, drained	1 cup
Medium Cheddar cheese, grated	1 cup
Carrots, grated	½ cup
Onion, finely chopped	½ cup

Preheat oven to 400°. Grease the baking pan.

In a mixing bowl, whisk together the flour mix, cornmeal, xanthan gum, Egg Replacer, sugar, baking soda, baking powder, and salt.

In a smaller bowl, blend the yogurt, beaten eggs, melted margarine, and orange juice or water. Add to the dry mix and stir until blended. Stir in the corn, cheese, carrots, and onion. Spoon the batter into the prepared pan and bake 30–35 minutes, or until the bread springs back when gently pressed. Cut into squares and serve warm or at room temperature.

Makes 15 squares.

Nutrients per serving: Calories 140, Fat 5g, Carbohydrate 19g, Cholesterol 35mg, Sodium 230mg, Fiber 1g, Protein 4g.
Dietary exchanges: Bread 1, Fat 1, Vegetable 1.

Date Nut Loaf

325°

A reader in Canada sent in this recipe for a sweet bread, saying, "It's my husband's favorite." It is a bit fussy to make but well worth the trouble. This stays moist and keeps well if you can stop the family from nibbling.

INGREDIENTS	ONE LOAF
Pitted dates, chopped	1 cup
Baking soda	1 teaspoon
Boiling water	¾ cup
Light Bean Flour Mix (page 40)	1½ cups
Xanthan gum	¾ teaspoon
Salt	¾ teaspoon
Baking powder	2 teaspoons
Eggs	2
Brown sugar	¾ cup
Vegetable oil	2 tablespoons
Vanilla flavoring	1 teaspoon
Chopped walnuts	½ cup

Preheat oven to 325°. Grease one 9" × 5" or one 8½" × 4½" loaf pan, line the bottom with wax paper, and grease the paper.

Place the dates and baking soda in a large mixing bowl and cover with the boiling water. Let cool.

Meanwhile, combine the flour mix, salt, xanthan gum, and baking powder. Set aside.

Beat the eggs well; add the brown sugar and oil. Add to the cooled date mixture. Add the dry ingredients, beating until smooth. Fold in the vanilla and nuts. Pour into the prepared pan and bake for approximately 45 minutes for the larger pan, 55–60 minutes for the smaller. Tip from the pan and remove the paper while still hot. Cool before cutting.

Nutrients per slice: Calories 150, Fat 4g, Carbohydrate 25g, Cholesterol 25mg, Sodium 240mg, Fiber 2g, Protein 4g.
Dietary exchanges: Bread 1½, Fat ½.

Elizabeth's Favorite Banana Bread 350°

Children often do not want nuts in their bread, so Elizabeth's mother sent in her daughter's favorite recipe for a sweet bread. I made a few revisions and added the nutty taste by using a bit of garbanzo bean flour. The real secret to success with this bread is to have the bananas very ripe.

INGREDIENTS	8½" × 4½" LOAF PAN
Gluten-free Flour Mix (page 40)	2 cups
Garbanzo flour	¼ cup
Baking powder	1 teaspoon
Xanthan gum	½ teaspoon
Bananas, large and ripe	3
Brown sugar	¾ cup
Salt	¼ teaspoon
Eggs, beaten	2
Margarine or butter	¼ cup (½ stick)
Baking soda	1 teaspoon
Water	2 tablespoons

Preheat oven to 350°. Grease the loaf pan and dust with rice flour.

In a medium bowl, whisk together the flour mix, garbanzo flour, baking powder, and xanthan gum. Set aside.

Mash the bananas in a large mixing bowl. Add the brown sugar, salt, and beaten eggs. Beat with a mixing spoon until well blended. Melt the margarine and stir into the mixture.

Dissolve the baking soda in the water and add to the mixture. Finally, stir in the dry ingredients and beat just until smooth. Spoon into the prepared pan and bake 45 minutes. Cool before slicing.

Nutrients per slice: Calories 150, Fat 3g, Carbohydrate 29g, Cholesterol 25mg, Sodium 160mg, Fiber 1g.
Dietary exchanges: Bread 2.

Four Flour Banana Nut Bread 350°

One of my testers created this bread using the new Four Flour Bean Mix and my original Best Banana Bread recipe. This new bread looks and tastes more like wheat bread than any other. The color is appetizing, the texture is even, and the taste is super.

INGREDIENTS	8 1/2" × 4 1/2" LOAF PAN
Four Flour Bean Mix (page 40)	1¾ cups
Xanthan gum	1 teaspoon (heaping)
Baking soda	¾ teaspoon
Baking powder	½ teaspoon
Salt	½ teaspoon
Butter Flavor Crisco	⅓ cup
Sugar	⅔ cup
Eggs, well beaten	2
Mashed banana	½ cup
Chopped pecans	½ cup

Preheat oven to 350°. Grease the loaf pan and dust with rice flour.

In a medium bowl, whisk together the flour mix, xanthan gum, baking soda, baking powder, and salt. Set aside.

In the bowl of your mixer, cream the Crisco and sugar. Add the well-beaten eggs and beat until blended. Add the dry mix alternately with the mashed banana in 3 parts. Beat after each addition until the batter is smooth. Stir in the nuts.

Spoon the batter into the prepared pan. Bake 50–60 minutes. Turn out immediately. Cool before slicing.

Nutrients per slice: Calories 140, Fat 7g, Carbohydrate 20g, Cholesterol 35mg, Sodium 150mg, Fiber 1g.
Dietary exchanges: Bread 1, Fat 1.

Pumpkin Tea Bread 375°

So good it's almost a cake, this bread can be served for brunch, tea, or at a party. The pumpkin keeps it moist, and the combination of cream cheese and butter makes it rich.

INGREDIENTS	TWO 8½" × 4½" LOAF PANS
Four Flour Bean Mix (page 40)	2 cups
Xanthan gum	½ teaspoon (rounded)
Baking powder	3 teaspoons
Baking soda	1 teaspoon
Pumpkin pie spice	2 teaspoons
Dried orange peel	1 teaspoon
Salt	½ teaspoon
Margarine or butter	½ cup (1 stick)
Cream cheese	One (3-ounce) package
White sugar	1 cup
Brown sugar	½ cup
Eggs	2
Pumpkin, canned	1 cup
Orange juice	½ cup (scant)
Chopped pecans	¾ cup

Preheat oven to 375°. Grease two loaf pans and line the bottom of each with a piece of waxed paper. Grease the paper and dust with rice flour.

In a medium bowl, whisk together the flour mix, xanthan gum, baking powder, baking soda, pumpkin pie spice, orange peel, and salt. Set aside.

In the bowl of your mixer, cream the margarine, cream cheese, and both sugars until smooth. Add the eggs, one at a time, beating well after each addition. Add the pumpkin and orange juice. Mix well. With a spoon, stir in the dry ingredients until just mixed and then fold in the nuts.

Spoon the batter into the prepared pans and bake about 1 hour or until a tester comes out clean. Cool the loaves in the pans for about 10 minutes before turning out and removing the paper from the bottom. Allow the loaves to cool completely before cutting.

Nutrients per slice: Calories 230, Fat 11g, Carbohydrate 32g, Cholesterol 30mg, Sodium 280mg, Fiber 1g, Protein 3g.
Dietary exchanges: Bread 2, Fat 2.

Chocolate-Cherry Loaf 350°

A wonderful chocolate bread to serve at that special luncheon or to eat plain as a snack. With a bit of cheese, this can be dessert. The amount of chocolate chips can vary according to your taste. I prefer the smaller amount, but a true chocolate lover will probably choose the larger.

INGREDIENTS	ONE 9" × 5" LOAF PAN
Four Flour Bean Mix (page 40)	2 cups
Xanthan gum	1½ teaspoons
Egg Replacer (optional)	1 teaspoon
Sugar	½ cup
Baking soda	1 teaspoon
Baking powder	1 teaspoon
Salt	¼ teaspoon
Chopped walnuts	1 cup
Semisweet chocolate chips	¾ to 1 cup
Margarine or butter	4 tablespoons
Eggs	2

	ONE 9" × 5"
INGREDIENTS	LOAF PAN
Milk or nondairy liquid	¾ cup
Cherry fruit spread	½ cup
Cherry or vanilla flavoring	1 teaspoon

Preheat oven to 350°. Grease the loaf pan and dust with rice flour.

In a mixing bowl, whisk together the flour mix, xanthan gum, Egg Replacer, sugar, baking soda, salt, and chopped walnuts. Set aside.

Melt the chocolate chips and margarine in a saucepan over low heat or in a microwaveable bowl on low in the microwave. In a medium bowl, whisk the eggs lightly. Add the milk, fruit spread, and flavoring. Beat until well blended. Add this and the chocolate mixture to the dry ingredients and beat just until moistened.

Spoon into the prepared pan and bake for 50–60 minutes or until a tester inserted in the center comes out clean. Cool about 5 minutes before turning out from the pan. Cool completely before slicing.

VARIATION:

CHOCOLATE-RASPBERRY LOAF: Substitute raspberry fruit spread for the cherry. Use pecans instead of walnuts.

Nutrients per slice: Calories 230, Fat 9g, Carbohydrate 37g, Cholesterol 30mg, Sodium 160mg, Fiber 1g, Protein 4g.
Dietary exchanges: Bread 2, Fat 1½.

Pineapple Walnut Loaf

Great for snacking, this sweet bread could be served at a luncheon or in place of dessert at dinner. For a more tropical taste, replace the walnuts with toasted macadamia nuts.

INGREDIENTS	9" × 5" LOAF PAN
Featherlight Rice Flour Mix (page 40)	2 cups
Xanthan gum	1½ teaspoons
Egg Replacer	1 teaspoon
Sugar	½ cup
Baking soda	1 teaspoon
Baking powder	1 teaspoon
Salt	¼ teaspoon
Chopped walnuts or macadamia nuts	1 cup
Eggs	2
Milk or nondairy liquid	¾ cup
Pineapple fruit spread	½ cup
Pineapple, black walnut, or vanilla flavoring	1 teaspoon
Margarine or butter, melted	4 tablespoons

Preheat oven to 350°. Grease the loaf pan and dust with rice flour.

In the mixing bowl, whisk together the flour mix, xanthan gum, Egg Replacer, sugar, baking soda, baking powder, salt, and nuts. Set aside.

In a bowl, whisk the eggs lightly. Add the milk, fruit spread, and flavoring. Beat until well blended. Add this and the melted margarine to the flour mix and beat just until moistened.

Spoon into the prepared pan and bake for 50–60 minutes or until a tester comes out clean. Cool for 5 minutes before turning out of the pan.

Nutrients per slice: Calories 110, Fat 6g, Carbohydrate 12g, Cholesterol 25mg, Sodium 150mg, Fiber 0g, Protein 2g.
Dietary exchanges: Bread 1, Fat 1.

YEAST-FREE LOAF BREAD RECIPES FROM OTHER BOOKS IN THE GLUTEN-FREE GOURMET SERIES

The self-rising or yeast-free loaf breads in my first three books were almost all of the sweet bread or "tea bread" type, while in this book most of them are all-purpose breads that can also be made into sandwiches or toasted for breakfast. Here is a list of recipes in my other books.

BREADS	BASE	BOOK	PAGE
African Squash Bread	Rice	MORE	78
Almond-Cheese Bread	Rice	MORE	82
Applesauce Bread	Rice	F&H	97
Best Banana Bread	Rice	GFG	38
Caraway Soda Bread	Rice	MORE	77
Cranberry-Nut Bread	Rice	MORE	79
Grated Apple Loaf	Rice	MORE	81
Lentil Sesame Bread	Rice	GFG	38
Potato Quick Bread	Potato	GFG	35
Potato Rice Sponge Bread	Rice	GFG	34
Pumpkin Bread	Rice	GFG	38
Spiced Banana Loaf	Bean	F&H	98

Rolls and Buns

Bean-Based Rolls

Sesame Bean Buns
Four Flour Crumpets (with three
  variations)
Dinner Rolls
Egg-free Bean Flour Buns

Bean/Rice–Based Rolls

Touch o' Bean English Muffins
Egg-free Touch o' Bean English Muffins

Rice-Based Rolls

Crusty French Rolls
Hamburger Buns
Crumpets
Egg-free Crumpets

Yeast-free Rolls and Buns

Devonshire Scones
Orange Crumpets
Perky Popovers

Rolls and Buns Recipes from Other Books in the Gluten-free Gourmet Series

When we first started making yeast breads, we found that they were more successful when baked in small pans or muffin tins. Although we now know how to make breads in larger-sized pans than we originally used, these buns and rolls using the small-size pans or English muffin rings will ensure success for even the novice baker.

If you've never worked with yeast before, this is a good way to start. These recipes require no bread maker or even a heavy-duty mixer. A handheld electric beater will be strong enough for all of them. And you can be sure to end up with bread that you can be proud of—and it will be good to eat.

Even if you are a good cook, there are several recipes here that you will use over and over. My favorite is the crumpet, so good that I have repeated it here and varied it in many ways with different flours and flavorings.

I have also included several recipes for those who are yeast intolerant and a couple for celiacs with egg and lactose allergies.

Some of the flour mixes are old favorites, but others are new. To find the formulas and mixing recipes, turn to page 40.

In my three earlier books I gave only a few recipes for rolls and buns. The crumpets are repeated here, but for the others please check the list at the end of this chapter.

Sesame Bean Buns

If you want a taste of the Sesame Bean Bread but are still not confident of your ability to make "real bread," try these easy-to-make, easy-to-bake, and easy-to-eat buns.

INGREDIENTS	6 BUNS	12 BUNS
Light Bean Flour Mix (page 40)	1½ cups	3 cups
Xanthan gum	1 teaspoon (rounded)	2 teaspoons (rounded)
Baking powder	1½ teaspoons	3 teaspoons
Salt	½ teaspoon	1 teaspoon
Sesame seeds	1 tablespoon	2 tablespoons
Egg Replacer	1½ teaspoons	3 teaspoons
Brown sugar, divided	2 tablespoons	4 tablespoons
Lukewarm water	1 cup	2 cups
Dry yeast granules	2¼ teaspoons	2¼ teaspoons
Dough enhancer or vinegar	½ teaspoon	1 teaspoon
Molasses	2 teaspoons	4 teaspoons
Eggs	1	2
Margarine or butter	2 tablespoons	4 tablespoons

Place 6 (12) English muffin rings on 1 (2) cookie sheet(s) and grease the rings with vegetable oil spray.

In a medium bowl, whisk together the flour mix, xanthan gum, baking powder, salt, sesame seeds, and Egg Replacer. Set aside.

Place 1 teaspoon of the brown sugar in the water and add the yeast to let foam.

Place the rest of the sugar in a large mixing bowl and add the dough enhancer, molasses, egg(s), and margarine (cut into small pieces). Beat with a hand mixer until well blended. Add the yeast water and beat again. Spoon in half of the dry ingredients and beat until smooth. Add the remaining ingredients and beat with a spoon until smooth. Spoon into the prepared rings, cover with a paper towel, and let rise for 25–35 minutes for rapid-rising yeast, 45–60 minutes for regular yeast.

Bake in a preheated 375° oven for 22–25 minutes. Remove the rings while still hot. Cool the buns before cutting.

Nutrients per bun: Calories 210, Fat 6g, Carbohydrate 33g, Cholesterol 35mg, Sodium 350mg, Fiber 2g, Protein 5g.
Dietary exchanges: Bread 2, Fat 1.

Four Flour Crumpets (with three variations)

375°

My old favorite, the easy-to-make crumpet, takes on a whole new flavor with this flour combination. See the variations using wild rice flour, quinoa, or some sesame seeds.

INGREDIENTS	6 BUNS	12 BUNS
Four Flour Bean Mix (page 40)	1½ cups	3 cups
Brown rice flour	2 tablespoons	4 tablespoons
Xanthan gum	1 teaspoon	2 teaspoons
Baking powder	1½ teaspoons	3 teaspoons
Egg Replacer	1 teaspoon	2 teaspoons
Salt	½ teaspoon	1 teaspoon
Unflavored gelatin (optional)	1 teaspoon	2 teaspoons
Dry yeast granules	2¼ teaspoons	2¼ teaspoons
Warm water	1 cup	2 cups
Brown sugar, divided	1½ tablespoons	3 tablespoons
Dough enhancer or vinegar	½ teaspoon	1 teaspoon
Eggs	1	2
Margarine or butter, melted	2½ tablespoons	5 tablespoons

Place 6 (12) muffin rings on 1 (2) cookie sheet(s) and grease them with vegetable oil spray.

In a medium bowl, whisk together the flour mix, brown rice flour, xanthan gum, baking powder, Egg Replacer, salt, and gelatin (if using). Set aside.

To the warm water, add the yeast and 1 teaspoon of the sugar. Put the remaining sugar in a large mixing bowl. Add the dough enhancer, egg(s), and melted margarine. Beat slightly with a hand mixer. When the yeast has foamed slightly, add that liquid to the mixing bowl. Beat in half of the dry ingredients. With a spoon, stir in the remaining mix and beat until smooth.

Spoon the batter into the prepared rings. Cover lightly and let rise in a warm place until the buns double in bulk (25–35 minutes for rapid-rising yeast, 45–60 minutes for regular yeast). Bake in a preheated 375° oven for 18 to 20 minutes. Remove the rings while still hot.

VARIATIONS:

SESAME SEED BUNS: Add 1 (2) tablespoon(s) sesame seeds to the dry ingredients.

WILD RICE BUNS: Substitute wild rice flour for the brown rice flour.

QUINOA BUNS: Substitute quinoa flour for the brown rice flour.

Nutrients per bun: Calories 210, Fat 6g, Carbohydrate 34g, Cholesterol 35mg, Sodium 350mg, Fiber 2g, Protein 5g.
Dietary exchanges: Bread 2, Fat 1.

Dinner Rolls

Is your mouth watering for one of those soft, yeasty dinner rolls you remember from before your diagnosis? Are you throwing a party and want to impress the guests? You can, you know.

If our bread dough were like that of wheat bread, it would be simple to form rolls such as we see on the bakery shelves—the cloverleaf, dinner roll, knots, or crescents. But since it's more like a cake batter, it's almost impossible to shape, so our rolls can be formed only by dropping the dough onto a baking sheet. Almost every one of the yeast bread doughs from the Yeast Breads section can be made into rolls in this way.

1 recipe (any size) bread dough

Grease a cookie sheet and drop the dough from a mixing spoon in oval-shaped mounds about 12 to the sheet. Let rise in a warm place about 25–30 minutes for rapid-rising yeast and 45–60 minutes for regular yeast. Bake in a preheated 400° oven for about 20–22 minutes. Remove from the pan while still warm.

Egg-free Bean Flour Buns 375°

I wondered if the bean flour (which contains more protein than rice flours) would make a good bun, so I converted my original Crumpet recipe (page 178) to egg free. I discovered that this raised higher, was more tender than the rice bun, and had a delicious flavor. I added sesame seeds for flavor, as I do in the bean bread, but this can be eliminated.

INGREDIENTS	6 BUNS	12 BUNS
Light Bean Flour Mix (page 40)	1½ cups	3 cups
Xanthan gum	1 teaspoon	2 teaspoons
Baking powder	1½ teaspoons	3 teaspoons
Unflavored gelatin	2 teaspoons	4 teaspoons
Salt	½ teaspoon	1 teaspoon
Brown sugar, divided	1½ tablespoons	3 tablespoons
Warm water	1 cup	2 cups
Dry yeast granules	2¼ teaspoons	2¼ teaspoons
Sesame seeds (optional)	1½ tablespoons	3 tablespoons
Egg Replacer	1 tablespoon	2 tablespoons
Cool water	¼ cup	½ cup
Dough enhancer or vinegar	1 teaspoon	1½ teaspoons
Margarine or butter, melted	3 tablespoons	6 tablespoons

Place 6 (12) English muffin rings on 1 (2) cookie sheet(s) and grease the rings with vegetable oil spray.

In a medium bowl, combine the flour mix, xanthan gum, baking powder, gelatin, salt, and sesame seeds (if using). Set aside. Place ½ tablespoon of the sugar in a measuring cup; add the warm water and the yeast. Set aside to foam. Dissolve the Egg Replacer in the cool water and stir until it is slightly thick, like egg whites.

In a large mixing bowl, place the remaining sugar, the dissolved Egg Replacer, the dough enhancer, and the melted margarine. With a hand electric mixer, beat the ingre-

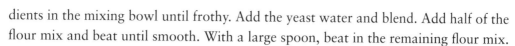

dients in the mixing bowl until frothy. Add the yeast water and blend. Add half of the flour mix and beat until smooth. With a large spoon, beat in the remaining flour mix.

Spoon into the prepared rings. Cover and let rise until almost double in bulk (25–35 minutes for rapid-rising yeast, 45–50 minutes for regular yeast). Bake in a preheated 375° oven for 22 minutes. Remove the rings while still hot.

Nutrients per bun: Calories 210, Fat 7g, Carbohydrate 32g, Cholesterol 0mg, Sodium 360mg, Fiber 2g, Protein 5g.
Dietary exchanges: Bread 2, Fat 1.

Touch o' Bean English Muffins 375°

With garbanzo bean flour added to the rice flour and one of the nut butters replacing the shortening, these buns are a sure taste winner.

INGREDIENTS	6 MUFFINS	12 MUFFINS
Featherlight Rice Flour Mix (page 40)	1½ cups	3 cups
Garbanzo bean flour	¼ cup	½ cup
Xanthan gum	1 teaspoon (rounded)	2 teaspoons (rounded)
Baking powder	1½ teaspoons	3 teaspoons
Unflavored gelatin	2 teaspoons	4 teaspoons
Salt	½ teaspoon	1 teaspoon
NutQuik or almond meal	1 tablespoon	2 tablespoons
Egg Replacer	1 teaspoon	2 teaspoons
Brown sugar, divided	1½ tablespoons	3 tablespoons
Lukewarm water	1 cup plus 2 tablespoons	2¼ cups

INGREDIENTS	**6** MUFFINS	**12** MUFFINS
Dry yeast granules	2¼ teaspoons	2¼ teaspoons
Eggs	1	2
Dough enhancer or vinegar	½ teaspoon	1 teaspoon
Honey	1 teaspoon	2 teaspoons
Nut butter (almond, cashew, filbert, sesame, or peanut)	¼ cup	½ cup

Place 6 (12) English muffin rings on 1 (2) cookie sheet(s) and grease the rings with vegetable oil spray.

In a medium bowl, whisk together the flour mix, garbanzo bean flour, xanthan gum, baking powder, gelatin, salt, NutQuik, and Egg Replacer. Set aside.

Put 1 teaspoon brown sugar in the lukewarm water and add the yeast. Set aside to foam.

In a mixing bowl, break the egg(s) and add the remaining brown sugar, dough enhancer, honey, and nut butter. Beat with a hand mixer until well blended. Add the yeast water and mix well.

Add half of the dry ingredients and beat until smooth. Stir in the remaining flour and beat with a spoon until smooth. Spoon the batter into the prepared rings. Cover lightly and let rise for 25–35 minutes for rapid-rising yeast, 45–60 minutes for regular yeast. Bake in a preheated 375° oven for 22–25 minutes. Remove the rings while still hot.

Nutrients per bun: Calories 240, Fat 7g, Carbohydrate 40g, Cholesterol 35mg, Sodium 300mg, Fiber 3g, Protein 6g.
Dietary exchanges: Bread 2½, Fat 1.

Egg-free Touch o' Bean English Muffins 375°

In many egg-free rice flour recipes there is not enough protein to make the breads rise, but with the addition of the high-protein bean flour, this is no longer a problem. The flavor of this bread is delicious, with just a touch of the nutty bean, augmented with the protein-rich NutQuik or almond meal while using the almond, peanut, cashew, filbert, or sesame butter as the fat.

INGREDIENTS	6 MUFFINS	12 MUFFINS
Featherlight Rice Flour Mix (page 40)	1½ cups	3 cups
Garbanzo bean flour	¼ cup	½ cup
Xanthan gum	1 teaspoon (rounded)	2 teaspoons (rounded)
Baking powder	1½ teaspoons	3 teaspoons
Unflavored gelatin	2 teaspoons	4 teaspoons
Salt	½ teaspoon	1 teaspoon
NutQuik or almond meal	1 tablespoon	2 tablespoons
Egg Replacer	4 teaspoons	8 teaspoons
Cool water	¼ cup	½ cup
Brown sugar, divided	1½ tablespoons	3 tablespoons
Lukewarm water	1 cup plus 2 tablespoons	2¼ cups
Dry yeast granules	2¼ teaspoons	2¼ teaspoons
Dough enhancer or vinegar	½ teaspoon	1 teaspoon
Nut butter (almond, cashew, filbert, sesame, or peanut)	¼ cup	½ cup
Molasses	1 teaspoon	2 teaspoons

Place 6 (12) English muffin rings on 1 (2) cookie sheet(s) and grease the rings with vegetable oil spray.

In a medium bowl, whisk together the flour mix, garbanzo bean flour, xanthan gum, baking powder, gelatin, salt, and NutQuik. Set aside.

Place the Egg Replacer in the cool water and whisk until it thickens to egg white consistency. Measure ½ tablespoon of the brown sugar into the warm water and add the yeast. Set aside.

In a large mixing bowl, place the rest of the sugar, the dough enhancer, nut butter, and molasses. With a hand mixer, beat slightly. Add the Egg Replacer liquid and beat again. Add the yeast water and blend on low. Spoon in half of the dry ingredients and beat until smooth. Add the remaining flour and beat with a spoon until blended.

Spoon into the prepared rings, cover, and let rise for about 25–30 minutes for rapid-rising yeast or 45–60 minutes for regular yeast. Bake in a preheated 375° oven for 22–25 minutes. Remove the rings while still hot.

Nutrients per bun: Calories 230, Fat 6g, Carbohydrate 41g, Cholesterol 0mg, Sodium 290mg, Fiber 3g, Protein 5g.
Dietary exchanges: Bread 2½, Fat 1.

Crusty French Rolls 425°

Crusty on the outside, chewy on the inside, these rolls taste and crunch like their wheat counterparts. They're easy to make if you have some of the French Bread/Pizza Mix on your shelf.

DRY INGREDIENTS	6 ROLLS	12 ROLLS
French Bread/Pizza Mix (page 190)	1¾ cups	3½ cups
Dry yeast granules	1 tablespoon	1 tablespoon
Dry milk powder or nondairy substitute	3 tablespoons	6 tablespoons
Salt	½ teaspoon	1 teaspoon
Baking powder	½ teaspoon	1 teaspoon
WET INGREDIENTS		
Egg whites	2	4
Dough enhancer or vinegar	1 teaspoon	2 teaspoons
Vegetable oil	1½ tablespoons	3 tablespoons
Warm water (more or less)	⅔ cup	1⅓ cups

Grease 1 (2) cookie sheet(s) with vegetable oil spray. Dust with fine cornmeal.

In the bowl of a heavy-duty mixer, combine the dry ingredients. Blend gently with the mixer on low. In a bowl, whisk together the egg whites, dough enhancer, and vegetable oil. Add most of the warm water.

Add the liquids to the dry ingredients and blend. If the dough is too thick, add more water until the dough seems thick enough that it will spoon out into roll shape. Turn the mixer to high and beat for 2½ minutes.

Spoon onto the prepared cookie sheets and form into French roll shape. Cover lightly and let rise in a warm place until double in size (about 35 minutes for rapid-rising yeast, 60 or more minutes for regular yeast). Bake in a preheated 425° oven for 20–22 minutes.

Nutrients per bun: Calories 210, Fat 4g, Carbohydrate 40g, Cholesterol 0mg, Sodium 250mg, Fiber 1g, Protein 4g.
Dietary exchanges: Bread 2½, Fat 1.

Hamburger Buns

375°

If you've been craving hamburgers but your buns crumble at the first bite, mix these easily with a handheld electric mixer. These springy buns will never crumble around your filling and will stay fresh tasting and tender for several days. The secret is the new rice flour formula and the method of mixing.

INGREDIENTS	6 BUNS	12 BUNS
Featherlight Rice Flour Mix (page 40)	1½ cups	3 cups
Xanthan gum	1 teaspoon	2 teaspoons
Egg Replacer (optional)	1 teaspoon	2 teaspoons
Unflavored gelatin	1 teaspoon	2 teaspoons
Baking powder	1½ teaspoons	1 tablespoon
Salt	½ teaspoon	1 teaspoon
Sugar, divided	1½ tablespoons	3 tablespoons
Warm water	1 cup	2 cups
Dry yeast granules	2¼ teaspoons	2¼ teaspoons
Dough enhancer or vinegar	1 teaspoon	1½ teaspoons
Eggs	1	2
Vegetable oil	2 tablespoons	4 tablespoons

Place 6 (12) muffin rings on 1 (2) cookie sheet(s) and grease with vegetable oil spray.

In a medium bowl, whisk together the flour mix, xanthan gum, Egg Replacer (if using), gelatin, baking powder, and salt. Set aside. Add 1 teaspoon of the sugar to the warm water and sprinkle on the yeast. Set aside to foam slightly.

In a large mixing bowl, blend together at low speed of a hand mixer the remaining sugar, dough enhancer, egg(s), and vegetable oil. Add the yeast mixture. Beat in half of the dry ingredients. With a mixing spoon, stir in the remaining flour and beat until smooth.

Spoon the batter into the prepared rings. Cover lightly and let rise in a warm place until double in size (20–25 minutes for rapid-rising yeast, 40–45 minutes for regular yeast). Bake in a preheated 375° oven for 20–22 minutes.

Nutrients per bun: Calories 200, Fat 6g, Carbohydrate 34g, Cholesterol 35mg, Sodium 310mg, Fiber 1g, Protein 3g.
Dietary exchanges: Bread 2, Fat 1.

Crumpets

This is another of my five-star recipes—so good it deserves a place in any bread book. These buns are easy to make and don't require a heavy-duty mixer; any handheld electric mixer will work. The dough is very forgiving, and the bun can serve as a hamburger bun, bread for sandwiches, or a base for gravies or a combination of melted cheese and seafood. Or spread with butter and sprinkle with garlic salt to toast for garlic bread.

INGREDIENTS	6 BUNS	12 BUNS
Gluten-free Flour Mix (page 40)	1½ cups	3 cups
Xanthan gum	1 teaspoon	2 teaspoons
Baking powder	1½ teaspoons	3 teaspoons
Unflavored gelatin (optional)	1 teaspoon	2 teaspoons
Egg Replacer (optional)	1½ teaspoons	3 teaspoons
Salt	½ teaspoon	1 teaspoon
Sugar, divided	1½ tablespoons	3 tablespoons
Water, lukewarm	1 cup	2 cups
Dry yeast granules	2¼ teaspoons	2¼ teaspoons
Eggs	1	2
Dough enhancer or vinegar	½ teaspoon	1 teaspoon
Margarine or butter, melted	3 tablespoons	6 tablespoons

Place 6 (12) English muffin rings on 1 (2) cookie sheet(s) and grease with vegetable oil spray.

In a medium bowl, whisk together the flour mix, xanthan gum, baking powder, unflavored gelatin (if using), Egg Replacer (if using), and salt. Set aside.

Add 1 teaspoon of the sugar to the warm water and stir in the yeast. Set aside.

Place the remaining sugar in a mixing bowl and add the egg(s), dough enhancer, and melted margarine. Blend with a hand mixer. Add the yeast mixture and blend again. Add half of the flour mixture and beat until smooth. Stir in the remaining flour and beat with a spoon until smooth. Spoon into the prepared rings. Cover and let rise in a warm place until the batter doubles in size (20–25 minutes for rapid-rising yeast, 40–50 minutes for regular yeast).

Place in a preheated 375° oven and bake for 18–20 minutes, or until browned lightly and pulled slightly from the ring edges. Remove the rings while still warm.

Nutrients per bun: Calories 220, Fat 6g, Carbohydrate 34g, Cholesterol 35mg, Sodium 310mg, Fiber 1g, Protein 3g.
Dietary exchanges: Bread 2, Fat 1.

Egg-free Crumpets 375°

When a reader wrote that her daughter had been diagnosed as intolerant of gluten, eggs, and lactose, I wanted to help her create some kind of bread to satisfy the girl's craving. I turned to my old standby, the crumpet recipe. This needed a few changes but turned out tasty and springy, the way a bread should feel. By increasing the unflavored gelatin and Egg Replacer and adding some NutQuik, the protein in the egg was replaced with other proteins so the yeast had something to work on.

Note: *If allergic to soy or corn, substitute vegetable oil for the margarine.*

INGREDIENTS	6 BUNS	12 BUNS
Gluten-free Flour Mix (page 40)	1½ cups	3 cups
Xanthan gum	1 teaspoon	2 teaspoons
Baking powder	1 teaspoon	2 teaspoons
Unflavored gelatin	2 teaspoons	4 teaspoons
Salt	½ teaspoon	1 teaspoon
NutQuik or almond meal	1½ tablespoons	3 tablespoons
Egg Replacer	1 tablespoon	2 tablespoons
Cool water	¼ cup	½ cup
Sugar, divided	1½ tablespoons	3 tablespoons

INGREDIENTS	6 BUNS	12 BUNS
Warm water	1 cup	2 cups
Dry yeast granules	2¼ teaspoons	2¼ teaspoons
Vinegar	1 teaspoon	1 teaspoon
Margarine, melted	3 tablespoons	6 tablespoons

Place 6 (12) English muffin rings on 1 (2) cookie sheet(s) and grease with vegetable oil spray.

In a medium bowl, whisk together the flour mix, xanthan gum, baking powder, unflavored gelatin, salt, and NutQuik. Set aside.

Dissolve the Egg Replacer in the cool water. Place ½ tablespoon of the sugar in a measuring cup. Add the warm water and yeast. Set aside.

In a large mixing bowl, place the remaining sugar, the dissolved Egg Replacer, vinegar, and melted margarine. With a hand mixer, beat the ingredients in the mixing bowl until frothy. Add the yeast mixture and blend. Add half of the flour mixture and beat until smooth. With a large spoon, beat in the remaining flour. Spoon into the prepared rings. Cover and let rise in a warm place until double in size (35 minutes if using rapid-rising yeast; 60 minutes or more if using regular yeast).

Bake in a preheated 375° oven for 22–25 minutes, or until slightly browned. Remove the rings while still warm.

Nutrients per bun: Calories 220, Fat 7g, Carbohydrate 32g, Cholesterol 0mg, Sodium 310mg, Fiber 1g, Protein 3g.
Dietary exchanges: Bread 2, Fat 1½.

Devonshire Scones
(Egg and Yeast Free)

400°

These light and tender biscuits are great with jam, or use them as shortcake with fresh fruit.

INGREDIENTS	10 TO 12 SCONES	20 TO 24 SCONES
White rice flour	1 cup	2 cups
Tapioca flour	½ cup	1 cup
Xanthan gum	½ teaspoon	1 teaspoon
Baking powder	2 teaspoons	4 teaspoons
Baking soda	1 teaspoon	2 teaspoons
White sugar	2 tablespoons	¼ cup
Brown sugar	2 tablespoons	¼ cup
Butter or margarine	4 tablespoons (½ stick)	8 tablespoons (1 stick)
Plain yogurt	½ cup	1 cup

Preheat oven to 400°. Grease 1 (2) baking sheet(s).

In a medium mixing bowl, whisk together the flours, xanthan gum, baking powder, baking soda, and sugars. Add the butter and cut in with fork (or rub with your fingers) until the mixture resembles coarse meal.

Stir in as much of the yogurt as you need for the dough to form a soft ball. Place on a rice-floured board and knead slightly. Roll out the dough to ¾ inch thick. Cut into rounds with a 2½-inch cookie cutter and place the rounds on the prepared baking sheet. Bake for 10 to 12 minutes.

Nutrients per bun: Calories 120, Fat 4g, Carbohydrate 20g, Cholesterol 10mg, Sodium 150mg, Fiber 0g, Protein 1g.
Dietary exchanges: Bread 1, Fat 1.

Orange Crumpets
(Yeast and Lactose Free)

Tasty and delicate, this yeast-free bun can serve as sandwich bread or as a base for creamy toppings for those who can't have yeast. It's also wonderful toasted for breakfast or topped with fresh berries for dessert.

DRY INGREDIENTS	6 BUNS	12 BUNS
Four Flour Bean Mix (page 40)	1½ cups	3 cups
Xanthan gum	1 teaspoon	2 teaspoons
Baking powder	1½ teaspoons	3 teaspoons
Baking soda	½ teaspoon	1 teaspoon
Salt	½ teaspoon	1 teaspoon
Egg Replacer	1 teaspoon	2 teaspoons
Sugar	1½ tablespoons	3 tablespoons

WET INGREDIENTS		
Eggs or liquid egg substitute	1 or ¼ cup substitute	2 or ½ cup substitute
Margarine, melted	3 tablespoons	6 tablespoons
Dough enhancer	1 teaspoon	2 teaspoons
Orange juice	1 cup	2 cups

Preheat oven to 375°. Place 6 (12) English muffin rings on 1 (2) cookie sheet(s) and grease with vegetable oil spray.

In a medium bowl, whisk together the dry ingredients.

In a mixing bowl, using a hand mixer, beat the egg(s), melted margarine, and dough enhancer. Add the orange juice. Spoon in half of the dry ingredients and beat until smooth. Add the remaining and beat with a spoon until incorporated. Spoon into the prepared rings and bake for 18–20 minutes. Remove the rings while still warm.

Nutrients per bun: Calories 230, Fat 7g, Carbohydrate 37g, Cholesterol 50mg, Sodium 330mg, Fiber 2g, Protein 4g.
Dietary exchanges: Bread 2, Fat 1.

Perky Popovers

If you want raves for something easy, just serve these at your next dinner. Although they are better straight from the oven, they can be made ahead and reheated on a baking sheet at 375° for about 5 minutes.

These are also good split and topped with chicken à la king for an entree or used cold and stuffed with a seafood filling such as tuna fish or crab meat.

Note: It's important to have all the ingredients at room temperature and to heat the pan in the oven while whirling the ingredients in your food processor.

INGREDIENTS	6 POPOVERS	12 POPOVERS
Butter or margarine, melted	1 tablespoon	2 tablespoons
Gluten-free Flour Mix (page 40)	1 cup	2 cups
Xanthan gum	¼ teaspoon	½ teaspoon
Almond meal or NutQuik	1 tablespoon	2 tablespoons
Salt	¼ teaspoon	½ teaspoon
Milk	1 cup	2 cups
Eggs	2	4

Preheat oven to 400°. Coat the custard cups or popover pan cups with the melted butter. Place the pans to heat in oven while you process the dough.

Combine the flour mix, xanthan gum, almond meal, and salt. Place in a food processor or blender. Add the milk and eggs, and process until smooth. Pour into the hot pans, dividing the thin dough equally. Bake for 45 minutes. Serve hot.

Nutrients per bun: Calories 190, Fat 7g, Carbohydrate 25g, Cholesterol 80mg, Sodium 170mg, Fiber 1g, Protein 6g.
Dietary exchanges: Bread 1½, Fat 1.

ROLLS AND BUNS RECIPES FROM OTHER BOOKS IN THE GLUTEN-FREE GOURMET SERIES

These recipes from my earlier books (see page 107 for title abbreviations) are basically rice based, and I still use them frequently. Although the names may be similar, they have not been repeated in this book.

ROLLS AND BUNS	BASE	BOOK	PAGE
English Muffins	Rice	GFG	104
English Tea Scones	Rice	MORE	80
Ginger-Orange Rolls	Rice	MORE	76
Salem Crumpets	Bean/Rice	F&H	95
Sticky Pecan Rolls	Rice	GFG	27
Popovers	Rice/Potato	GFG	44

Specialty Breads

French Bread/Pizza Mix

Rice-Based Specialty Breads

Seasoned Pizza Crust
Pita Bread
Quick Bagels
Sarah's Bagels
Bread Sticks
Pretzel Sticks

Bean-Based Specialty
  Breads

New Focaccia

Corn-Based Specialty
  Breads

Southern Spoon Bread

Specialty Bread Recipes from
  Other Books in the Gluten-
  free Gourmet Series

If you're like me, pizza, bagels, and focaccia are breads you thought you would never be able to eat again when you looked at that list of no-nos after you were first diagnosed. Breads seemed to head the list, and anything that resembled bread followed right behind.

It was frightening and frustrating, wasn't it? Even though I had never eaten much bread before my diagnosis, I still didn't like the idea of forever doing without. And I especially balked at the idea of never again having a pizza. I discovered that others felt the same way, and for my first book I begged recipes from some who had already developed them and added two of my own. Soon after the book came out, a cry went up from the bagel lovers, claiming I had left them out.

The recipes in this section are not the first I've offered for some of these breads, but they are all new and improved in taste, texture, and ease of making. For most of them I use a French Bread/Pizza Mix (page 190) that I always keep on hand. This saves a lot of time and mess when I have a craving for pizza, pretzels, or bagels. For the other new-formula flour mixes that I use here, please turn to page 40.

If you want to use a favorite specialty bread recipe from my other books, you will find them listed at the end of this chapter.

French Bread/Pizza Mix

A container of this on hand will save a lot of time in making not only French bread and pizzas but many other recipes. This bread mix, unlike most of the flour mixes, contains xanthan gum and other ingredients, so it takes very little work to finish making your dough or batters.

INGREDIENTS	6 CUPS MIX	12 CUPS MIX
White rice flour	3½ cups	7 cups
Tapioca flour	2½ cups	5 cups
Xanthan gum	2 tablespoons	¼ cup
Unflavored gelatin	2 (7-gram) packets	4 (7-gram) packets
Egg Replacer	2 tablespoons	¼ cup
Sugar (white)	¼ cup	½ cup

Stir together well or place in a plastic bag and tumble. Store on your pantry shelf; no need to refrigerate.

Seasoned Pizza Crust

400°

With a bag of French Bread/Pizza Mix on hand, this is so easy to make, you can have pizza anytime you wish. It tastes like the real thing! If desired, add a bit of onion salt or garlic salt for more flavor.

To freeze for later use, bake for the first 10 minutes, cool, and then wrap and freeze. To use, thaw completely, then top and bake. I have let this thaw in the refrigerator overnight and baked the next morning.

Note: If you can't find Italian Pizza Seasoning, use Italian Spice Mix or pinches of your favorite pizza spices.

DRY INGREDIENTS	1 CRUST	2 CRUSTS
French Bread/Pizza Mix (page 190)	1½ cups	3 cups
Dry milk powder or nondairy substitute (try almond meal)	3 tablespoons	⅓ cup
Italian Pizza Seasoning	¾ teaspoon	1½ teaspoons
Salt	½ teaspoon	1 teaspoon
Dry yeast granules	2½ teaspoons	2½ teaspoons

WET INGREDIENTS		
Egg whites	2	4
Olive oil or vegetable oil	1½ tablespoons	3 tablespoons
Dough enhancer or vinegar	½ teaspoon	1 teaspoon
Warm water (more or less)	¾ cup	1½ cups

Preheat oven to 400°. Lightly grease 1 (2) cookie sheets or round (solid-bottom) pizza pan(s).

Blend the dry ingredients in a medium bowl. Set aside.

Place the wet ingredients in the bowl of your heavy-duty mixer and blend. (Reserve some of the water.) Turn the mixer to low and add the flour mix. Add more water if needed to get a firm dough that can still be spread. Beat on high for 3½ minutes.

Spoon the dough onto the prepared sheet(s) and spread in circle(s) about 12 inches in diameter, making sure the edges are raised to contain the sauce. (I do this with a thin spatula, turning the pan and forcing the dough to thin out except at the edges.)

Let rise about 10 minutes and then bake for 10 minutes while preparing your toppings. Spread on your choice of pizza sauces, cheeses, and meats. Bake again about 22–25 minutes.

Makes 12-inch, thick pizza crusts or 14-inch, thin crusts. Each pizza serves 6 to 8.

Nutrients per serving: Calories 200, Fat 5g, Carbohydrate 35g, Cholesterol 5mg, Sodium 220mg, Fiber 1g, Protein 4g.
Dietary exchanges: Bread 2, Fat 1.

Pita Bread

Hand-patted into flat rounds, this bread is a delicious alternative to bread slices for stuffing or filling. There are other names for this: pocket bread, Armenian flatbread, and Arab bread. These are sometimes stuffed and sometimes used for scooping food. The bread below may not always form the perfect pocket, but it can slit for filling. Whether you use it for scooping or prefer it stuffed, you'll find it a tasty addition to your bread choices.

DRY INGREDIENTS	SIX 6-INCH ROUNDS	TWELVE 6-INCH ROUNDS
French Bread/Pizza Mix (page 190)	2 cups	4 cups
Almond meal	2 tablespoons	¼ cup
Salt	½ teaspoon	1 teaspoon
Sugar	1½ tablespoons	3 tablespoons
WET INGREDIENTS		
Dry yeast granules	4 teaspoons	4 teaspoons
Warm water	½ cup	1 cup
Sugar	1 teaspoon	1 teaspoon
Shortening	2 tablespoons	¼ cup
Hot water	¼ cup	½ cup
Egg whites	2	4

Grease 2 cookie sheets.

In the bowl of your heavy-duty mixer, blend the dry ingredients with the paddle (not the dough hook).

Dissolve the yeast in the warm water with the 1 teaspoon of sugar added. Set aside to foam. Melt the shortening in the hot water. Pour both into the dry ingredients and blend on low. Add the egg whites and blend. Turn the mixer to high and beat for 3½ minutes.

With a well-greased hand, pluck a ball of dough the size of a duck egg and roll, then pat to about a 6-inch round approximately ¼ inch thick or less. Place on the prepared cookie sheets. Repeat 5 (or 11) times until all the dough is used. Let rise about 30 minutes for rapid-rising yeast or 60 minutes for regular yeast (or until about 50 percent higher).

Bake in a preheated 525° oven for 5–6 minutes.

High altitude: Add up to 2 tablespoons (4 tablespoons) more flour or use less water so that the dough can be handled.

Nutrients per serving: Calories 260, Fat 6g, Carbohydrate 48g, Cholesterol 0mg, Sodium 200mg, Fiber 2g, Protein 4g.
Dietary exchanges: Bread 3, Fat 1.

Quick Bagels

425°

These are easy to stir up and are slightly lighter and more flavorful than the usual bagel, but they keep springy for days and taste delicious.

Note: An easy egg wash can be made by using 1 tablespoon liquid egg substitute and 1 teaspoon water. Or use lightly whipped egg white.

DRY INGREDIENTS	8 BAGELS	12 BAGELS
French Bread/Pizza Mix (page 190)	2¼ cups	3⅓ cups
Almond meal or dry milk powder	2 tablespoons	3 tablespoons
Salt	½ teaspoon	¾ teaspoon
Sugar (optional)	1½ tablespoons	2¼ tablespoons
WET INGREDIENTS		
Dry yeast granules	2¼ teaspoons	2¼ teaspoons
Warm water	½ cup	¾ cup
Sugar	1 teaspoon	1 teaspoon
Shortening	2 tablespoons	3 tablespoons
Hot water	¼ cup	⅓ cup
Egg whites	2	3
FOR ROLLING AND TOPPING		
Sweet rice flour	as needed	as needed
Egg wash (see Note)		

Grease one cookie sheet for 8 bagels; two for 12 bagels.

Place the dry ingredients in the bowl of a heavy-duty mixer and blend with the heavy mixing blade (not the dough hook).

Dissolve the yeast in the warm water with the teaspoon of sugar added. Melt the shortening in the hot water. Pour both into the dry ingredients and blend on low. Add the egg whites and blend again. Turn the mixer to high and beat for 3½ minutes. (This dough should be firm enough to pluck out with greased hands and roll. If not that thick, add sweet rice flour, 1 tablespoon at a time, until the desired consistency is achieved.)

Form bagels by dividing the dough into 8 (12) pieces. Working with greased hands, roll into balls larger than golf balls but smaller than tennis balls. Flatten the balls to about ½ inch thick. Create the hole by poking a finger through the center and enlarging. Place on the cookie sheet(s), brush with egg wash, cover with plastic wrap, and let rise until they are puffy and almost double in bulk (about 30–40 minutes for rapid-rising yeast, 60 minutes for regular yeast).

Ten minutes before they have finished rising, preheat the oven to 425°.

In a large low pan, bring 3 inches of water plus 1 teaspoon sugar to a boil. Drop in the bagels 4 at a time. Cook for 1 minute, turning at 30 seconds. Drain and replace on the cookie sheet. Repeat, keeping the water at a low boil. Bake for 20 minutes. Cool slightly before eating.

Note: *To freshen old bagels, slice them in half, then microwave for 25 seconds on high. They will taste as if they've come fresh from the oven.*

VARIATIONS: Changes are for the small recipe. Increase proportionally for the larger recipe.

CINNAMON: Add 2 tablespoons sugar and a scant teaspoon cinnamon to the dry ingredients.

CINNAMON-RAISIN: Add 2 tablespoons sugar and 1 teaspoon cinnamon to the dry ingredients. After the dough has finished beating, stir in about a handful (⅓ cup) raisins.

Nutrients per serving: Calories 210, Fat 4g, Carbohydrate 40g, Cholesterol 0mg, Sodium 190mg, Fiber 1g, Protein 3g.
Dietary exchanges: Bread 3, Fat 1.

Sarah's Bagels

425°

This recipe was given to me by Sarah's mother, a fine cook. Tasters tell me this is the closest to a real bagel they've had. The recipe can be mixed at night, placed in the refrigerator, and pulled out to shape and rise in the morning. I made a few changes to the original recipe, but my results were much as I tasted when I shared Sarah's.

DRY INGREDIENTS	8 BAGELS	16 BAGELS
Rice flour	1 cup	2 cups
Tapioca flour	1 cup	2 cups
Dry milk powder	2 tablespoons	¼ cup
Xanthan gum	1¾ teaspoons	3½ teaspoons
Salt	1 teaspoon	1¾ teaspoons
Sugar	1 tablespoon	2 tablespoons

WET INGREDIENTS		
Sugar	1 teaspoon	1 teaspoon
Warm water (110° to 115°)	½ cup	1 cup
Dry yeast granules	1 tablespoon	1 tablespoon
Shortening	2 tablespoons	¼ cup
Hot water	¼ cup	½ cup
Egg whites	2	4
Extra rice flour (as needed)		

When measuring the flours, tap the measure to be sure to have a full, heavy cup. Place these and the rest of the dry ingredients in the bowl of a heavy-duty mixer equipped with the dough hook.

Place the sugar in the warm water and stir in the yeast. Dissolve the shortening in the hot water.

With the mixer on low, blend the dry ingredients. Pour in the shortening and hot water, and blend to mix. Add the egg whites and blend again; then add the yeast mixture. Check the dough to be sure it is the right consistency. It should be thick enough to be able to shape with greased hands. If too thin, add the extra rice flour, 1 tablespoon at a time. If too thick, add water, 1 tablespoon at a time. Beat on high for 4 minutes.

Shaping bagels: At this point the dough can be formed into bagels or placed in the refrigerator for use later or the next morning.

Prepare 1 (2) cookie sheet(s) by greasing with vegetable oil spray and sprinkling lightly with cornmeal. Form the bagels by dividing the dough into 8 (16) pieces. Working with greased hands, roll into balls larger than golf balls but smaller than tennis balls. Flatten the balls to about ½ inch thick. Create the hole by poking a finger through the center and enlarging. Place on the cookie sheet(s), cover with plastic wrap, and let rise until they are puffy and almost doubled in size (about 30 minutes for rapid-rising yeast, 60 minutes or more for regular yeast).

Ten minutes before they have finished rising, preheat the oven to 425°.

In a large pan, bring 3 inches of water plus 1 teaspoon sugar to a boil. Drop in the bagels 4 at a time. Cook for 1 minute, turning at 30 seconds. Drain and replace on the cookie sheet(s). Repeat, keeping the water at a low boil. Bake for 20 minutes. Cool slightly before eating.

VARIATIONS: Amounts given are for the small recipe; increase proportionally for the larger recipe.

CINNAMON: Add 2 tablespoons sugar and a scant teaspoon cinnamon to the dry ingredients.

CINNAMON-RAISIN: Add 2 tablespoons sugar and 1 teaspoon cinnamon to the dry ingredients. After the dough has finished beating, stir in a handful of raisins (⅓ cup).

Nutrients per serving: Calories 170, Fat 4g, Carbohydrate 32g, Cholesterol 0mg, Sodium 290mg, Fiber 1g, Protein 3g.
Dietary exchanges: Bread 2, Fat 1.

Bread Sticks 400°

Try these for an impressive treat with your Italian dinner or as a marvelous dry bread when traveling. They will last for weeks.

DRY INGREDIENTS

French Bread/Pizza Mix (page 190)	1¾ cups
Dry yeast granules	1 tablespoon
Buttermilk powder or nondairy substitute	3 tablespoons
Salt	½ teaspoon
Baking powder	½ teaspoon

WET INGREDIENTS

Egg whites	2
Dough enhancer or vinegar	½ teaspoon
Vegetable oil	1½ tablespoons
Warm water (more or less)	⅔ cup

Preheat oven to 400°. To avoid overbrowning the bottom of the sticks, use insulated cookie sheets or line 2 cookie sheets with aluminum foil. Grease with vegetable oil spray.

Cut ½ inch from the bottom corner of a 1-gallon plastic freezer bag.

In the bowl of a heavy-duty mixer, combine the dry ingredients. In a bowl, beat the egg whites, dough enhancer, and oil slightly with a fork. Add most of the warm water. Add to the dry ingredients and beat on high for 3 minutes. Check after a few seconds of mixing to see if the dough needs more water. It should be as thick as cookie dough but not dry or forming a ball.

Spoon the dough into the prepared bag and squeeze onto the cookie sheets in 2 straight lines about 4½ inches long. Let rise about 10 minutes for rapid-rising yeast or 20 minutes for regular yeast.

Bake for 10 minutes, reversing the position of the sheets halfway through baking. *Makes 3½ dozen.*

VARIATIONS:

SESAME STICKS: Brush the sticks with an egg wash and sprinkle on sesame seeds.

ROSEMARY BREAD STICKS: After mixing, stir in 1 tablespoon chopped fresh rosemary.

Nutrients per stick: Calories 30, Fat .5g, Carbohydrate 6g, Cholesterol 0mg, Sodium 30mg, Fiber 0g, Protein 1g.
Dietary exchanges: Bread ½.

Pretzel Sticks

Pretzel sticks are so handy for traveling, for nibbling in a car, or for just plain snacking that all celiacs should be able to make them if they have some French Bread/Pizza Mix on hand.

Note: *An easy egg wash is about 1 tablespoon liquid egg substitute thinned with ½ teaspoon water. Otherwise use 1 tablespoon beaten egg.*

DRY INGREDIENTS

French Bread/Pizza Mix (page 190)	1¾ cups
Dry yeast granules	1 tablespoon
Almond meal or dry milk powder	1 tablespoon
Salt	½ teaspoon
Baking powder	½ teaspoon

WET INGREDIENTS

Egg whites	2
Dough enhancer or vinegar	½ teaspoon
Vegetable oil	1½ tablespoons
Honey (optional)	1 tablespoon
Warm water (more or less)	⅔ cup
Egg wash (see Note)	
Coarse sea salt for sprinkling	

Grease 2 cookie sheets with vegetable oil spray. To avoid overbrowning the bottom of the sticks, use insulated cookie sheets or line 2 cookie sheets with aluminum foil. Clip ¼ inch from the bottom corner of a heavy 1-gallon plastic freezer bag.

In the bowl of a heavy duty-mixer, combine the dry ingredients. In a medium bowl, beat the egg whites slightly with a fork. Add the dough enhancer, oil, and honey (if using) and whisk again. Add most of the warm water.

Pour the wet ingredients into the dry ingredients in the mixer and beat on high for

3 minutes, checking after about 30 seconds to see if more water is needed. The dough should be thicker than for our bread but not dry or forming a ball.

Spoon the dough into the prepared bag and squeeze onto the cookie sheets in straight lines about 3 inches long. Brush lightly with egg wash and sprinkle on the salt. Let rise about 20 minutes for rapid-rising yeast or 40–45 minutes for regular yeast.

Bake in a preheated 425° oven for 10 minutes, or until the sticks are a warm rich brown and are hard. If not crisp enough when cool, return to a 200° oven for up to 30 minutes.

Makes about 8 dozen.

Nutrients per stick: Calories 15, Fat 15g, Carbohydrate 3g, Cholesterol 0mg, Sodium 15mg, Fiber 0g, Protein 0g.
Dietary exchanges: Bread ½.

New Focaccia

Enjoy compliments when you serve this seasoned Italian flatbread topped with your favorite cheeses, meats, or vegetables as suggested below. Serve this with soups or stews or by itself as a snack.

DRY INGREDIENTS	9" × 13" CAKE PAN	10" × 15" JELLY ROLL PAN
Four Flour Bean Mix (page 40)	1½ cups	2 cups
Xanthan gum	1 teaspoon	1½ teaspoons
Salt	⅓ teaspoon	½ teaspoon
Egg Replacer	1 teaspoon	1 teaspoon
Unflavored gelatin	1 teaspoon	1 teaspoon
Sugar	2 teaspoons	3 teaspoons
Almond meal or dry milk powder	2¼ tablespoons	3 tablespoons
Dried minced onion	2½ teaspoons	3 teaspoons

Italian Pizza Seasoning
  (or snipped fresh rosemary)
	1½ teaspoons
	  (1 to 2 tablespoons)
		2 teaspoons
		  (1 to 2 tablespoons)

Dry yeast granules	2¼ teaspoons	2¼ teaspoons
WET INGREDIENTS		
Liquid egg substitute (or eggs)	⅓ cup (1 plus 1 white)	½ cup (2)
Dough enhancer or vinegar	½ teaspoon	½ teaspoon
Olive oil	3 tablespoons	4 tablespoons
Warm water (more or less)	1 cup	1¼ cup

Preheat oven to 400°. Grease your chosen pan.

In a medium bowl, whisk together the dry ingredients. Set aside.

In the bowl of your heavy-duty mixer, beat the egg substitute, dough enhancer, and olive oil. Add most of the water. With the mixer on low, spoon in the dry ingredients. Check to be sure the dough is the right consistency (like cake batter). Add water as necessary. Turn the mixer to high and beat 3½ minutes. Spoon into the prepared pan. Let rise about 10 minutes while preparing the topping (see below).

Top and bake for 35–40 minutes, or until the bread showing through the topping is a nice brown.

Makes 9 (12) servings.

VARIATIONS:

HAM AND CHEESE TOPPING: Mix together and spread on top of the dough before cooking.

¾ (1) cup chopped cooked ham

¾ (1) cup grated Monterey Jack cheese

¼ (⅓) cup chopped onion

One (2.25-ounce) can chopped olives

2 garlic cloves, minced

¼ (⅓) cup chopped fresh parsley

2½ (3) tablespoons olive oil

SIMPLE CHEESE TOPPING: Sprinkle on onion salt, Parmesan cheese, and a few tablespoons olive oil.

FRESH VEGETABLE TOPPING: Sprinkle on 2 diced tomatoes and ¼ cup chopped onion. Sprinkle on salt, pepper, fresh rosemary, and 2 tablespoons olive oil. Add other vegetables as desired.

ONION AND POPPY SEED TOPPING: Drizzle on 1 tablespoon olive oil and scatter on 1 cup chopped onion. Sprinkle with ¼ cup Parmesan cheese and 2 teaspoons poppy seeds. Sprinkle lightly with salt.

Nutrients per serving: Calories 160, Fat 6g, Carbohydrate 22g, Cholesterol 25mg, Sodium 110mg, Fiber 1g, Protein 4g.
Dietary exchanges: Bread ½, Fat 1.

Southern Spoon Bread

375°

This is not truly a bread but more of a side dish to be served with main dishes when you need a starch but have no gravy or sauce. Try it with baked chicken, meat loaf, or casseroles.

INGREDIENTS	1-QUART CASSEROLE	2-QUART CASSEROLE
Eggs, separated	2 large	4 large
Milk or nondairy liquid	1½ cups	3 cups
Yellow cornmeal	½ cup	1 cup
Margarine or butter	2 tablespoons	4 tablespoons
Salt	½ teaspoon	1 teaspoon
Ground black pepper	⅛ teaspoon	¼ teaspoon
Baking powder	½ teaspoon	1 teaspoon
Parmesan cheese (optional)	½ tablespoon	1 tablespoon

Preheat oven to 375°. Grease your chosen casserole.

Separate eggs, placing whites in the bowl of your mixer and the yolks in a small bowl. Beat the yolks and set aside.

In a medium saucepan, heat the milk almost to a boil over medium heat. Using a wire whisk, gradually beat in the cornmeal. Cook for 2 minutes, stirring constantly. Whisk in the margarine, salt, and pepper. Beat several tablespoons of the cornmeal into the egg yolks and then blend this into the hot cornmeal. Remove from stove and stir in the baking powder and cheese (if using).

Beat the egg whites until stiff peaks form. Stir about ¼ cup egg whites into the cornmeal mix. Gradually fold in the remaining whites. Spoon into the prepared casserole and bake for 30–35 minutes or until a tester comes out clean. Serve hot.

The small recipe serves 3; the large recipe serves 6.

Nutrients per serving: Calories 236, Fat 12g, Carbohydrate 22g, Cholesterol 151mg, Sodium 586mg, Fiber 3g, Protein 10g.
Dietary exchanges: Milk ½, Bread 1, Meat ½, Fat 2.

SPECIALTY BREAD RECIPES FROM OTHER BOOKS IN THE GLUTEN-FREE GOURMET SERIES

Here are the twelve specialty breads from my first three books (see page 107 for title abbreviations).

Breads	Base	Book	Page
Arab Pocket Bread (Pita Bread)	Rice	More	73
Bagels	Rice	F&H	104
Bean Flour Crêpes	Bean	F&H	232
Bread Sticks	Rice	GFG	31
Breakfast Focaccia	Rice	F&H	106
Crêpes	Rice	GFG	108
Flaky Breakfast Rusks	Rice	More	86
Focaccia	Rice	F&H	97
GF Flour Tortillas	Rice	F&H	234
Orange Corn Bread	Corn	GFG	46
Pretzels	Rice	More	41
Swedish Hardtack	Rice	More	85

Muffins

Minute Muffin Mix

Minute Muffins

   Nut or Fruit Muffins
   Lemon Muffins
   Lemon–Poppy Seed Muffins
   Blueberry Muffins
   Almond-Banana Muffins
   Apple-Spice Muffins
   Apple-Pecan Muffins
Sweet Potato–Cranberry Muffins

Apple–Peanut Butter Muffins
Chocolate Macadamia Nut Muffins
Date-Walnut Muffins
Spiced Banana Nut Muffins
Streusel-Topped Apple Muffins

Muffin Recipes from Other
   Books in the Gluten-free
   Gourmet Series

Muffins have been a substitute bread for celiacs since before the time of our yeast breads. They were easy to make and turned out well in their small pans when other bread types failed. Using more eggs, sugar, and shortening also ensured that they would be tasty even if the texture left a lot to be desired.

With all the wonderful-tasting breads, I don't rely on muffins as bread but now use them as a treat or an addition to a meal.

Since I created many muffin recipes in my other books, several of them basic bread replacers, this book contains only special muffins to appeal to everyone. Serve these as I do: at family gatherings or parties. (Or just keep them for yourself for treats.)

I have also added a basic muffin mix from which you can make the suggested seven variations or dream up dozens of your own.

Most of these recipes use the new bean and sorghum flour mix. Please turn to page 210 for the formula.

You will find a list of my earlier muffin recipes at the end of this chapter.

Minute Muffin Mix

Keep this mix handy to make a variety of muffins.

INGREDIENTS	6-CUP MIX (6 BATCHES)	12-CUP MIX (12 BATCHES)
Garfava bean flour	1½ cups	3 cups
Sorghum flour	½ cup	1 cup
Cornstarch	2 cups	4 cups
Tapioca flour	2 cups	4 cups
Baking soda	2½ teaspoons	5 teaspoons
Baking powder	3 tablespoons	6 tablespoons
Salt	2 teaspoons	4 teaspoons
Egg Replacer	1 tablespoon	2 tablespoons
Sugar	⅔ cup	1⅓ cups
Powdered vanilla	1 tablespoon (rounded)	2 tablespoons (rounded)

Blend the dry ingredients well and store on a pantry shelf. No need to refrigerate. (Place these directions on the bag or container.)

To make muffins: Preheat oven to 375°. Place 1 cup mix in a bowl. Beat together 1 egg plus 1 white or ⅓ cup liquid egg substitute, 2 tablespoons oil or melted butter or margarine, plus ½ cup liquid (buttermilk, milk, nondairy liquid, fruit juice, or carbonated drink). Pour into flour mix and beat until smooth. Spoon into 6 (12) greased muffin tins and bake for 12–15 minutes.

Makes 6 (12) muffins.

Minute Muffins

Using the handy Minute Muffin Mix on page 210, you can whip up a variety of muffins in no time at all.

INGREDIENTS	**6** MUFFINS	**12** MUFFINS
Minute Muffin Mix	1 cup	2 cups
Egg (or liquid egg substitute)	1 plus 1 white (⅓ cup)	2 plus 2 whites (⅔ cup)
Oil or melted butter or margarine	2 tablespoons	4 tablespoons
Buttermilk, milk, nondairy liquid, fruit juice, or carbonated drink	½ cup	1 cup

Preheat oven to 375°. Grease the muffin tins or line with paper cups and grease lightly with vegetable oil spray.

Place the muffin mix in a bowl. In another bowl, beat together the egg(s) and white(s) (or the liquid egg substitute), oil (or melted butter or margarine), and the liquid.

Pour the liquid mixture into the flour mixture and beat until smooth. Spoon into the greased muffin tins and bake for 12–15 minutes.

VARIATIONS:

NUT OR FRUIT MUFFINS: Add 2 (4) tablespoons raisins, nuts, mashed banana, kiwi, chopped dates, or fresh grated apple.

LEMON MUFFINS: Add 1 (2) tablespoon(s) lemon zest to the dry ingredients. Use 1½ (3) tablespoons lemon juice as part of the liquid.

LEMON–POPPY SEED MUFFINS: Add ½ (1) teaspoon lemon zest and 2 (4) teaspoons poppy seeds to the dry ingredients.

BLUEBERRY MUFFINS: Add 2 (4) tablespoons fresh blueberries to the dry ingredients.

ALMOND-BANANA MUFFINS: Add 1 (2) tablespoons almond meal to the dry ingredients. Use water for the liquid and, after the mix is beaten, fold in ½ (1) banana, chopped.

APPLE-SPICE MUFFINS: Add ¾ (1½) teaspoon(s) apple pie spice to the dry ingredients. Use apple juice for the liquid, and after mixing, fold in 2 tablespoons chopped fresh apple.

APPLE-PECAN MUFFINS: Add 2 (4) tablespoons almond meal and 2 (4) tablespoons chopped pecans to the dry ingredients. Use apple juice for the liquid.

Nutrients per basic muffin: Calories 160, Fat 6g, Carbohydrate 23g, Cholesterol 35mg, Sodium 250mg, Fiber 1g, Protein 4g.
Dietary exchanges: Bread 1½, Fat 1.

Sweet Potato–Cranberry Muffins 375°

Delicious enough for any party; easy enough for the family dinner. These muffins received raves from my tasters for their tart, sweet taste and a texture that rivals any wheat muffin.

DRY INGREDIENTS	6 MUFFINS	12 MUFFINS
Four Flour Bean Mix (page 40)	¾ cup	1½ cups
Xanthan gum	½ teaspoon	1 teaspoon
Sugar	¼ cup	½ cup
Egg Replacer	1 teaspoon	2 teaspoons
Baking powder	1 teaspoon	2 teaspoons
Salt	½ teaspoon (scant)	¾ teaspoon
Pumpkin pie spice	½ teaspoon	1 teaspoon

WET INGREDIENTS		
Egg	1	2
Milk or nondairy substitute	¼ cup	½ cup
Cold mashed sweet potatoes	¼ cup	½ cup
Margarine or butter, melted	2 tablespoons	4 tablespoons
Cranberries (fresh or frozen), chopped	½ cup	1 cup

Preheat oven to 375°. Grease the muffin tins or line with paper cups and grease lightly with vegetable oil spray.

In a mixing bowl, combine the dry ingredients. In a smaller bowl, combine the egg(s), milk, sweet potatoes, and margarine. Beat with a fork or spoon until well blended and smooth. Stir into the dry ingredients until just moistened. Stir in the cranberries.

Fill the muffin cups ⅔ full and bake for 20–24 minutes or until a tester inserted in the center comes out clean. Cool in the pan for about 10 minutes before removing. Serve warm or at room temperature.

Nutrients per muffin: Calories 160, Fat 5g, Carbohydrate 27g, Cholesterol 35mg, Sodium 330mg, Fiber 1g, Protein 3g.
Dietary exchanges: Bread 2, Fat 1.

Apple–Peanut Butter Muffins

400°

Deliciously different, these muffins can pass any taste test, so don't be afraid to serve them for your next family dinner or party.

INGREDIENTS	8 MUFFINS	16 MUFFINS
Four Flour Bean Mix (page 40)	1 cup	2 cups
Xanthan gum	½ teaspoon	1 teaspoon
Baking powder	½ teaspoon	1 teaspoon
Baking soda	½ teaspoon	1 teaspoon
Salt	¼ teaspoon	½ teaspoon
Apple, peeled, cored, and chopped	1	2
Honey	¼ cup	½ cup
Peanut butter, extra chunky	¼ cup	½ cup
Eggs (or liquid substitute)	2 (or ½ cup)	4 (or 1 cup)
Vegetable oil	3 tablespoons	⅓ cup
Brown sugar	2 tablespoons	¼ cup
Fruit juice (apple, orange, or other)	1 tablespoon	2 tablespoons
Vanilla flavoring	½ teaspoon	1 teaspoon

Preheat oven to 400°. Line the muffin tins with paper cups and coat with vegetable oil spray.

In a medium bowl, whisk together the flour mix, xanthan gum, baking powder, baking soda, and salt. Set aside.

In a mixing bowl, using an electric mixer, beat the apple, honey, peanut butter, eggs, oil, sugar, fruit juice, and vanilla until fairly smooth. Beat in the flour mixture with a spoon, then divide the batter into the prepared muffin cups. Bake 20 minutes or until a tester inserted in the center comes out clean.

Nutrients per muffin: Calories 230, Fat 11g, Carbohydrate 30g, Cholesterol 55mg, Sodium 230mg, Fiber 2g, Protein 5g.
Dietary exchanges: Bread 2, Fat 2.

Chocolate Macadamia Nut Muffins 400°

This chocolate muffin is almost like a dessert. Use it for your bread at a luncheon or, if you have a school-age child, send it to school as a treat for the whole class. It does not have to be buttered.

INGREDIENTS	**12** MUFFINS	**24** MUFFINS
Four Flour Bean Mix (page 40)	1¼ cups	2½ cups
Xanthan gum	½ teaspoon	1 teaspoon
Cocoa powder	2½ tablespoons	⅓ cup
Baking soda	1 teaspoon	2 teaspoons
Baking powder	1 teaspoon	2 teaspoons
Salt	¼ teaspoon	½ teaspoon
Sugar	3 tablespoons	⅓ cup
Margarine or butter, melted	3 tablespoons	⅓ cup
Buttermilk	⅔ cup	1⅓ cup
Eggs, beaten with whisk	2	4
Vanilla flavoring	1 teaspoon	2 teaspoons
Macadamia nuts, chopped	½ cup	1 cup

Preheat oven to 400°. Grease the muffin tins or line with paper cups.

In a mixing bowl, whisk together the flour mix, xanthan gum, cocoa, baking soda, baking powder, salt, and sugar.

In another bowl, combine the margarine, buttermilk, beaten eggs, and vanilla. Stir and add to the flour mixture until just moistened. (Don't beat.) Fold in the nuts and spoon into the prepared cups.

Bake for 13–15 minutes or until a tester inserted in the center comes out clean. Cool slightly in muffin pans to avoid breaking when removing.

High altitude: Decrease the baking powder by ¼ (½) teaspoon. Decrease the baking soda by ¼ (½) teaspoon.

Nutrients per muffin: Calories 160, Fat 9g, Carbohydrate 16g, Cholesterol 35mg, Sodium 240mg, Fiber 1g, Protein 4g.
Dietary exchanges: Bread 1, Fat 2.

Date-Walnut Muffins

400°

The pumpkin or squash base keeps these wonderfully spicy muffins moist. Serve them for brunches, teas, or mid-morning snacks. No one will guess they're gluten-free.

INGREDIENTS	8 TO 10 MUFFINS	18 TO 20 MUFFINS
Four Flour Bean Mix (page 40)	1 cup	2 cups
Xanthan gum (optional)	¼ teaspoon	½ teaspoon
Baking powder	1 teaspoon	2 teaspoons
Baking soda	¼ teaspoon	½ teaspoon
Pumpkin pie spice	1 teaspoon	2 teaspoons
Sugar	1½ tablespoons	3 tablespoons
Salt	¼ teaspoon	½ teaspoon
Pitted dates, chopped	⅓ cup	¾ cup
Chopped walnuts	⅓ cup	¾ cup
Margarine, melted	4 tablespoons (½ stick)	8 tablespoons (1 stick)
Pumpkin, cooked, or junior squash	6 tablespoons	¾ cup
Buttermilk	¼ cup	½ cup
Eggs, slightly beaten	1	2
Molasses	1½ tablespoons	3 tablespoons
Vanilla flavoring	½ teaspoon	1 teaspoon

Preheat oven to 400°. Grease the muffin tins or line with paper cups and spray with vegetable oil spray.

In a mixing bowl, whisk together the flour mix, xanthan gum (if using), baking powder, baking soda, pumpkin pie spice, sugar, and salt. Add the chopped dates and walnuts, and tumble to cover them with flour.

In a medium bowl, blend together the melted margarine, pumpkin, buttermilk, beaten egg(s), molasses, and vanilla. Make a well in the center of the flour mixture and pour in the liquids, stirring until just combined. Spoon the batter into the prepared cups and bake 20–25 minutes (usually 22). Serve warm or at room temperature.

Nutrients per muffin: Calories 150, Fat 7g, Carbohydrate 20g, Cholesterol 20mg, Sodium 190mg, Fiber 2g, Protein 3g.
Dietary exchanges: Bread 1, Fat 1.

Spiced Banana Nut Muffins   375°

Sorghum flour brings a new flavor to the familiar banana nut muffins. And because sorghum is already sweet, the sugar can be drastically reduced. These also stay together well, so the xanthan gum is optional.

INGREDIENTS	10 TO 12 MUFFINS	20 TO 24 MUFFINS
Sorghum flour	¾ cup	1½ cups
Tapioca flour	½ cup	1 cup
Cornstarch	¼ cup	½ cup
Salt	¼ teaspoon	½ teaspoon
Xanthan gum (optional)	¼ teaspoon	½ teaspoon
Baking powder	1 teaspoon (rounded)	2½ teaspoons
Baking soda	½ teaspoon	1 teaspoon
Sugar	1 tablespoon	2 tablespoons
Dried orange or lemon peel	½ teaspoon	1 teaspoon
Apple pie spice	½ teaspoon	1 teaspoon
Eggs	1 plus 1 white	2 plus 2 whites
Vegetable oil	2 tablespoons	¼ cup
Fruit juice (orange, apple, or other)	½ cup	1 cup
Mashed banana	½ cup (1 large)	1 cup (2 large)
Chopped nuts (walnut, pecan)	2 tablespoons	¼ cup

Preheat oven to 375°. Grease the muffin tins or use paper liners and spray with vegetable oil spray.

In your mixing bowl, whisk together the sorghum flour, tapioca flour, cornstarch, salt, xanthan gum (if using), baking powder, baking soda, sugar, orange peel, and apple pie spice.

In a small bowl, whisk the egg(s) and white(s) with the oil. Stir in the juice and mashed banana. Pour this into the flour mix and stir until just blended. (Do not overmix or beat.) Stir in the nuts and spoon into the prepared pans.

Bake for 15 minutes or until a tester inserted in the center comes out clean. Serve warm or cool.

Nutrients per muffin: Calories 210, Fat 5g, Carbohydrate 42g, Cholesterol 35mg, Sodium 320mg, Fiber 4g, Protein 5g.
Dietary exchanges: Bread 2½, Fat 1.

Streusel-Topped Apple Muffins 375°

This rich muffin can be used as bread at a luncheon or dinner when made without the topping. With the streusel, it is a mid-morning treat or late-evening snack.

	6 TO 8 MUFFINS	12 TO 15 MUFFINS
TOPPING		
Sugar	2 tablespoons	¼ cup
Chopped walnuts	2 tablespoons	¼ cup
Apple pie spice	¼ teaspoon	½ teaspoon
Butter or margarine	½ tablespoon	1 tablespoon
BATTER		
Four Flour Bean Mix (page 40)	1 cup	2 cups
Xanthan gum	½ teaspoon	1 teaspoon
Baking powder	1 teaspoon	2 teaspoons
Baking soda	½ teaspoon	1 teaspoon
Salt	¼ teaspoon	½ teaspoon
Sugar	¼ cup	½ cup
Apple pie spice	¾ teaspoon	1½ teaspoons
Eggs	1	2
Sour cream or nondairy substitute	¼ cup	½ cup
Butter or margarine, melted	2 tablespoons	4 tablespoons
Peeled, cored, and grated apple	¾ cup (1 medium)	1½ cups (2 medium)
Chopped walnuts	¼ cup	½ cup

Preheat oven to 375°. Grease the muffin tins with vegetable oil spray.

If using the topping, make the streusel by blending the sugar, walnuts, spice, and butter in a small bowl. Set aside.

In a mixing bowl, whisk together the flour mix, xanthan gum, baking powder, baking soda, salt, sugar, and spice. Set aside.

In a smaller bowl, blend the egg(s), sour cream, and melted butter. Mix in the apple. Stir into the flour mixture. Add the nuts and spoon into the prepared muffin cups. Sprinkle on the topping and bake about 20–22 minutes. Serve warm or cold.

High altitude: Add 1 tablespoon more per cup of flour mix and reduce the baking powder by ⅛ (¼) teaspoon.

Nutrients per muffin: Calories 190, Fat 8g, Carbohydrate 26g, Cholesterol 30mg, Sodium 250 mg, Fiber 1g, Protein 3g.
Dietary exchanges: Bread 1½, Fat 1½.

MUFFIN RECIPES FROM OTHER BOOKS IN THE GLUTEN-FREE GOURMET SERIES

Most of the following muffin recipes in my first three books were rice based. Many of them can substitute for breads because they are not sweet.

MUFFINS	BASE	BOOK	PAGE
Boston Brown Bread Muffins	Bean	F&H	100
Cream-Filled Squash Gems	Rice	MORE	78
Cranberry or Blueberry Muffins	Rice	MORE	83
Fresh Apple Muffins	Rice	F&H	102
Fruit and Fiber Muffins	Rice	MORE	83
Kasha (Buckwheat) Muffins	Rice	GFG	41
Kiwi Muffins	Rice	MORE	84
My Favorite High-Fiber Muffins	Bean	F&H	102
Quick and Easy Muffins	Rice	GFG	40
Spicy Corn Muffins	Rice	F&H	103
Sugar-free White Corn Muffins	Corn	GFG	41
Vegetable Garden Muffins	Rice	F&H	101
Yellow Corn Muffins	Corn	GFG	45

Breakfast Breads

Bette's Best Waffle and
    Pancake Mix

Pancakes and Waffles

Bette's Bean Waffles
    Macadamia Waffles
Ricotta Waffles
Belgian Waffles
Zucchini Pancakes

Rolls and Buns

Cinnamon Pecan Sticky Buns
    Cinnamon Rolls
Caramel Pecan Rolls (Yeast-free)
    Cinnamon Rolls (Yeast-free)
Frankly Fabulous Fruit Danish
St. Lucia Buns

Orange Coffee Rolls
    Raisin-Nut Coffee Rolls
    Fruited Coffee Rolls
Hot Cross Buns

Breads

Breakfast Focaccia
Raisin Cinnamon English Muffins

Biscuits

Baking Powder Biscuits
Sweet Fruited Scones

Breakfast Bread Recipes
    from Other Books in the
    Gluten-free Gourmet Series

Most of us probably thought we had given up on breakfast breads when we started the gluten-free diet. And that was quite true two decades ago. After all, what can you do with rice cakes to make them taste like anything but rice cakes?

With the introduction of xanthan gum and yeast doughs, we've come to expect toast for breakfast (or rolls, Danish, or English muffins). In this section you will find even more of those breakfast breads that are so much like the "rest of the world" eats. And for those who can't have yeast I have included several yeast-free recipes.

Many of the flour mixes are new to this book. To find the formulas for them, turn to page 40.

Many of the breakfast breads in my former books are not repeated here. They are listed at the end of this chapter.

Bette's Best Waffle and Pancake Mix

Keep this mix on hand for wonderfully crispy waffles anytime. Or use a bit more water and make delicious pancakes in seconds.

INGREDIENTS	FOR 4 SMALL BATCHES	FOR 4 LARGE BATCHES
Four Flour Bean Mix (page 40)	5 cups	10 cups
Xanthan gum	2 teaspoons	4 teaspoons
Dry milk powder or almond meal	1 cup	2 cups
Egg Replacer	4 teaspoons	3 scant tablespoons
Baking powder	3 rounded tablespoons	7 scant tablespoons
Salt	2 teaspoons	4 teaspoons
Brown sugar	¾ cup	1½ cups
Butter Flavor Crisco or other solid shortening	1 cup	2 cups

In a large bowl, whisk together the flour mix, xanthan gum, milk powder, Egg Replacer, baking powder, salt, and brown sugar. Cut in the shortening with a pastry cutter until well incorporated. Store in a covered plastic container in the refrigerator.

To use for waffles: Place 1¾ cups in a mixing bowl. Separate 2 eggs. Beat the yolk in 1 cup water. Beat the egg whites to soft peaks. Beat the egg water into the mix until smooth. Gently fold in the whites. Bake on a hot waffle iron. *Makes 4 to 5 waffles.*

To use for pancakes: Place 1¾ cups in a mixing bowl. Beat 2 eggs into 1¼ cups water. Beat the liquid into the mix until smooth. Cook on a hot griddle.

Makes 8 to 10 pancakes.

Nutrients per waffle: Calories 290, Fat 13g, Carbohydrate 36g, Cholesterol 85mg, Sodium 320mg, Fiber 2g, Protein 6g.
Dietary exchanges: Bread 2, Fat 2½.

Bette's Bean Waffles

It is always a good test when the family prefers the gluten-free bread to a wheat one. These waffles passed the test so well that my daughter asked for the recipe. These taste like the wheat ones you might remember—only better. A mix can be made of the dry ingredients and stored for easy making anytime. See page 224.

DRY INGREDIENTS	4 TO 5 WAFFLES	8 TO 10 WAFFLES
Four Flour Bean Mix (page 40)	1¼ cups	2½ cups
Xanthan gum	½ teaspoon	1 teaspoon
Dry milk powder or nondairy substitute (I use almond meal)	¼ cup	½ cup
Egg Replacer	1 teaspoon	2 teaspoons
Baking powder	2½ teaspoons	5 teaspoons
Salt	½ teaspoon	1 teaspoon
Brown sugar	3 tablespoons	6 tablespoons
Shortening (Butter Flavor Crisco)	¼ cup (4 tablespoons)	½ cup (8 tablespoons)
WET INGREDIENTS		
Eggs, separated	2	4
Milk (or water) or substitute (more or less)	1 cup	2 cups

Combine the flour mix, xanthan gum, milk powder, Egg Replacer, baking powder, salt, and brown sugar in your mixing bowl. Cut in the shortening with a pastry cutter or fork.

Beat the egg yolks until light. Beat the whites to soft peaks. Set aside.

Add most of the liquid to the dry mix until well incorporated. Use the remaining as needed to get the consistency of cake batter. Stir in the egg yolks. Gently fold in the whites. Spoon onto a hot waffle iron and bake.

VARIATION:

MACADAMIA WAFFLES: If you don't use the almond meal, add 3 (or 6) table-spoons macadamia nuts that have been chopped and toasted in a 350° oven for about 5 minutes.

Nutrients per waffle: Calories 310, Fat 15g, Carbohydrate 39g, Cholesterol 90mg, Sodium 460mg, Fiber 2g, Protein 7g.
Dietary exchanges: Bread 3, Fat 3.

Ricotta Waffles

I've been making the Rice-Ricotta Pancakes (from The Gluten-free Gourmet*) as a favorite of the family and guests for years, but now I realize the recipe can be adapted to make delicious waffles. Eat them for breakfast, brunch, or supper. Or use them for the "cake" in your berry shortcakes.*

DRY INGREDIENTS	6 SIX-INCH WAFFLES	12 SIX-INCH WAFFLES
Gluten-free Flour Mix (page 40)	1 cup	2 cups
Xanthan gum	½ teaspoon	1 teaspoon
Sugar	1 tablespoon	2 tablespoons
Salt	½ teaspoon	1 teaspoon
Baking powder	2 teaspoons	4 teaspoons
WET INGREDIENTS		
Eggs (or liquid egg substitute)	3 (¾ cup)	6 (1½ cups)
Ricotta cheese	¾ cup	1½ cups
Vegetable oil or melted shortening	3 tablespoons	6 tablespoons
Milk or nondairy substitute	1¼ cups	2½ cups

In a small bowl, whisk together the dry ingredients. Set aside.

In a large mixing bowl, beat the eggs, ricotta cheese, and vegetable oil until smooth. Add the dry ingredients alternately with the milk, beating after each addition. Pour onto a hot waffle iron and bake according to your waffle iron's directions.

Nutrients per waffle: Calories 290, Fat 16g, Carbohydrate 27g, Cholesterol 130mg, Sodium 390mg, Fiber 0g, Protein 10g.
Dietary exchanges: Milk 1, Bread 1, Fat 2.

Belgian Waffles

This light, crisp waffle with a strong vanilla flavor tastes like the real thing even with our flours. They also freeze well to use later as a waffle topped with fruit and ice cream or with meat in curry sauce.

DRY INGREDIENTS	6 TO 8 SIX-INCH WAFFLES	12 TO 14 SIX-INCH WAFFLES
Rice flour (white or brown)	1 cup	2 cups
Soy flour	½ cup	1 cup
Potato starch flour	½ cup	1 cup
Salt	½ teaspoon	1 teaspoon
Baking powder	5 teaspoons	3 tablespoons
Sugar	1 tablespoon	2 tablespoons
WET INGREDIENTS		
Eggs	1 plus 3 whites	2 plus 6 whites
Vegetable oil	¼ cup	½ cup
Milk or nondairy liquid	1½ cups	3 cups
Vanilla flavoring	2½ teaspoons	5 teaspoons

In a medium bowl, whisk together the dry ingredients. Set aside.

Break the eggs, placing the whites in a bowl suitable for beating. Place the egg yolk(s) in a mixing bowl and beat together with the oil, milk, and vanilla. Stir in the dry ingredients until blended. Beat the egg whites until soft peaks form and fold them gently into the batter. Don't overbeat.

Bake on a heated Belgian waffle iron. Serve hot topped with fresh fruit (strawberries are the usual topping) and whipped cream.

Nutrients per waffle: Calories 240, Fat 9g, Carbohydrate 34g, Cholesterol 30mg, Sodium 410mg, Fiber 1g, Protein 5g.
Dietary exchanges: Bread 2, Fat 2.

Zucchini Pancakes

For a Sunday breakfast or a luncheon treat, try these very different pancakes. Serve them with sausage and a fruit for a meal.

INGREDIENTS	**14 PANCAKES**
Zucchini (medium size)	3 (about 1 pound)
Salt, divided	¾ teaspoon
Finely chopped onion	½ cup
Butter or margarine, melted	1 tablespoon
Eggs, slightly beaten	2
Four-Flour Bean Mix (page 40)	¼ cup
Ground pepper	⅛ teaspoon
Oil for frying	

Grate the zucchini finely, place in a colander, and sprinkle on ½ teaspoon salt. Set aside for about 30 minutes, then squeeze as much liquid from the zucchini as you can.

In a small frying pan, sauté the onion in the butter until translucent. Transfer to a mixing bowl and add the zucchini. Stir in the eggs, flour, remaining salt, and pepper.

Drop on a clean, oiled frypan in rounded tablespoonfuls. Flatten and cook about 1 minute on each side. Serve immediately.

Serves 5 to 6.

Nutrients per pancake: Calories 35, Fat 1.5g, Carbohydrate 3g, Cholesterol 30mg, Sodium 135mg, Fiber 1g, Protein 2g.
Dietary exchanges: Bread 1.

Cinnamon Pecan Sticky Buns

If you've been missing those breakfast rolls that make your mouth water at the bakery, search no further. These light, fluffy, easy-to-make buns will satisfy any craving.

TOPPING	12 BUNS	24 BUNS
Margarine or butter, melted	¼ cup	½ cup
Brown sugar	¼ cup	½ cup
Cinnamon	1 teaspoon	2 teaspoons
Pecans, chopped	½ cup	1 cup
DRY INGREDIENTS		
Featherlight Rice Flour Mix (page 40)	2 cups	4 cups
Xanthan gum	1¼ teaspoons	2½ teaspoons
Salt	½ teaspoon	1 teaspoon
Unflavored gelatin	1 teaspoon	2 teaspoons
Egg Replacer	1 teaspoon	2 teaspoons
Sugar (or to taste)	⅓ cup	⅔ cup
Almond meal or NutQuik	3 tablespoons	⅓ cup (rounded)
Dry yeast granules	2¼ teaspoons	2¼ teaspoons
WET INGREDIENTS		
Potato Buds	2 teaspoons	4 teaspoons
Warm water (more or less)	1 cup	2 cups
Margarine or butter, melted	⅓ cup	⅔ cups
Dough enhancer or vinegar	½ teaspoon	1 teaspoon
Honey	2 teaspoons	4 teaspoons
Eggs	3	6

Prepare your muffin tins by dividing the margarine into the cups and adding the brown sugar blended with the cinnamon. Sprinkle on the nuts. Set aside.

In the bowl of your mixer, place the dry ingredients and blend with the mixing blade (not the dough hook). Blend the Potato Buds with the water. Add to the dry ingredients with the margarine, dough enhancer, and honey and blend. Break in the eggs and beat on high for 2½ minutes.

Divide the soft dough into the prepared tins. Let rise about 25–35 minutes, or until almost doubled in bulk. Bake in a preheated 375° oven for 20 minutes. Turn out from the pans while still warm. Serve warm or cold.

VARIATION:

CINNAMON ROLLS: Omit the pecans but add ½ (1) teaspoon more cinnamon to the topping ingredients.

Nutrients per roll: Calories 290, Fat 15g, Carbohydrate 36g, Cholesterol 55mg, Sodium 220mg, Fiber 1g, Protein 4g.
Dietary exchanges: Bread 2, Fat 3.

Caramel Pecan Rolls
(Yeast-free)

425°

A tasty breakfast treat for those who can't have yeast. The basis for this is the new buttermilk biscuit recipe. Just spread on a topping of butter, brown sugar, and a sprinkle of nuts.

DRY INGREDIENTS	6 ROLLS	12 ROLLS
Four Flour Bean Mix (page 40)	1 cup	2 cups
Xanthan gum	¼ teaspoon	½ teaspoon
Baking powder	1½ teaspoons	3 teaspoons
Baking soda	¼ teaspoon	½ teaspoon
Sugar	1 tablespoon	2 tablespoons
Salt	½ (scant) teaspoon	1 (scant) teaspoon
Powdered egg white	2 teaspoons	4 teaspoons
WET INGREDIENTS		
Shortening (chilled)	3 tablespoons	6 tablespoons
Buttermilk	½ cup	1 cup
TOPPING		
Butter or margarine, softened	1 tablespoon	2 tablespoons
Brown sugar	1½ tablespoons	3 tablespoons
Chopped pecans	2 tablespoons	¼ cup

Preheat oven to 425°. Generously grease your muffin tin(s).

In a mixing bowl, whisk together the dry ingredients. With a pastry blender or two knives, cut the shortening into the flour mixture until coarse crumbs form. Add the buttermilk (reserving some in case the dough is too sticky) and mix gently until a ball forms.

Place the dough on a lightly rice-floured surface and pat (or roll) to about a

¾ inch thickness in an oblong shape. Spread on the softened butter or margarine and sprinkle on the brown sugar and nuts. Because this dough does not roll very well it is best to cut into 3 lengthwise strips. Using a spatula, place 1 strip on top of the next; repeat until you have the 3 in a pile. Cut through the dough crosswise into 6 sections (12 for the large recipe). Fold them gently and place cut side up in the muffin tins.

Bake for 12 to 15 minutes. Serve warm. If necessary, reheat in the microwave.

VARIATION:

CINNAMON ROLLS (Yeast-free): Add ½ teaspoon cinnamon (or to taste) to the brown sugar. Omit the nuts.

Nutrients per roll: Calories 200, Fat 10g, Carbohydrate 25g, Cholesterol 0mg, Sodium 380mg, Fiber 1g, Protein 3g.
Dietary exchanges: Bread 1½, Fat 2.

Frankly Fabulous Fruit Danish 375°

Serve these to anyone with no apology for being gluten free. For the filling, use any jam or preserves you like (apricot, cherry, raspberry, pineapple, or others) or purchase gluten-free lemon curd.

DRY INGREDIENTS	**8** ROLLS	**12** ROLLS
Four Flour Bean Mix (page 40)	2 cups	3 cups
Xanthan gum	1½ teaspoons	2¼ teaspoons
Egg Replacer (optional)	1 teaspoon	1½ teaspoons
Unflavored gelatin	1 teaspoon	1½ teaspoons
Salt	½ teaspoon	¾ teaspoon
Sugar	⅓ cup	½ cup
NutQuik, almond meal, or dry milk powder	3 tablespoons	4½ tablespoons
Dried lemon peel	1 teaspoon	1½ teaspoons
Dry yeast powder	2¼ teaspoons	2¼ teaspoons
WET INGREDIENTS		
Eggs	2 plus 1 yolk	3 plus 1 yolk
Margarine or butter	4 tablespoons	6 tablespoons
Dough enhancer or vinegar	1 teaspoon	1½ teaspoons
Honey	1 tablespoon	1½ tablespoons
Instant potato flakes	1 teaspoon	1 teaspoon
Warm water	1 cup	1½ cups
Jam or preserves	½ cup	⅔ cup
ICING		
Confectioners' sugar	½ cup	¾ cup
Orange juice (more or less)	1 tablespoon	1½ tablespoons
Almonds, sliced (optional)	½ cup	¾ cup

Grease 2 cookie sheets. Set aside.

In a medium bowl, whisk together the dry ingredients. Set aside.

In the bowl of your mixer, place the eggs plus yolk, margarine, dough enhancer, and honey, and blend on low. Dissolve the potato flakes in the warm water and add to the mixing bowl. With the mixer on low, blend in the dry ingredients. Turn the mixer to high and beat for 2 minutes.

Spoon the batter onto the cookie sheets in 8 (12) rounds and swirl a circle depression in each round. Fill with approximately 1 tablespoon of the desired filling. Cover the rolls and let rise until the batter doubles (or swells up around the filling), approximately 25–30 minutes for rapid-rising yeast and 40–60 minutes for regular yeast.

Bake in a preheated oven at 375° for 20–23 minutes or until slightly browned. Do not overbake or the filling will be dry.

To make the icing, combine the confectioners' sugar and juice until it is a consistency suitable for dribbling on the Danish while still warm. For an extra-special topping, add a sprinkle of sliced almonds.

Nutrients per roll: Calories 430, Fat 15g, Carbohydrate 69g, Cholesterol 80mg, Sodium 240mg, Fiber 3g, Protein 9g.
Dietary exchanges: Bread 4, Fat 3.

St. Lucia Buns

375°

These saffron buns are a special treat at Christmas in Swedish homes, but you don't have to be Scandinavian to enjoy them. I followed a recipe for the buns using the new Four-Flour Bean Mix, and the neighborhood Scandinavian bakery said they were very close to theirs in taste.

Note: *The buns can be shaped in X's, twists, triangles, or braids, but I suggest the snail shapes described below as the easiest for our soft dough.*

DRY INGREDIENTS	8 BUNS	12 BUNS
Four Flour Bean Mix (page 40)	2 cups	3 cups
Xanthan gum	1½ teaspoons	2¼ teaspoons
Egg Replacer (optional)	1 teaspoon	1½ teaspoons
Unflavored gelatin	1 teaspoon	1½ teaspoons
Salt	½ teaspoon (rounded)	¾ teaspoon
Almond meal (or finely ground almonds)	¼ cup	⅓ cup
Dry yeast granules	2¼ teaspoons	2¼ teaspoons
WET INGREDIENTS		
Ground saffron or crushed saffron threads	¼ teaspoon	⅓ teaspoon
Eggs	2	3
Butter or margarine	4 tablespoons	6 tablespoons
Dough enhancer or vinegar	1 teaspoon	1½ teaspoons
Potato flakes	1 teaspoon	1½ teaspoons
Warm water (more or less)	¾ cup	1 cup plus 2 tablespoons
Golden raisins	¼ cup plus 8	⅓ cup plus 12

Grease 1 (2) large cookie sheets.

In a medium bowl, whisk together the dry ingredients. Set aside.

In the bowl of your mixer, place the saffron, eggs, butter, and dough enhancer. Beat until well blended. Dissolve the potato flakes in the warm water and add to the mixing bowl. With the mixer on low, blend in the dry ingredients. Turn the mixer to high and beat for 3½ minutes. Stir in the raisins except for the 8 (12) saved for decorating.

To shape the buns in a traditional "snail" shape, place the dough in a plastic bag with the corner clipped about ½ inch. Squeeze the dough in about a 4-inch circle and continue circling and filling in the center (like a snail). This should make 8 (12) buns. In the center of each, place a raisin. Brush with an egg wash if you wish (see below). Let the buns rise until doubled in size (about 20–30 minutes for rapid-rising yeast and 45–60 minutes for regular yeast).

Place in a preheated 375° oven and bake for 20–22 minutes.

Optional egg wash: Thin a beaten egg with water or use liquid egg substitute. Because our dough is soft, you can eliminate the egg wash and brush the buns with melted butter after baking, while the buns are still hot.

Nutrients per bun: Calories 250, Fat 10g, Carbohydrate 34g, Cholesterol 55mg, Sodium 250mg, Fiber 3g, Protein 6g.
Dietary exchanges: Bread 2, Fat 2.

Orange Coffee Rolls

425°

Serve with pride this yeast-rising coffee cake filled with flavor and topped with an orange icing. Made ahead and heated in the microwave, it will taste as if it just came from the oven.

DRY INGREDIENTS	9-INCH ROUND PAN
Four Flour Bean Mix (page 40)	2¾ cups
Xanthan gum	2 teaspoons
Egg Replacer	1½ teaspoons
Unflavored gelatin	1½ teaspoons
Salt	¾ teaspoon
Baking soda	¼ teaspoon
Brown sugar	⅓ cup
NutQuik or almond meal	¼ cup
Orange zest	2 tablespoons (1 orange)
Dry yeast granules	2¼ teaspoons
WET INGREDIENTS	
Liquid egg substitute	¾ cup or 3 eggs
Vegetable oil	2 tablespoons
Ricotta cheese	¼ cup
Dough enhancer or vinegar	1 teaspoon (scant)
Orange juice (more or less)	1 cup
GLAZING AND ICING	
Liquid egg substitute	1 tablespoon
Confectioners' sugar	1 cup
Orange juice	1 to 2 tablespoons

Grease a 9-inch springform pan and dust lightly with rice flour.

In a medium bowl, whisk together the dry ingredients, including the yeast.

In the bowl of your heavy-duty mixer, combine the egg substitute, oil, cheese, and dough enhancer. Beat on low until well combined. Add most of the orange juice (warmed to 110°). The remaining juice should be added as needed, 1 tablespoon at a time, to make a dough slightly thicker than the usual bread dough, which is like cake batter. This should be thick enough to spoon out and hold its shape as separate buns.

With the mixer on low, slowly add the dry ingredients to the liquid in the mixer. Turn the mixer to high and beat for 3½ minutes. Spoon the dough into the prepared pan in 9 bun-shaped spoonfuls, separating them slightly in the bottom of the pan. (As they bake, they will retain the bun-shaped look.) Glaze the unbaked dough by smoothing on (with your fingers) the liquid egg substitute (or beaten egg, if desired). Let rise until almost doubled in bulk, 20–30 minutes for rapid-rising yeast or 45–60 minutes for regular yeast. Bake in a preheated 425° oven for 25–30 minutes, covering after 10 minutes with aluminum foil.

While still hot, remove the ring. Ice with the confectioners' sugar mixed with enough orange juice to make the desired consistency. Serve warm by cutting into wedges.

Makes 12 servings.

VARIATIONS:

RAISIN-NUT COFFEE ROLLS: Add ⅓ cup raisins and ⅓ cup chopped nuts to the dough after mixing.

FRUITED COFFEE ROLLS: Add ½ cup diced citron to the dough after mixing.

Nutrients per roll: Calories 250, Fat 7g, Carbohydrate 43g, Cholesterol 55mg, Sodium 200mg, Fiber 2g, Protein 6g.
Dietary exchanges: Bread 2½, Fat 1½.

Hot Cross Buns

These will taste so much like the hot cross buns you tasted before your diagnosis, you'll think they have to be made of wheat flour!

DRY INGREDIENTS	**9** BUNS	**15** BUNS
Four Flour Bean Mix (page 40)	2 cups	3 cups
Xanthan gum	1½ teaspoons	2¼ teaspoons
Unflavored gelatin	1 teaspoon	1½ teaspoons
Salt	½ teaspoon	¾ teaspoon
Brown sugar	3 tablespoons	4½ tablespoons
Cinnamon or cardamom	¾ teaspoon	1 teaspoon (rounded)
Egg Replacer	1 teaspoon	1½ teaspoons
Almond meal, dry milk powder, or nondairy substitute	2 tablespoons	3 tablespoons

WET INGREDIENTS		
Eggs	2	3
Margarine or butter	2 tablespoons	3 tablespoons
Dough enhancer or vinegar	¾ teaspoon	1 teaspoon
Dry yeast granules	2¼ teaspoons	2¼ teaspoons
Warm water	¾ cup	1 cup plus 2 tablespoons
Raisins, dried cranberries, or citron (or a combination)	⅓ cup	½ cup

ICING		
Confectioners' sugar	¾ cup	1 cup
Orange juice or milk	1 to 2 tablespoons	1 to 2 tablespoons

Grease an 8-inch square pan (9 buns) or a 9" × 13" pan (15 buns). Dust with rice flour.

In a small bowl, combine the dry ingredients. Set aside.

In the bowl of a heavy-duty mixer, place the eggs, margarine (cut into small chunks), and dough enhancer. Beat at medium speed until the eggs are frothy.

Dissolve the yeast in the water and add to the egg mixture. With the mixer on low, spoon in the dry ingredients. Beat on high for 2 minutes. Stir in the fruit and spoon into the prepared pan in round, bun-shaped spoonfuls. For an 8-inch pan make 3 rows of 3 buns; in a larger pan, make 5 rows of 3 buns. Cover and let rise about 35 minutes for rapid-rising yeast or about 60 minutes for regular yeast, or until almost double in bulk.

Bake in a preheated 380° oven for approximately 28 minutes. For a finishing touch, combine the confectioners' sugar and orange juice and pipe the icing in the form of a cross on each bun when slightly cool.

Nutrients per bun: Calories 190, Fat 4g, Carbohydrate 34g, Cholesterol 30mg, Sodium 180mg, Fiber 2g, Protein 5g.
Dietary exchanges: Bread 2, Fat 1.

Breakfast Focaccia

This sweetened bread, cooked in a flat pan and topped with fruit preserves (or canned pie filling) that melt into the dough, is easy to make and should delight family or friends at breakfast or brunch.

DRY INGREDIENTS	9" × 13" CAKE PAN	10" × 15" JELLY ROLL PAN
Four Flour Bean Mix (page 40)	1½ cups	2 cups
Xanthan gum	1 teaspoon	1½ teaspoons
Salt	½ teaspoon	½ teaspoon
Egg Replacer	1 teaspoon	1 teaspoon
Unflavored gelatin	1 teaspoon	1 teaspoon
Sugar	4 tablespoons	5½ tablespoons
Almond meal or dry milk powder	2¼ tablespoons	3 tablespoons
Lemon or orange peel	1 teaspoon	1½ teaspoons
Dry yeast granules	2¼ teaspoons	2¼ teaspoons
WET INGREDIENTS		
Liquid egg substitute (or eggs)	⅓ cup (1)	½ cup (2)
Dough enhancer	½ teaspoon	½ teaspoon
Margarine or butter	4 tablespoons	5½ tablespoons
Warm water (more or less)	¾ cup	1 cup
TOPPING		
Margarine or butter, melted	1 tablespoon	1½ tablespoons
Fruit preserves	¾ cup	1 cup

Preheat oven to 400°. Grease your chosen pan.

In a medium bowl, whisk together the dry ingredients, including the yeast. Set aside.

In the bowl of your mixer, beat the egg substitute, dough enhancer, margarine (cut in chunks), and most of the water. With the mixer on low, spoon in the flour mix. Test to see if the dough is the right consistency (like cake batter). Add water as necessary. Turn the mixer to high and beat 3½ minutes. Spoon into the prepared pan and smooth evenly.

Drizzle the melted margarine over the top, then gently spoon on the preserves in even dabs. Let the dough rise about 10 minutes. Bake for 35–40 minutes, or until the bread showing through the topping is a nice brown. Serve warm or at room temperature.

Makes 9 (12) servings.

Nutrients per serving: Calories 260, Fat 8g, Carbohydrate 44g, Cholesterol 0mg, Sodium 220mg, Fiber 2g, Protein 4g.
Dietary exchanges: Bread 2½, Fat 1½.

Raisin Cinnamon English Muffins
(Rice-free, Lactose-free)

Sorghum flour, cinnamon, and raisins make this English muffin a sweet breakfast treat. It's easy to make with a hand electric mixer, and by using a rapid-rising yeast, you can make and bake this in less than an hour.

Note: For a more solid muffin, add ¼ cup instant dry powdered milk to the dry ingredients.

DRY INGREDIENTS	6 MUFFINS	12 MUFFINS
Sorghum flour	¾ cup	1½ cups
Potato starch	½ cup	1 cup
Tapioca starch	¼ cup	½ cup
Xanthan gum	1 teaspoon	2 teaspoons
Baking powder	1½ teaspoons	3 teaspoons
Salt	½ teaspoon	1 teaspoon
Cinnamon	½ teaspoon	1 teaspoon
Dried lemon or orange peel (optional)	½ teaspoon	1 teaspoon
Raisins	¼ cup	½ cup
WET INGREDIENTS		
Sugar	1 tablespoon	2 tablespoons
Water, lukewarm	1 cup	2 cups
Dry yeast granules	2¼ teaspoons	2¼ teaspoons
Egg(s)	1	2
Dough enhancer or vinegar	½ teaspoon	1 teaspoon
Margarine or butter, melted	1½ tablespoons	3 tablespoons

Place 6 (12) English muffin rings on 1 (2) cookie sheet(s) and grease the rings with vegetable oil spray.

In a medium mixing bowl, whisk together the sorghum flour, potato starch, tapioca starch, xanthan gum, baking powder, salt, cinnamon, and dried lemon peel (if using). Set aside.

Stir 1 teaspoon sugar into the water and add the yeast. Set aside.

In a large mixing bowl, place the remaining sugar, egg(s), dough enhancer, and melted margarine. Beat with a hand mixer until the egg(s) are foamy. Add the yeast water and beat slightly. Spoon in half of the flour mixture. Beat until well blended and smooth. Add the remaining flour mixture and beat slightly. Stir in the raisins. Spoon into the prepared rings. Cover with paper toweling and let rise for 25–35 minutes for rapid-rising yeast or 45–60 minutes for regular yeast, until almost double in bulk. Bake in a preheated 375° oven for 20 minutes. Cool slightly before removing from the rings.

Nutrients per muffin: Calories 210, Fat 5g, Carbohydrate 42g, Cholesterol 35mg, Sodium 320mg, Fiber 4g, Protein 5g.
Dietary exchanges: Bread 2½, Fat 1.

Baking Powder Biscuits

Delicate and light, these biscuits taste more like the wheat biscuits I remember. Using the optional powdered egg whites makes them lighter; you have a choice of milk or a nondairy substitute for the liquid.

DRY INGREDIENTS	6 BISCUITS	12 BISCUITS
Four Flour Bean Mix (page 40)	1 cup	2 cups
Xanthan gum	⅛ teaspoon	¼ teaspoon
Baking powder	2 teaspoons (scant)	4 teaspoons (scant)
Baking soda	¼ teaspoon	½ teaspoon
Sugar	1 tablespoon	2 tablespoons
Salt	½ teaspoon	1 teaspoon
Powdered egg white (optional)	2 teaspoons	4 teaspoons
WET INGREDIENTS		
Margarine or shortening	3 tablespoons	6 tablespoons
Milk or nondairy substitute	⅓ cup	⅔ cup
Vinegar	1 teaspoon	2 teaspoons

Preheat oven to 425°.

In a mixing bowl, whisk together the dry ingredients. With a pastry blender or two knives, cut the margarine into the flour mixture until coarse crumbs form. Add the milk to which you have added the vinegar, mixing in just enough until a ball forms.

Place the dough on a surface lightly coated with rice flour and pat out to ¾ inch thick. Cut with a biscuit cutter (or a glass dipped in flour). Place the biscuits on an ungreased baking sheet, leaving at least 1 inch between them. Bake for 12–15 minutes.

Nutrients per biscuit: Calories 150, Fat 7g, Carbohydrate 21g, Cholesterol 0mg, Sodium 430mg, Fiber 1g, Protein 2g.
Dietary exchanges: Bread 1, Fat 1.

Sweet Fruited Scones 375°

These are as flaky as biscuits but sweeter and fruit-flavored. Mix them up in minutes, bake immediately, and eat hot from the oven. Use them at breakfast as a sweet roll, pair with a luncheon salad, or eat alone as a snack anytime. Day-old scones will microwave to taste like freshly baked.

DRY INGREDIENTS	8 WEDGES
Gluten-free Flour Mix (page 40)	2 cups
Xanthan gum	1 teaspoon (rounded)
Egg Replacer (optional)	3 teaspoons
Sugar	¼ cup
Baking powder	4 teaspoons
Baking soda	1 teaspoon
Dried orange peel	1 teaspoon
Salt	½ teaspoon

OTHER INGREDIENTS	
Butter or margarine	5½ tablespoons
Sweetened dried cranberries	½ cup
Sliced almonds, chopped	½ cup
Eggs, beaten slightly (or liquid egg substitute)	2
Buttermilk	½ cup

TOPPING	
Buttermilk-egg mixture, reserved from mix	2 tablespoons
Sugar	½ teaspoon

Preheat the oven to 375°. Grease a cookie sheet.

In the mixing bowl, combine the dry ingredients. With a fork or pastry blender, cut in the butter until the mixture resembles coarse crumbs. Stir in the cranberries and almonds.

In a cup measure, mix the beaten eggs and buttermilk. Pour all but about 2 tablespoons into the flour mix. Blend gently until all the flour is moistened. It will be a soft ball. Spoon onto the cookie sheet and gently pat into an 8-inch circle about ½ to ¾ inch thick. Moisten the top with the remaining buttermilk-egg mixture and sprinkle on the sugar. Cut into 8 wedges and separate slightly.

Bake for about 18 minutes or until light golden brown. Serve warm with butter and jam.

Nutrients per scone: Calories 310, Fat 14g, Carbohydrate 45g, Cholesterol 75mg, Sodium 590mg, Fiber 2g, Protein 6g.
Dietary exchanges: Bread 2½, Fat 2½.

BREAKFAST BREAD RECIPES FROM OTHER BOOKS IN THE GLUTEN-FREE GOURMET SERIES

My first three books contained several breakfast breads that differ so much from the breads in this book that I am still using them often. I hope you will want to try them (see p. 107 for book title abbreviations).

BREAKFAST BREADS	BASE	BOOK	PAGE
Buttermilk Pancakes	Rice	GFG	106
Buttermilk Waffles	Rice	GFG	107
Crêpes	Rice	GFG	113
Drop Scones	Rice	MORE	88
Dutch Babies	Rice	GFG	114
Fruited Breakfast Torte	Rice	MORE	91
Raised Doughnuts	Rice	MORE	89
Rice-Ricotta Pancakes	Rice	GFG	106
Rice-Soy Waffles	Rice	GFG	108
Surprise Doughnut Holes	Potato	GFG	113

Crackers

Rice-Based Crackers

Rice-itz
Hi Ho Crackers (Mock)
Sesame Wafers
Cheese Nips

Bean-Based Crackers

Graham Crackers

Cracker Recipes from Other Books in the Gluten-free Gourmet Series

*C*rackers are one of the wheat flour products I most missed when starting my diet. I did so enjoy the salty little nips with juice or wine—or, as I often did, eating them for lunch, slathered with a gooey mix of tuna fish, mayonnaise, and pickle relish. I'd pile it as high as I could get it to stay and make a lunch of a few crackers with a lot of the tuna fish mix.

I'm not sure if I was unconsciously avoiding huge amounts of gluten in the crackers or if I just liked the nourishment that the tuna and mayonnaise gave me. Now I eat the crackers just by themselves (counting calories!) and enjoy them. I even carry them to parties and other places where hors d'oeuvres may be served so that I can have my own tidbit to crunch.

I've given many good cracker recipes in former books, but these new and different ones should add variety to your collection. Cracker recipes from my earlier books in the Gluten-free Gourmet series are listed at the end of this chapter.

Rice-itz

Not quite the Ritz we may remember but as close as I've ever tasted. They are easy to make, for you just roll them out thin on the baking sheet and then score to size.

Note: *You can substitute pecan meal or finely ground pecans for the almond meal.*

INGREDIENTS

Rice flour (white)	¾ cup
Tapioca flour	½ cup
Xanthan gum	1½ teaspoons
Salt	½ teaspoon
Unflavored gelatin	1 teaspoon
Egg Replacer	1 teaspoon
Sugar	1 tablespoon
Almond meal	⅓ cup
Butter (no substitute)	5 tablespoons
Milk (whole or 2%) (no substitutes)	½ cup
Dry yeast granules	2¼ teaspoons (1 packet)
Olive oil (for brushing)	2 teaspoons
Salt (for sprinkling)	

Preheat oven to 350°. Grease an 11" × 17" baking sheet with vegetable oil spray.

In a small bowl, combine the rice flour, tapioca flour, xanthan gum, gelatin, Egg Replacer, sugar, and almond meal. Set aside.

In a medium saucepan, melt the butter and add the milk. Warm to about 120°. Stir in 1 tablespoon of the flour mix and the yeast. Let set until the yeast foams slightly.

Add the remaining flour mix and blend. The mixture may be crumbly. Work it with your hands, adding a bit of warm water (if necessary) until you can form a ball.

Place on the baking sheet and cover with plastic wrap, then roll the dough with a rolling pin until it fills the sheet and is even in depth (about ⅛ inch). Remove the plastic wrap and brush the dough with olive oil. Sprinkle with salt. Score into 1-inch squares.

Bake about 20 minutes, turning the baking sheet at the halfway point to allow the crackers to brown evenly. They should be a toasty brown for best taste. Cool before breaking apart. Stored in an airtight container, these will keep several weeks.

Makes about 175 crackers.

Nutrients per cracker: Calories 10, Fat .5g, Carbohydrate 1g, Cholesterol 0mg, Sodium 5mg, Fiber 0g, Protein 0g.

Hi Ho Crackers (Mock)

375°

A great traveler! This slightly sweet rice cracker is the closest I've come to making a plain cracker that tastes like the Hi Hos I remember. They go well with any dip or cheese, but you can also eat them alone as a flavorful, almost sugarless cookie.

INGREDIENTS

French Bread/Pizza Mix (page 190)	1½ cups
Baking powder	1 teaspoon
Baking soda	½ teaspoon
Salt	½ teaspoon
Butter	4 tablespoons
Ice water	6 to 7 tablespoons
Olive oil for brushing	1 tablespoon
Coarse salt	

Preheat oven to 375°. Grease a cookie sheet with vegetable oil spray.

In a medium bowl, whisk together the flour mix, baking powder, baking soda, and salt. Cut in the butter until the texture is crumbly. Add the water, 1 tablespoon at a time, until the dough forms a firm ball.

Place on the prepared cookie sheet, cover with plastic wrap, and roll with a rolling pin until the dough is no more than ⅛ inch thick. (This should cover the cookie sheet.) Score into 1½-inch squares, brush with the olive oil, sprinkle with coarse salt, and prick each cracker with a fork 3 times. If you prefer round wafers, roll the dough out between sheets of waxed paper, sprinkle with salt, and cut with a small round cookie cutter. Place the crackers on cookie sheets approximately ½ inch apart. Bake 15–20 minutes. Cool and store in an airtight container.

Makes about 65 crackers.

Nutrients per cracker: Calories 20, Fat .5g, Carbohydrate 3g, Cholesterol 0mg, Sodium 30mg, Fiber 0g, Protein 0g.

Sesame Wafers

300°

These crispy, sesame-flavored crackers have a wonderful nip to them. The cayenne pepper can be eliminated for plain sesame wafers.

INGREDIENTS

French Bread/Pizza Mix (page 190)	1 cup
Salt	½ teaspoon
Cayenne pepper	⅛ teaspoon
Butter Flavor Crisco	3 tablespoons
Butter or margarine	3 tablespoons
Toasted sesame seeds	½ cup
Ice water	2 tablespoons (more or less)
Coarse or regular salt for sprinkling (optional)	

Preheat oven to 300°.

In a medium bowl, whisk together the flour mix, salt, and cayenne pepper. Cut in the Crisco and butter to form coarse crumbs. Stir in the sesame seeds. Sprinkle in the ice water, using only what is necessary to form a ball.

Place on a cookie sheet, cover with plastic, and roll out to ⅛ inch thickness overall. (This will almost fill the sheet.) Score into 1½-inch squares. If you prefer round wafers, divide the dough in half, roll each section out between sheets of waxed paper, and cut with a small round cookie cutter. Place the crackers on cookie sheets approximately ½ inch apart. Sprinkle with salt if desired.

Bake for 25–30 minutes or until very lightly colored.

Makes about 6 dozen.

Nutrients per cracker: Calories 20, Fat ½g, Carbohydrate 3g, Cholesterol ½mg, Sodium 30mg, Fiber 0g, Protein 0g.

Cheese Nips 400°

A reader with a lot of imagination created these wonderfully nippy cheese snacks using my original Cheese Sticks recipe and rolling the dough very thinly.

INGREDIENTS

Butter or margarine	2 tablespoons
Egg	1 large
Salt	½ teaspoon
Pepper	⅛ teaspoon
Grated sharp cheddar cheese	2 cups
Rice flour	¾ cup
Potato starch flour	¼ cup
Xanthan gum	1 teaspoon
Salt for sprinkling (optional)	

Preheat oven to 400°.

In a mixer, beat the butter until creamy. Add the egg, salt, and pepper, and beat until blended. Beat in the cheese, a third at a time, until combined. Stir in the flours and xanthan gum until thoroughly blended. Work the dough into a ball. If the dough doesn't stick together, add cold water, 1 tablespoon at a time, until a ball can be formed. Don't worry about overworking.

Divide the dough in half. Place 1 ball on a baking sheet, cover with plastic wrap, and roll as thin as possible. Repeat with the other half. Sprinkle with salt, if desired, and cut with a pastry wheel into 1-inch squares. Bake for 4–6 minutes, until deep golden.

Makes about 12 dozen Nips.

Nutrients per cracker: Calories 10, Fat ½g, Carbohydrate 1g, Cholesterol 5mg, Sodium 20mg, Fiber 0g, Protein 0g.

Graham Crackers

These egg-free, rice-free new crackers taste so much like the real graham crackers that I didn't call them "mock." Like all graham crackers, these keep well, so are great for traveling for they can serve as bread or cookie. At home, use these crushed for graham cracker crusts.

INGREDIENTS

Four Flour Bean Mix (page 40)	2 cups
Xanthan gum	1 teaspoon
Salt	1½ teaspoons
Cinnamon	1 teaspoon (rounded)
Baking powder	2½ teaspoons
Margarine or butter	¾ cup (1½ sticks)
Honey	¼ cup
Brown sugar	1 cup
Vanilla flavoring	1 teaspoon
Water	1 to 2 tablespoons
Cornstarch for rolling	As needed

In a medium bowl, whisk together the flour mix, xanthan gum, salt, cinnamon, and baking powder. Set aside.

In a large mixing bowl, beat together the margarine, honey, brown sugar, and vanilla. Add the dry ingredients alternately with the water, using just enough to hold the batter in a dough ball that will handle easily. Refrigerate for at least 1 hour.

Preheat the oven to 325°. Lightly grease two 12" × 15" baking sheets.

Using half the dough, work in some cornstarch if necessary to form a ball that isn't sticky. (The dough can take handling.) Roll out on a cornstarch-dusted piece of plastic wrap to a rectangle about 13 inches thick. Transfer to the prepared baking sheet by placing the sheet over the dough, holding the wrap, and flipping the whole piece of dough onto the baking sheet. Continue rolling out the dough until it completely covers the sheet and is about ⅛ inch thick or the thickness of pastry dough. Cut with a pastry wheel into 3-inch squares. Prick each square with a fork 5 times.

Bake for about 30 minutes, removing the crackers around the edges if they get too brown. Repeat with the other half of the dough.

Makes about 5 dozen.

Nutrients per cracker: Calories 50, Fat 2.5g, Carbohydrate 8g, Cholesterol 0mg, Sodium 95mg, Fiber 0g, Protein 0g.
Dietary exchanges: Bread ½, Fat ½.

CRACKER RECIPES FROM OTHER BOOKS IN THE GLUTEN-FREE GOURMET SERIES

CRACKERS	BASE	BOOK	PAGE
Cheese Crackers	Rice	F&H	203
Cheese Crisps	Rice	MORE	188
Cheese Sticks	Rice	GFG	121
Corn Chips	Rice	MORE	186
Italian Cheese Straws	Rice	MORE	187
Mock Graham Crackers	Rice	MORE	87
Onion Crackers	Bean and Rice	F&H	202
Pecan Wafers	Rice	MORE	185
Rice-free Graham Crackers	Bean	F&H	99
Sesame Thins	Rice	MORE	184

Leftovers

Dried Bread Crumbs
Apple Celery Dressing
Maple Pecan Bread Pudding
   Vanilla Sauce
Lemon Sauce Bread Pudding
Quick Bread Pudding
Banana Bread Pudding with Caramel
  Sauce

Since my diagnosis, when bread became a coveted (and expensive) item, I'm conscious of every crumb and save the dried crusts and slices as closely as old Mother Hubbard.

Having fresh bread in the house means toast and sandwiches; having leftover bread means stuffing for poultry, bread crumbs for topping casseroles, and a filler for meat loaf. And following the practice of my English mother, when a loaf goes stale and I need dessert, I turn it into the old-fashioned, homey bread pudding.

Even fresh loaves that turn out heavy, lopsided, or unpalatable can be rescued and used in one of the following recipes.

Dried Bread Crumbs

A good way to use up those end pieces of bread, any bread machine failures, and those stale muffins is to make dried bread crumbs and store them in the freezer. Pull them out to make pie and cheesecake shells, mock graham cracker crusts, or toppings for casseroles.

Preheat the oven to 200°. Have handy a cookie sheet with slightly raised sides. Crumble the bread or muffins onto the sheet. Bake for 1 hour, and then turn off the oven and let the bread crumbs remain for another hour (or overnight).

To make even finer crumbs, place in a food processor and whirl to the desired texture. Store in the freezer. These need not be defrosted to use if they are whirled until they are fine.

Apple Celery Dressing 375°

This is a tasty and different side dish for pork or poultry that makes use of leftover bread. Just cut up your stale bread into cubes and freeze. Pull them out when you want to stuff a turkey or put this dressing in the pan beside your pork roast or under those chicken pieces when you bake them.

INGREDIENTS	6 TO 8 SERVINGS	10 TO 15 SERVINGS
Dried bread cubes	2½ cups	5 cups
Poultry seasoning	1 to 2 teaspoons	2 to 3½ teaspoons
Margarine or butter	4 tablespoons (½ stick)	8 tablespoons (1 stick)
Apple, peeled, cored, and diced	1 large	2 large
Celery, diced	1 cup	2 cups
Onion, chopped	½ cup	1 cup
Eggs, beaten	1	2
Chicken broth (more or less)	1 cup	2 cups
Salt (or to taste)	1 teaspoon	2 teaspoons

Place the bread cubes in a large mixing bowl. Stir in the poultry seasoning.

In a large skillet, melt the margarine and sauté the apple, celery, and onion until the onion and apple are translucent. Add to the bread cubes with the egg. Mix in the chicken broth, a little at a time, until the texture of the dressing is moist. If baking separately, you will probably want a moist mixture. If you are stuffing a fowl or placing next to a pork roast, you might wish a drier dressing because the juices from the meat will add to the moisture. Salt to taste.

To bake separately, place in a 2- (4-) quart greased casserole and bake in a preheated 375° oven for 1 hour.

Nutrients per serving: Calories 110, Fat 7g, Carbohydrate 9g, Cholesterol 40mg, Sodium 490mg, Fiber 1g, Protein 3g.
Dietary exchanges: Bread 1, Fat 1.

Maple Pecan Bread Pudding 325°

Fantastic! This old standby from my childhood has now come full circle. We had a lot of leftover bread on the farm, and Mother made this very earthy dessert using the extra milk from the cow and eggs from our chickens. It went out of style when bread became a store-bought item, but in the last few years I've seen it served on cruise ships and at pricey restaurants. And diners love it. This pudding is similar to one served on the Mississippi River steamboats. It is usually topped with a vanilla sauce like the one below.

INGREDIENTS	1-QUART CASSEROLE	2-QUART CASSEROLE
White or sweet gluten-free bread cubes	2 cups	4 cups
Pecans, chopped	3 tablespoons	⅓ cup
Orange juice	¼ cup	½ cup
Eggs	2 medium	3 large
Light cream or nondairy creamer	1 cup	2 cups
Sugar	¼ cup	½ cup
Vanilla flavoring	½ teaspoon	1 teaspoon
Maple syrup	¼ cup	½ cup
Allspice	¼ teaspoon	½ teaspoon
Cloves	⅛ teaspoon	¼ teaspoon
Cinnamon	½ teaspoon	1 teaspoon

Preheat oven to 325°. Butter the chosen casserole.

In the greased casserole, place the bread cubes and sprinkle on the pecans. Pour on the orange juice.

In a medium bowl, beat the eggs slightly and add the cream, sugar, vanilla, maple syrup, and spices. Stir and pour this over the bread. Bake for 35 minutes. Serve warm or at room temperature topped with cream, milk, or the vanilla sauce below.

VANILLA SAUCE

¼ cup sugar

1 tablespoon cornstarch

1 cup water

2 to 3 tablespoons butter

⅛ teaspoon salt

1 to 2 teaspoons vanilla flavoring (or 1 tablespoon rum)

Combine the sugar, cornstarch, and water in the top of a double boiler.

Cook over hot water until thickened. Remove from heat and stir in the butter, salt, and vanilla.

Makes approximately 1 cup.

Nutrients per serving: Calories 220, Fat 9g, Carbohydrate 34g, Cholesterol 90mg, Sodium 75mg, Fiber 3g, Protein 3g.
Dietary exchanges: Bread 2, Fat 2.

Lemon Sauce Bread Pudding 325°

A delicious way to use up some of your extra white or French bread. The delicate lemon sauce taste needs only a dab of whipped topping to become an elegant dessert.

INGREDIENTS	4 TO 5 SERVINGS	8 TO 10 SERVINGS
Gluten-free white or French bread, cubed	2¼ cups	4½ cups
Frozen lemonade concentrate	¼ cup	½ cup
Butter or margarine	4 tablespoons (½ stick)	8 tablespoons (1 stick)

INGREDIENTS	4 TO 5 SERVINGS	8 TO 10 SERVINGS
Eggs (or liquid egg substitute)	3 plus 1 white (½ cup)	5 plus 3 whites (1 cup)
Sugar	½ cup	1 cup
Milk or nondairy creamer	1 cup	2 cups
Salt	⅛ teaspoon	¼ teaspoon
Whipped topping (optional)		

Preheat oven to 325°. Grease a 2- (4-) quart baking dish with butter.

Spread the bread on the bottom of the baking dish.

In the top of a double boiler, combine 3 (6) tablespoons of the lemonade concentrate, butter, and half the sugar. Set over simmering water, stirring until the butter melts. Beat 1 (2) egg(s) and 1 (2) white(s) in a mixing bowl. Add a little of the hot mix to the eggs and then pour the mixture back into the hot mix. Cook, stirring constantly, until the sauce is thickened enough to coat the back of a spoon. Pour this over the bread.

Whisk together the remaining lemonade concentrate, the remaining sugar, the remaining eggs, milk, and salt Pour this mixture over the bread and lemon sauce. Let stand for 10 minutes.

Cover and bake 30 minutes. Uncover and bake about 30 minutes more, until golden. Serve hot or at room temperature. If you don't use the whipped topping, a dusting of confectioners' sugar will dress up the dessert.

Nutrients per serving: Calories 310, Fat 16g, Carbohydrate 39g, Cholesterol 155mg, Sodium 250mg, Fiber 1g, Protein 5g.
Dietary exchanges: Bread 2, Fat 3.

Quick Bread Pudding 350°

This easy bread pudding can be put together in minutes and varied to suit any taste. Raisins may be substituted for other dried fruit, or add a bit of lemon zest. Use either brown or white sugar. Or for a delightfully rich pudding, use a gluten-free, flavored nondairy liquid.

INGREDIENTS	5 TO 6 SERVINGS	10 TO 12 SERVINGS
Gluten-free bread, cake, or muffin, crumbled	2 cups	4 cups
Dried cranberries or cherries	¼ cup	½ cup
Milk or nondairy liquid	2 cups	4 cups
Margarine or butter	4 tablespoons (½ stick)	8 tablespoons (1 stick)
Sugar (or to taste)	½ cup	1 cup
Gluten-free flavoring (vanilla or other)	1 teaspoon	2 teaspoons
Cinnamon	½ teaspoon	1 teaspoon
Eggs (or liquid egg substitute)	2	4
Whipped topping		

Preheat oven to 350°. Butter a 1½- (3-) quart casserole.

Spread the crumbled bread on the bottom and top with the dried cranberries or cherries.

In a medium saucepan over low heat, combine the milk, margarine, sugar, flavoring, and cinnamon. Heat until the margarine melts. Remove from heat and pour over the bread. Beat the eggs slightly, pour into the casserole, and stir lightly. Bake for 45 minutes. Serve warm or cold with whipped cream or nondairy whipped topping.

Nutrients per serving: Calories 250, Fat 12g, Carbohydrate 3g, Cholesterol 100mg, Sodium 170mg, Fiber 0g, Protein 6g.
Dietary exchanges: Bread 2, Fat 2.

Banana Bread Pudding
with Caramel Sauce

375°

The caramel sauce, banana, and rum make this simple dessert into company fare.

INGREDIENTS	4 TO 6 SERVINGS	8 TO 12 SERVINGS
Gluten-free white or sweet bread, cubed	2¼ cups	4½ cups
Margarine or butter, melted	2 tablespoons	4 tablespoons
Eggs (or liquid substitute)	2 (½ cup)	4 (1 cup)
Milk or nondairy liquid	1½ cups	3 cups
Brown sugar	¼ cup	½ cup
Vanilla flavoring	2 teaspoons	1 tablespoon
Cinnamon	¼ teaspoon	½ teaspoon
Nutmeg	¼ teaspoon	½ teaspoon
Salt	¼ teaspoon	½ teaspoon
Bananas, peeled and sliced	1	2
Rum (optional)	1 tablespoon	2 tablespoons
SAUCE		
Margarine or butter	3 tablespoons	6 tablespoons
Brown sugar	2 tablespoons	¼ cup
Cornstarch	1 tablespoon	2 tablespoons
Milk or nondairy substitute	¾ cup	1½ cups
Dark corn syrup	¼ cup	½ cup
Vanilla flavoring	1 teaspoon	2 teaspoons

Preheat oven to 375°. Butter a 2- (4-) quart casserole or baking dish and put in the bread cubes. Pour in the butter and toss to coat.

In a medium bowl, lightly beat the eggs. Add the milk, sugar, flavoring, cinnamon, nutmeg, and salt. Stir in the bananas and add the rum (if using). Pour the liquid over the bread cubes and stir. Bake, uncovered, for 40 minutes or until a knife inserted in the center comes out clean.

Sauce: Melt the margarine in a small saucepan while the pudding is baking. Combine brown sugar and cornstarch and add to the saucepan. Stir in the milk and corn syrup, and cook over medium heat until the mixture comes to a full boil. Boil for 1 minute. Remove from heat and stir in vanilla. Serve the warm sauce over warm pudding.

Nutrients per serving: Calories 270, Fat 13g, Carbohydrate 33g, Cholesterol 110mg, Sodium 270mg, Fiber 1g, Protein 4g.
Dietary exchanges: Bread 2, Fat 2½.

Where to Find Gluten-free Baking Supplies

For those of us who have to live gluten or wheat free, baking our own breads is often very frustrating because few of the supplies are carried at the corner grocery store. Some can be found in Asian markets, the neighborhood health food store, or even a local grocery that carries some special items. But by far the largest amount of our baking needs have to be special-ordered from one of the following suppliers who feature gluten-free flours and the necessary xanthan or guar gums.

Today there are many more suppliers, some specializing in gluten-free goods, so you should find your needs close to home. But a few flours featured in this book are so unusual that they probably haven't reached regular markets yet. Garfava, bean, and sorghum flours will have to be special-ordered for a time, until the health food stores carry them on a regular basis.

AUTHENTIC FOODS (Garfava flour, brown and white rice flour, tapioca starch, potato flour and potato starch, xanthan gum, maple sugar, vanilla powder, rye flavor powder): 1850 West 169th Street, Suite B, Gardena, CA 90247; phone (800) 806-4737 or (310) 366-7612; fax (310) 366-6938. Accepts orders by phone, mail, or fax. Write for complete product list. Some products can be found in health food stores.

BOB'S RED MILL NATURAL FOODS (xanthan and guar gums, wheat-free flours, legume flours): 5209 S.E. International Way, Milwaukie, OR 97222; phone (503) 654-3215; fax (503) 653-1339. Accepts orders by mail, phone, or fax. Write for an order form. Some products can be found in health food stores and in health sections of grocery stores.

CYBROS, INC. (white rice flour and tapioca flour): P.O. Box 851, Waukesha, WI 53187-0851; phone (800) 876-2253. Accepts orders by mail or phone. Products can also be found in health food stores.

DE-RO-MA (Food Intolerance Centre) (gluten-free flours): 1118 Berlier, Laval, Quebec H7L 3R9, Canada; phone (514) 990-5694 or (800) 363-DIET; fax (450) 629-4781. Call, fax, or write for their full catalog.

DIETARY SPECIALTIES, INC. (xanthan and guar gums, flavorings, dough enhancer): 865 Centennial Ave., Piscataway, NJ 08854; phone (888) 636-8123. Accepts orders by phone or mail. Write or phone for list of products.

EL PETO PRODUCTS (bean, rice, quinoa, millet, and other gluten-free flours milled especially for them by The Mill Stone): 41 Shoemaker Street, Kitchener, Ontario N2E 3G9, Canada; phone (800) 387-4064; fax (519) 748-5279; e-mail: elpeto@golden.net. Order by phone, fax, mail, or e-mail. Some products can be found in specialty markets and health food stores.

ENER-G FOODS, INC. (xanthan gum, methocel, dough enhancer, almond meal, and tapioca, bean, rice, and other gluten-free flours; Bette Hagman's GF Gourmet Flour Mix; Egg Replacer; Lacto-Free): P.O. Box 24723, Seattle, WA 98124-0723; phone (800) 331-5222. Accepts orders by phone, mail, or secure Web site: www.ener-g.com. Phone for a catalog of their long list. Products can be found in some health food stores and specialty markets.

THE GLUTEN FREE PANTRY, INC. (xanthan and guar gums, dough enhancer, a long list of gluten-free flours including white, brown, and wild rice, garbanzo bean, several corn flours, and more): P.O. Box 840, Glastonbury, CT 06033; phone (800) 291-8386 or (860) 633-3826; fax (860) 633-6853; Web site www.glutenfree.com. Write or phone for their free catalog. Accepts orders by phone, mail, or fax.

GRAIN PROCESS ENTERPRISES, LTD. (Romano, navy, garbanzo bean, yellow pea, and other gluten-free flours including rice, buckwheat, millet, tapioca, potato, and arrowroot; xanthan and guar gums): 39 Golden Gate Court, Scarborough, Ontario M1P 3A4, Canada; phone (416) 291-3226; fax (416) 291-2159. Write or phone for their list. Takes orders by mail, phone, or fax. Some products can be found in health food stores.

JOWAR FOODS (sorghum flour): 113 Hickory Street, Hereford, TX 79045; phone (806) 363-9070; fax (806) 364-1984. Accepts orders by phone, mail, or fax. Sorghum flour can be found in some health food stores and specialty markets.

KING ARTHUR FLOUR (rice and tapioca flours, potato starch, xanthan gum): P.O. Box 876, Norwich, VT 05055; phone (800) 827-6836. Accepts orders by phone or mail. Please request King Arthur Flour Baker's catalog.

KINNIKINNICK FOODS (xanthan and guar gums; rice, corn, potato, and soya flours; other baking supplies): 10306-112 Street, Edmonton, Alberta T5K 1N1, Canada; phone (403) 424-2900, toll free 1-877-503-4466; fax (403) 421-0456, e-mail: info@ kinnikinnick.com; Web site www.kinnikinnick.com. Accepts orders via phone, mail, fax, and secure Web site. Offers home delivery of all products to most areas in North America.

MISS ROBEN'S (gluten-free flours including sorghum and Gluten-free Flour Mix, xanthan and guar gums, and other baking supplies): P.O. Box 1149, Frederick, MD 21702; phone (800) 891-0083; fax (301) 631-5954; e-mail: misroben@msn.com. Accepts orders by mail, phone, e-mail, or fax.

NANCY'S NATURAL FOODS (long list of gluten-free flours including sorghum and bean, xanthan and guar gums, milk powders and substitutes): 266 N.W. First Avenue, Ste. A, Canby, OR 97013; phone (503) 266-3306; fax (503) 266-3306; e-mail: nnfoods@juno.com. Accepts orders by phone, mail, and e-mail. Ask for their long list of gluten-free baking supplies.

THE REALLY GREAT FOOD CO. (rice and tapioca flours, xanthan gum): P.O. Box 319, Malverne, NY 11565; phone (800) 593-5377; fax (516) 593-9522. Accepts orders by mail, phone, or fax. Call or write for a full product list.

SON'S MILLING (Romano bean flour and other gluten-free flours): Unit #23, 6809 Kirkpatrick Crescent, Faanichiton, BC V8M 1Z8, Canada; phone (250) 544-1733; fax (604) 389-6719. Accepts orders by phone, mail, or fax. Write or call for complete list. Some products may be found in health food stores.

SPECIALTY FOOD SHOP (long line of gluten-free flours, xanthan and guar gums, rice and corn bran): Radio Centre Plaza, Upper Level, 875 Main Street West, Hamilton, Ontario L8S 4P9, Canada; phone (800) SFS-7976 or (905) 528-4707; fax (905) 528-5625; e-mail: SFS@sickkids.on.ca. Accepts orders by phone, mail, fax, or e-mail. Write for product list. Also has retail stores in Hamilton and Toronto.

TAD ENTERPRISES (rice, potato, and tapioca flours, xanthan and guar gums): 9356 Pleasant, Tinley Park, IL 60477; phone (708) 429-2101; fax (708) 429-3954. Accepts orders by mail, phone, or fax. Write for an order form for complete list of products.

This list, offered for the reader's convenience, was updated at the time of publication of this book. I regret I cannot be responsible for later changes in names, addresses, or phone numbers, or for a company's removing some products from its line.

Index